THE THIRD WAVE

D0013087

THE THIRD WAVE

Democratization in
the Late Twentieth Century

By

SAMUEL P. HUNTINGTON

UNIVERSITY OF OKLAHOMA PRESS : NORMAN AND LONDON

OTHER BOOKS BY SAMUEL P. HUNTINGTON

The Soldier and the State: The Theory and Politics of Civil-Military Relations (Cambridge, MA, 1957)

The Common Defense: Strategic Programs in National Politics (New York, 1961)

Political Order in Changing Societies (New Haven, 1968)

American Politics: The Promise of Disharmony (Cambridge, MA, 1981)

Library of Congress Cataloging-in-Publication Data

Huntington, Samuel P.
The third wave : democratization in the late twentieth century/ Samuel P. Huntington.
p.   cm. — (The Julian J. Rothbaum distinguished lecture series ; v. 4)
Includes bibliographical references and index.
1. Democracy—History—20th century.   2. Authoritarianism—History—20th century.   3. World politics—1975–1985.   4. World politics—1985–1995.   I. Title.   II. Series.
JC421.H86   1991   90-50690
321.8'09'04—dc20   CIP
ISBN: 0-8061-2346-X (cloth)
ISBN: 0-8061-2516-0 (paper)

The Third Wave: Democratization in the Late Twentieth Century is Volume 4 in the Julian J. Rothbaum Distinguished Lecture Series.

This book was written under the auspices of the Harvard University Center for International Affairs and its John M. Olin Institute for Strategic Studies.

The paper in this book meets the guidelines for permanence and durability of the Committee on Production Guidelines for Book Longevity of the Council on Library Resources, Inc. ∞

4   5   6   7   8   9   10   11

THE THIRD WAVE

Democratization in
the Late Twentieth Century

By

SAMUEL P. HUNTINGTON

UNIVERSITY OF OKLAHOMA PRESS : NORMAN AND LONDON

OTHER BOOKS BY SAMUEL P. HUNTINGTON

*The Soldier and the State: The Theory and Politics of
Civil-Military Relations* (Cambridge, MA, 1957)

*The Common Defense: Strategic Programs in
National Politics* (New York, 1961)

Political Order in Changing Societies (New Haven, 1968)

American Politics: The Promise of Disharmony (Cambridge, MA, 1981)

Library of Congress Cataloging-in-Publication Data

Huntington, Samuel P.
    The third wave : democratization in the late twentieth century/
Samuel P. Huntington.
        p.   cm. — (The Julian J. Rothbaum distinguished lecture series ;
v. 4)
    Includes bibliographical references and index.
    1. Democracy—History—20th century.   2. Authoritarianism—His-
tory—20th century.   3. World politics—1975–1985. 4. World politics—
1985–1995.   I. Title.   II. Series.
JC421.H86   1991   90-50690
321.8′09′04—dc20   CIP
    ISBN: 0-8061-2346-X (cloth)
    ISBN: 0-8061-2516-0 (paper)

The Third Wave: Democratization in the Late Twentieth Century is Volume 4 in the Julian J. Rothbaum Distinguished Lecture Series.

This book was written under the auspices of the Harvard University Center for International Affairs and its John M. Olin Institute for Strategic Studies.

The paper in this book meets the guidelines for permanence and durability of the Committee on Production Guidelines for Book Longevity of the Council on Library Resources, Inc. ∞

4   5   6   7   8   9   10   11

THE THIRD WAVE

Democratization in
the Late Twentieth Century

By

SAMUEL P. HUNTINGTON

UNIVERSITY OF OKLAHOMA PRESS : NORMAN AND LONDON

OTHER BOOKS BY SAMUEL P. HUNTINGTON

The Soldier and the State: The Theory and Politics of
Civil-Military Relations (Cambridge, MA, 1957)

The Common Defense: Strategic Programs in
National Politics (New York, 1961)

Political Order in Changing Societies (New Haven, 1968)

American Politics: The Promise of Disharmony (Cambridge, MA, 1981)

Library of Congress Cataloging-in-Publication Data

Huntington, Samuel P.
   The third wave : democratization in the late twentieth century/
Samuel P. Huntington.
       p.   cm. —(The Julian J. Rothbaum distinguished lecture series ;
   v. 4)
   Includes bibliographical references and index.
   1. Democracy—History—20th century.   2. Authoritarianism—History—20th century.   3. World politics—1975–1985.   4. World politics—1985–1995.   I. Title.   II. Series.
JC421.H86   1991   90-50690
321.8'09'04—dc20   CIP
   ISBN: 0-8061-2346-X (cloth)
   ISBN: 0-8061-2516-0 (paper)

The Third Wave: Democratization in the Late Twentieth Century is Volume 4 in the Julian J. Rothbaum Distinguished Lecture Series.

This book was written under the auspices of the Harvard University Center for International Affairs and its John M. Olin Institute for Strategic Studies.

The paper in this book meets the guidelines for permanence and durability of the Committee on Production Guidelines for Book Longevity of the Council on Library Resources, Inc. ∞

4   5   6   7   8   9   10   11

To the memory of Warren and Anita

FIGURES

TABLES

CONTENTS

versity of Oklahoma for two terms and as a State Regent for Higher Education. In 1974 he was awarded the University's highest honor, the Distinguished Service Citation, and in 1986 he was inducted into the Oklahoma Hall of Fame.

The Rothbaum Lecture Series is devoted to the themes of representative government, democracy and education, and citizen participation in public affairs, values to which Julian J. Rothbaum has been committed throughout his life. His lifelong dedication to the University of Oklahoma, the state, and his country is a tribute to the ideals to which the Rothbaum Lecture Series is dedicated. The books in the series make an enduring contribution to an understanding of American democracy.

CARL B. ALBERT

Forty-sixth Speaker
of the
United States House of Representatives

FOREWORD

AMONG THE MANY GOOD THINGS that have happened to me in my life, there is none in which I take more pride than the establishment of the Carl Albert Congressional Research and Studies Center at the University of Oklahoma, and none in which I take more satisfaction than the Center's presentation of the Julian J. Rothbaum Distinguished Lecture Series. The series is a perpetually endowed program of the University of Oklahoma, created in honor of Julian J. Rothbaum by his wife, Irene, and son, Joel Jankowsky.

Julian J. Rothbaum, my close friend since our childhood days in southeastern Oklahoma, has long been a leader in Oklahoma civic affairs. He has served as a Regent of the Uni-

PREFACE

THIS BOOK IS ABOUT an important—perhaps the most important—global political development of the late twentieth century: the transition of some thirty countries from nondemocratic to democratic political systems. It is an effort to explain
why, how, and with what immediate consequences this wave
of democratization occurred between 1974 and 1990.

This book partakes of both theory and history, but it is neither a work of theory nor a work of history. It falls somewhere
in between; it is primarily explanatory. A good theory is pre-
cise, austere, elegant, and highlights the relations among a
few conceptual variables. Inevitably, no theory can explain
fully a single event or group of events. An explanation, in
contrast, is inevitably complex, dense, messy, and intellectually unsatisfying. It succeeds not by being austere but by being comprehensive. A good history describes chronologically
and analyzes convincingly a sequence of events and shows
why one event led to another. This study does not do that
either. It does not spell out the general course of democratization in the 1970s and 1980s, nor does it describe the democratizations of individual countries. It instead attempts to explain and to analyze a particular group of regime transitions
that occurred in a limited period of time. In social science jar-
gon, this study is neither nomothetic nor idiographic. Both
theorists and historians are hence likely to find it unsatisfy-

ing. It does not provide the generalizations the former trea-
sure or the depth the latter prefer.

In its approach this study thus differs significantly from
several of my other books. In these other works I tried to
develop generalizations or theories about the relations between key variables, such as political power and military
professionalism, political participation and political institutionalization, and political ideals and political behavior. The
propositions about these relationships were generally set
forth as timeless truths. In this book, however, the generalizations are limited to a discrete class of events of the 1970s
and 1980s. One key point in the book, indeed, is that the
democratizations of the third wave differed from those of earlier waves. In writing this book I was at times tempted to
propound timeless truths, such as "Replacements are more
violent than transformations." I would then have to remind
myself that my evidence came from the limited historical
cases I had studied and that I was writing an explanatory,
not a theoretical, work. So I had to abjure the timeless present tense and instead write in the past tense: "Replacements
were more violent than transformations." With a very few
exceptions, I have done this. In some cases, the universality
of the proposition seemed so clear I could not resist the temptation to state it in more timeless terms. In addition, however,
almost no proposition even applied to all third wave cases.
Hence the reader will find words like "tended to be," "generally," "almost always," and other such qualifiers scattered
throughout the text. In its final form, the above-cited proposition should read, "Replacements usually were more violent
than transformations."

This book was written in 1989 and 1990, as the class of
events with which it was concerned was still unfolding. The
book thus suffers all the problems of contemporaneity and
must be viewed as a preliminary assessment and explanation
of these regime transitions. The book draws on the works of
historians, political scientists, and other scholars who have

written detailed monographs on particular events. It also re-
lies extensively on journalistic reports of these events. When
the third wave of democratization comes to an end, a fuller,
more satisfactory explanation of this phenomenon will be
possible.

My previous study of political change, *Political Order in
Changing Societies*, focused on the problem of political stability. I wrote that book because I thought political order was
a good thing. My purpose was to develop a general social
science theory of why, how, and under what circumstances
order could and could not be achieved. The current book focuses on democratization. I have written it because I believe
that democracy is good in itself and that, as I argue in chapter
1, it has positive consequences for individual freedom, domestic stability, international peace, and the United States of
America. As in *Political Order*, I have attempted to keep my
analysis as detached as possible from my values; at least that
is the case in 95 percent of this book. It did seem to me, however, that it might be useful occasionally to spell out explicitly
the implications of my analysis for people wishing to democratize their societies. Consequently, at five places in the book
I have abandoned the role of social scientist, assumed that of
political consultant, and set forth some "Guidelines for Democratizers." If that makes me seem like an aspiring democratic Machiavelli, so be it.

The immediate stimulus to writing this book was the invitation to deliver the Julian J. Rothbaum Lectures at the University of Oklahoma in November 1989. In those lectures I set
forth the principal themes of the book without, of course, all
the empirical evidence to buttress those themes. The bulk of
the manuscript was written in late 1989 and in 1990, and I
have made no attempt to include in the analysis any events
that occurred after 1990. I am greatly indebted to the Carl Albert Congressional Research and Studies Center at the University of Oklahoma and to its director, Dr. Ronald M. Peters,
Jr., for inviting me to deliver these lectures. My wife, Nancy,

and I also want to record how much we appreciate the unfailing courtesy and hospitality we received at the University of Oklahoma from Dr. Peters, Julian and Irene Rothbaum, Joel Jankowsky, and Speaker and Mrs. Carl Albert.

While the lecture invitation precipitated the writing of this book, the material in it has been germinating in my mind for some time. In a few places in the manuscript, I have drawn on two previous articles: "Will More Countries Become Democratic?" (*Political Science Quarterly* 99, Summer 1984, pp. 191–218) and "The Modest Meaning of Democracy," in *Democracy in the Americas: Stopping the Pendulum*, edited by Robert A. Pastor (New York: Holmes and Meier, 1989, pp. 11–28). Between 1987 and 1990 a John M. Olin Fellowship in Democracy and Development made it possible for me to devote much more time and effort than would otherwise have been the case to research on the subject of this book.

Many people have also contributed both consciously and unwittingly to this manuscript. Since 1983 I have taught a course on modern democracy in the core curriculum at Harvard that has focused on the problems of democratic transitions. Both students and teaching assistants alike will recognize that much of the material in this book has come out of that course; my thinking on this subject is much better than it would have been as a result of their comments and criticisms. Mary Kiraly, Young Jo Lee, Kevin Marchioro, and Adam Posen provided indispensable help in researching the material in this book and in making order out of my files on this subject. Jeffrey Cimbalo not only performed these tasks but in addition carefully reviewed the accuracy of text and footnotes in the final stages of manuscript preparation. Juliet Blackett and Amy Englehardt applied their very considerable word-processing skills to this manuscript, efficiently, rapidly, and accurately producing many drafts and seemingly endless revisions of drafts. The manuscript was read entirely or in part by several colleagues. Houchang Chehabi, Edwin Corr, Jorge Dominguez, Frances Hagopian, Eric Nordlinger, and

Tony Smith provided thoughtful, quite critical, and very constructive written comments. The members of the Harvard comparative politics discussion group helped with a lively discussion of the first half of the manuscript. Dankwart A. Rustow constructively identified four omissions from figure 1.1 in the hard-cover edition which have been corrected in this edition.

I am very grateful to all these people for their interest in my work and for the major contributions they made to improving the quality of my effort. In the end, however, I remain responsible for the argument, the evidence, and the errors of this study.

SAMUEL P. HUNTINGTON

Cambridge, Massachusetts

THE THIRD WAVE

CHAPTER 1

WHAT?

THE START OF THE THIRD WAVE

THE THIRD WAVE OF DEMOCRATIZATION in the modern world began, implausibly and unwittingly, at twenty-five minutes after midnight, Thursday, April 25, 1974, in Lisbon, Portugal, when a radio station played the song "Grandola Vila Morena." That broadcast was the go-ahead signal for the military units in and around Lisbon to carry out the plans for a coup d'etat that had been carefully drawn up by the young officers leading the Movimento das Forcas Armadas (MFA). The coup was carried out efficiently and successfully, with only minor resistance from the security police. Military units occupied key ministries, broadcasting stations, the post office, airports, and telephone exchanges. By late morning, crowds were flooding the streets, cheering the soldiers, and placing carnations in the barrels of their rifles. By late afternoon the deposed dictator, Marcello Caetano, had surrendered to the new military leaders of Portugal. The next day he flew into exile. So died the dictatorship that had been born in a similar military coup in 1926 and led for over thirty-five years by an austere civilian, António Salazar, working in close collaboration with Portugal's soldiers.[1]

The April 25 coup was an implausible beginning of a worldwide movement to democracy because coups d'etat more frequently overthrow democratic regimes than introduce them. It was an unwitting beginning because the installation of democracy, much less the triggering of a global democratic movement, was far from the minds of leaders of the coup. The death of the dictatorship did not ensure the birth of democracy. It did, however, unleash a huge array of popular, social, and political forces that had been effectively suppressed during the dictatorship. For eighteen months after the April coup, Portugal was in turmoil. The MFA officers split into competing conservative, moderate, and Marxist factions. The political parties covered an equally wide spectrum, from the hard-line Communist party on the left to fascist groups on the right. Six provisional governments succeeded each other, each exercising less authority than its predecessor. Coups and countercoups were attempted. Workers and peasants struck, demonstrated, and seized factories, farms, and media. Moderate parties won the national elections on the anniversary of the coup in 1975, but by the fall of that year civil war appeared possible between the conservative north and the radical south.

The revolutionary upheaval in Portugal seemed, in many respects, to be a replay of 1917 Russia, with Caetano as Nicholas II, the April coup as the February Revolution, the dominant groups in the MFA as the Bolsheviks, similar widespread economic turmoil and popular upheaval, and even the equivalent of the Kornilov conspiracy in General Spinola's unsuccessful right-wing coup attempt in March 1975. The resemblance was not lost on acute observers. In September 1974 Mário Soares, foreign minister of the provisional government and leader of the Portuguese Socialist party, met with Secretary of State Henry Kissinger in Washington. Kissinger berated Soares and other moderates for not acting more decisively to head off a Marxist-Leninist dictatorship.

"You are a Kerensky. . . . I believe your sincerity, but you are naive," Kissinger told Soares.

"I certainly don't want to be a Kerensky," replied Soares.

"Neither did Kerensky," shot back Kissinger.[2]

Portugal, however, turned out to be different from Russia. The Kerenskys won; democracy triumphed. Soares went on to become prime minister and later president. And the Lenin of the Portuguese revolution, the person who at the crucial moment deployed disciplined force to produce the political result he desired, was a taciturn prodemocracy colonel named António Ramalho Eanes who on November 25, 1975, crushed the radical leftist elements in the armed forces and ensured the future of democracy in Portugal.

The movement toward democracy in Portugal in 1974 and 1975 was dramatic but not unique. Less obvious democratic stirrings were occurring elsewhere. In 1973 in Brazil leaders of the outgoing government of Gen. Emílio Médici developed plans for political *distensão* or "decompression" and in 1974 Gen. Ernesto Geisel committed his new government to starting the process of political opening. In Spain Prime Minister Carlos Arias cautiously moved the Franco dictatorship in a liberalizing direction while the country awaited the death of the dictator. In Greece tensions were building up in the colonels' regime that led to its downfall in mid-1974 and, later that year, to the first democratically elected government in the new wave of transitions. During the following fifteen years this democratic wave became global in scope; about thirty countries shifted from authoritarianism to democracy, and at least a score of other countries were affected by the democratic wave.

THE MEANING OF DEMOCRACY

The transitions to democracy between 1974 and 1990 are the subject of this book. The first step in dealing with this subject is to clarify the meaning of democracy and democratization as they are used in this book.

The concept of democracy as a form of government goes back to the Greek philosophers. Its modern usage, however, dates from the revolutionary upheavals in Western society at the end of the eighteenth century. In the mid-twentieth century three general approaches emerged in the debates over the meaning of democracy. As a form of government, democracy has been defined in terms of sources of authority for government, purposes served by government, and procedures for constituting government.

Serious problems of ambiguity and imprecision arise when democracy is defined in terms of either source of authority or purposes, and a procedural definition is used in this study.[3] In other governmental systems people become leaders by reason of birth, lot, wealth, violence, cooptation, learning, appointment, or examination. The central procedure of democracy is the selection of leaders through competitive elections by the people they govern. The most important modern formulation of this concept of democracy was by Joseph Schumpeter in 1942. In his pathbreaking study, *Capitalism, Socialism, and Democracy*, Schumpeter spelled out the deficiencies of what he termed the "classical theory of democracy," which defined democracy in terms of "the will of the people" (source) and "the common good" (purpose). Effectively demolishing these approaches to the subject, Schumpeter advanced what he labeled "another theory of democracy." The "democratic method," he said, "is that institutional arrangement for arriving at political decisions in which individuals acquire the power to decide by means of a competitive struggle for the people's vote."[4]

For some while after World War II a debate went on between those determined, in the classical vein, to define democracy by source or purpose, and the growing number of theorists adhering to a procedural concept of democracy in the Schumpeterian mode. By the 1970s the debate was over, and Schumpeter had won. Theorists increasingly drew distinctions between rationalistic, utopian, idealistic definitions of democracy, on the one hand, and empirical, descriptive, institutional, and procedural definitions, on the other, and concluded that only the latter type of definition provided the analytical precision and empirical referents that make the concept a useful one. Sweeping discussions of democracy in terms of normative theory sharply declined, at least in American scholarly discussions, and were replaced by efforts to understand the nature of democratic institutions, how they function, and the reasons why they develop and collapse. The prevailing effort was to make democracy less of a "hurrah" word and more of a commonsense word.[5]

Following in the Schumpeterian tradition, this study defines a twentieth-century political system as democratic to the extent that its most powerful collective decision makers are selected through fair, honest, and periodic elections in which candidates freely compete for votes and in which virtually all the adult population is eligible to vote. So defined, democracy involves the two dimensions—contestation and participation—that Robert Dahl saw as critical to his realistic democracy or polyarchy. It also implies the existence of those civil and political freedoms to speak, publish, assemble, and organize that are necessary to political debate and the conduct of electoral campaigns.

This procedural definition of democracy provides a number of bench-marks—grouped largely along Dahl's two dimensions—that make it possible to judge to what extent political systems are democratic, to compare systems, and to analyze whether systems are becoming more or less democratic. To the extent, for instance, that a political system denies voting participation to part of its society—as the South African system did to the 70 percent of its population that was black, as Switzerland did to the 50 percent of its population that was female, or as the United States did to the 10 percent of its population that were southern blacks—it is undemocratic. Similarly, a system is undemocratic to the extent that no opposition is permitted in elections, or that the opposition is curbed or harassed in what it can do, or that opposition newspapers are censored or closed down, or that votes are manipulated or miscounted. In any society, the sustained failure of the major opposition political party to win office necessarily raises questions concerning the degree of competition permitted by the system. In the late 1980s, the free-and-fair-elections criterion of democracy became more useful by the increasing observation of elections by international groups. By 1990 the point had been reached where the first election in a democratizing country would only be generally accepted as legitimate if it was observed by one or more reasonably competent and detached teams of international observers, and if the observers certified the election as meeting minimal standards of honesty and fairness.

The procedural approach to democracy accords with the commonsense uses of the term. We all know that military coups, censorship, rigged elections, coercion and harassment of the opposition, jailing of political opponents, and prohibition of political meetings are incompatible with democracy. We all know also that informed political observers can apply the procedural conditions of democracy to existing world political systems and rather easily come up with a list of those countries that are clearly democratic, those that are clearly not, and those that fall somewhere in between, and that with minor exceptions different observers will compose identical lists. We all know also that we can make and do make judgments as to how governments change over time and that no one would dispute the proposition that Argentina, Brazil, and Uruguay were more democratic in 1986 than they were in 1976. Political regimes will never fit perfectly into intellectually defined boxes, and any system of classification has to accept the existence of ambiguous, borderline, and mixed cases. Historically, the Kuomintang (KMT) system on Taiwan, for instance, combined some elements of authoritarianism, democracy, and totalitarianism. In addition, governments that had democratic origins may end democracy by abolishing or severely limiting democratic procedures, as in Korea and Turkey in the late 1950s and in the Philippines in

1972. Yet with all its problems, the classification of regimes in terms of their degree of procedural democracy remains a relatively simple task.

If popular election of the top decision makers is the essence of democracy, then the critical point in the process of democratization is the replacement of a government that was not chosen this way by one that is selected in a free, open, and fair election. The overall process of democratization before and after that election, however, is usually complex and prolonged. It involves bringing about the end of the nondemocratic regime, the inauguration of the democratic regime, and then the consolidation of the democratic system. Liberalization, in contrast, is the partial opening of an authoritarian system short of choosing governmental leaders through freely competitive elections. Liberalizing authoritarian regimes may release political prisoners, open up some issues for public debate, loosen censorship, sponsor elections for offices that have little power, permit some renewal of civil society, and take other steps in a democratic direction, without submitting top decision makers to the electoral test. Liberalization may or may not lead to full-scale democratization.

Several additional points need to be made in defining democracy.

First, the definition of democracy in terms of elections is a minimal definition. To some people democracy has or should have much more sweeping and idealistic connotations. To them, "true democracy" means *liberté, egalité, fraternité*, effective citizen control over policy, responsible government, honesty and openness in politics, informed and rational deliberation, equal participation and power, and various other civic virtues. These are, for the most part, good things and people can, if they wish, define democracy in these terms. Doing so, however, raises all the problems that come up with the definitions of democracy by source or by purpose. Fuzzy norms do not yield useful analysis. Elections, open, free, and fair, are the essence of democracy, the inescapable sine qua non.

Governments produced by elections may be inefficient, corrupt, shortsighted, irresponsible, dominated by special interests, and incapable of adopting policies demanded by the public good. These qualities may make such governments undesirable but they do not make them undemocratic. Democracy is one public virtue, not the only one, and the relation of democracy to other public virtues and vices can only be understood if democracy is clearly distinguished from other characteristics of political systems.

Second, conceivably a society could choose its political leaders through democratic means, but these political leaders might not exercise real power. They may be simply the fronts or puppets of some other group. To the extent that the most powerful collective decision makers are not chosen through elections, the political system is not democratic. Implicit in the concept of democracy, however, are limitations on power. In democracies elected decision makers do not exercise total power. They share power with other groups in society. If those democratically elected decision makers become, however, simply a facade for the exercise of much greater power by a nondemocratically chosen group, then clearly that political system is not democratic. Legitimate questions may be raised, for instance, as to whether the elected governments in Japan in the late 1920s and in Guatemala in the late 1980s were sufficiently dominated by their military as not to be truly democratic. It is also, however, easy for critics of a government, whether from the left or the right, to allege that the elected officials are simply the "tools" of some other group or that they exercise their authority only on the sufferance of and within severe constraints set by some other group. Such allegations are often made, and they may be true. But they should not be judged to be true until they have been demonstrated to be true. That may be difficult, but it is not impossible.

A third issue concerns the fragility or stability of a democratic political system. One could incorporate into a definition of democracy a concept of stability or institutionalization. This typically refers to the degree to which the political system may be expected to remain in existence. Stability is a central dimension in the analysis of any political system. A political system may, however, be more or less democratic and more or less stable. Systems that may be appropriately classified as equally democratic may differ greatly in their stability. Thus, in its survey of freedom in the world published at the beginning of 1984, Freedom House quite reasonably classified both New Zealand and Nigeria as "free." When that judgment was made, freedom may well have been no less in the latter than it was in the former. It was, however, much less stable: a military coup on New Year's Day 1984 effectively ended Nigerian democracy. Democratic and nondemocratic systems may be created but they may or may not endure. The stability of a system differs from the nature of the system.[6]

Fourth, there is the issue of whether to treat democracy and nondemocracy as a dichotomous or continuous variable. Many analysts have preferred the latter approach and have developed measures of democracy combining indicators of fairness of elections, restrictions on political parties, freedom of the press, and other criteria. This approach is useful for some purposes, such as identifying variations in the degree of democracy among countries (United States, Sweden, France, Japan) that would normally be considered to be democratic or variations in the degree of authoritarianism in nondemocratic countries. It does, however, pose many problems, such as the weighting of indicators. A dichotomous approach better serves the purpose of this study because our concern is with the transition from a nondemocratic regime to a democratic one. Democracy has, moreover, been defined in this study by a single, relatively clear and widely accepted criterion. Even when analysts use somewhat different measures, their judgments as to which political systems are democratic and which are not correlate to an extremely high

degree.[7] This study will, consequently, treat democracy as a
dichotomous variable, recognizing that there will be some be-
twixt-and-between cases (e.g., Greece, 1915–36; Thailand,
1980–; Senegal, 1974–) that may be appropriately classified
"semidemocracies."

Fifth, nondemocratic regimes do not have electoral competition and widespread voting participation. Apart from these
shared negative characteristics they have little else in common. The category includes absolute monarchies, bureaucratic empires, oligarchies, aristocracies, constitutional regimes with limited suffrage, personal despotisms, fascist and
communist regimes, military dictatorships, and other types
of governance. Some of these forms were more prevalent in
previous eras; some are relatively modern. In particular, totalitarian regimes emerged in the twentieth century after the
beginning of democratization and attempt the mass mobilization of their citizenry to serve the purposes of the regime.
Social scientists have drawn an appropriate and important
distinction between these regimes and traditional nondemocratic authoritarian systems. The former are characterized by:
a single party, usually led by one man; a pervasive and powerful secret police; a highly developed ideology setting forth
the ideal society, which the totalitarian movement is committed to realizing; and government penetration and control
of mass communications and all or most social and economic
organizations. A traditional authoritarian system, on the
other hand, is characterized by a single leader or small group
of leaders, no party or a weak party, no mass mobilization,
possibly a "mentality" but no ideology , limited government,
"limited, not responsible, political pluralism," and no effort
to remake society and human nature.[8] This distinction between totalitarianism and authoritarianism is crucial to understanding twentieth-century politics. In order to avoid the
semantic awkwardness in repeated use of the term "nondemocratic," however, this study uses the term "authori-

tarian" to refer to all nondemocratic systems. Specific forms of nondemocratic or authoritarian regimes are referred to as one-party systems, totalitarian systems, personal dictatorships, military regimes, and the like.

THE WAVES OF DEMOCRATIZATION

Political systems with democratic characteristics are not limited to modern times. In many areas of the world tribal chiefs were elected for centuries and in some places democratic political institutions long existed at the village level. In addition, the concept of democracy was, of course, familiar to the ancient world. The democracy of the Greeks and the Romans, however, excluded women, slaves, and often other categories of people, such as resident aliens, from participation in political life. The extent to which ruling bodies were, in practice, responsible to even this restricted public was also often limited.

Modern democracy is not simply democracy of the village, the tribe, or the city-state; it is democracy of the nation-state and its emergence is associated with the development of the nation-state. The initial push toward democracy in the West occurred in the first half of the seventeenth century. Democratic ideas and democratic movements were an important, although not a central, feature of the English Revolution. The Fundamental Orders of Connecticut, adopted by the citizens of Hartford and neighboring towns on January 14, 1638, were the "first written constitution of modern democracy."[9] By and large, however, the Puritan upheavals did not leave a legacy of democratic institutions in either England or America. For over a century after 1660 government in both places tended to become even more closed and less broadly representative of the people than it had been earlier. In a variety of ways, an aristocratic and oligarchic resurgence occurred. In 1750 no democratic institutions at the national level existed in the Western world. In 1900 such institutions existed

Category	Number of Countries	First Wave	First Reverse	Second Wave	Second Reverse	Third Wave	Third Reverse?
L	3						
K	12						
J	6						
I	1						
H	9						
G	10						
F	3						
E	4						
D	5						
C	10						
B	1						
A	10						
Democratic Countries		33 (Max)	11 (Min)	52 (Max)	30 (Min)	65 (Max)	61 (Min)
Net Change		+33	-22	+41	-22	+35	-4
Total Countries = 74							

■ Democratic or semidemocratic phases
▨ Nondemocratic phases of previously democratic countries

Figure 1.1. Democratization Waves and Reverse Waves

in many countries. By the late twentieth century many more countries possessed democratic institutions. These institutions emerged in waves of democratization (see Figure 1.1). A wave of democratization is a group of transitions from nondemocratic to democratic regimes that occur within a specified period of time and that significantly outnumber transitions in the opposite direction during that period of time. A wave also usually involves liberalization or partial democratization in political systems that do not become fully democratic. Three waves of democratization have occurred in the modern world.[10] Each wave affected a relatively small number of countries, and during each wave some regime transitions occurred in a nondemocratic direction. In addition, not all transitions to democracy occurred during democratic waves. History is messy and political changes do not sort themselves into neat historical boxes. History is also not unidirectional. Each of the first two waves of democratization was followed by a reverse wave in which some but not all of

---

Note: Classification of countries in Figure 1.1:
(A) Australia, Canada, Finland, Iceland, Ireland, New Zealand, Sweden, Switzerland, United Kingdom, United States
(B) Chile
(C) Austria, Belgium, Colombia, Denmark, France, West Germany, Italy, Japan, Netherlands, Norway
(D) Argentina, Czechoslovakia, Greece, Hungary, Uruguay
(E) East Germany, Poland, Portugal, Spain
(F) Estonia, Latvia, Lithuania
(G) Botswana, Costa Rica, Gambia, Israel, Jamaica, Malaysia, Malta, Sri Lanka, Trinidad and Tobago, Venezuela
(H) Bolivia, Brazil, Ecuador, India, South Korea, Pakistan, Peru, Philippines, Turkey
(I) Nigeria
(J) Burma, Fiji, Ghana, Guyana, Indonesia, Lebanon
(K) Bulgaria, Dominican Republic, El Salvador, Guatemala, Honduras, Mongolia, Namibia, Nicaragua, Panama, Papua New Guinea, Romania, Senegal
(L) Haiti, Sudan, Suriname

the countries that had previously made the transition to democracy reverted to nondemocratic rule. It is often arbitrary to attempt to specify precisely when a regime transition occurs. It is also arbitrary to attempt to specify precisely the dates of democratization waves and reverse waves. It is, nonetheless, often useful to be arbitrary, and the dates of these waves of regime changes are more or less as follows:

First, long wave of democratization	1828–1926
First reverse wave	1922–42
Second, short wave of democratization	1943–62
Second reverse wave	1958–75
Third wave of democratization	1974–

The first wave of democratization. The first wave had its roots in the American and French revolutions. The actual emergence of national democratic institutions, however, is a nineteenth-century phenomenon. In most countries during that century democratic institutions developed gradually and it is, hence, difficult as well as arbitrary to specify a particular date after which a political system could be considered democratic. Jonathan Sunshine, however, sets forth two reasonable major criteria for when nineteenth-century political systems achieved minimal democratic qualifications in the context of that century: (1) 50 percent of adult males are eligible to vote; and (2) a responsible executive who either must maintain majority support in an elected parliament or is chosen in periodic popular elections. Adopting these criteria and applying them rather loosely, one can say that the United States began the first wave of democratization roughly about 1828.[11] The abolition of property qualifications in the older states and the admission of new states with universal manhood suffrage boosted to well over 50 percent the proportion of white males actually voting in the 1828 presidential election. In the following decades other countries gradually expanded the suffrage, reduced plural voting, introduced the secret ballot, and established the responsibility of prime ministers and cabinets to parliaments. Switzerland, the overseas English dominions, France, Great Britain, and several smaller European countries made the transition to democracy before the turn of the century. Shortly before World War I, Italy and Argentina introduced more or less democratic regimes. Following that war the newly independent Ireland and Iceland were democratic and a mass movement toward democracy occurred in the successor states to the Romanov, Hapsburg, and Hohenzollern empires. In the very early 1930s, after the first wave had effectively ended, Spain and Chile moved into the democratic column. All in all, in the course of a hundred years over thirty countries established at least minimal national democratic institutions. In the 1830s Tocqueville predicted this trend as it began. In 1920 James Bryce reviewed its history and speculated as to whether the "trend toward democracy now widely visible, is a natural trend, due to a general law of social progress." [12]

The first reverse wave. Even as Bryce speculated about its future, however, the democracy trend was tapering off and reversing. The dominant political development of the 1920s and the 1930s was the shift away from democracy and either the return to traditional forms of authoritarian rule or the introduction of new mass-based, more brutal and pervasive forms of totalitarianism. The reversals occurred largely in those countries that had adopted democratic forms just before or after World War I, where not only democracy was new but also, in many cases, the nation was new. Only one country, Greece, of the dozen countries that introduced democratic institutions before 1910 suffered a reversal after 1920. Only four of the seventeen countries that adopted democratic institutions between 1910 and 1931 maintained them throughout the 1920s and 1930s.

The first reverse wave began in 1922 with the March on Rome and Mussolini's easy disposal of Italy's fragile and rather corrupt democracy. In little over a decade fledgling democratic institutions in Lithuania, Poland, Latvia, and Estonia were overthrown by military coups. Countries such as Yugoslavia and Bulgaria that had never known real democracy were subjected to new forms of harsher dictatorship. The conquest of power by Hitler in 1933 ended German democracy, ensured the end of Austrian democracy the following year, and eventually of course produced the end of Czech democracy in 1938. Greek democracy, which had been unsettled by the National Schism in 1915, was finally buried in 1936. Portugal succumbed to a military coup in 1926 that led to the long Salazar dictatorship. Military takeovers occurred in Brazil and Argentina in 1930. Uruguay reverted to authoritarianism in 1933. A military coup in 1936 led to civil war and the death of the Spanish republic in 1939. The new and limited democracy introduced in Japan in the 1920s was supplanted by military rule in the early 1930s.

These regime changes reflected the rise of communist, fascist, and militaristic ideologies. In France, Britain, and other countries where democratic institutions remained in place, antidemocratic movements gained strength from the alienation of the 1920s and the depression of the 1930s. The war that had been fought to make the world safe for democracy had instead unleashed movements of both the Right and the Left that were intent on destroying it.

The second wave of democratization. Starting in World War II a second, short wave of democratization occurred. Allied occupation promoted inauguration of democratic institutions in West Germany, Italy, Austria, Japan, and Korea, while Soviet pressure snuffed out incipient democracy in Czechoslovakia and Hungary. In the late 1940s and early 1950s Turkey and Greece moved toward democracy. In Latin America Uruguay returned to democracy during the war and Brazil and Costa Rica shifted to democracy in the late 1940s. In four other Latin American countries—Argentina, Colombia, Peru, and Venezuela—elections in 1945 and 1946 ushered in popularly chosen governments. In all four countries, however, democratic practices did not last and dictatorships were in place by the early 1950s. In the later 1950s Argentina and Peru moved back toward limited democracy which was, however, highly unstable as a result of the conflict between the military and the populist Aprista and Peronista movements. Also in the late 1950s, in contrast, the elites in both Colombia and Venezuela negotiated arrangements to end the military dictatorships in those countries and to introduce democratic institutions that were to last.

Meanwhile, the beginning of the end of Western colonial rule produced a number of new states. In many no real effort was made to introduce democratic institutions. In some democracy was tenuous: in Pakistan, for instance, democratic institutions never really took hold and were formally abrogated in 1958. Malaysia became independent in 1957 and maintained its "quasi-democracy" except for a brief period, 1969–71, of emergency rule. Indonesia had a confused form of parliamentary democracy from 1950 to 1957. In a few new states—India, Sri Lanka, the Philippines, Israel—democratic institutions were sustained for a decade or more, and in 1960 Africa's largest state, Nigeria, began life as a democracy.

The second reverse wave. By the early 1960s the second wave of democratization had exhausted itself. By the late 1950s political development and regime transitions were taking on a heavily authoritarian cast.[13] The change was most dramatic in Latin America. The shift toward authoritarianism began in Peru in 1962 when the military intervened to alter the results of an election. The following year a civilian acceptable to the military was elected president, but he was displaced by a military coup in 1968. In 1964 military coups overthrew civilian governments in Brazil and Bolivia. Argentina followed suit in 1966 and Ecuador in 1972. In 1973 military regimes took over in Uruguay and Chile. The military governments of Brazil, Argentina, and, more debatably, Chile and Uruguay were examples, according to one theory, of a new type of political system, "bureaucratic authoritarianism."[14]

In Asia the military imposed a martial law regime in Paki-

stan in 1958. In the late 1950s Syngman Rhee began to undermine democratic procedures in Korea, and the democratic
regime that succeeded him in 1960 was overthrown by a military coup in 1961. This new "semiauthoritarian" regime was
legitimated by elections in 1963 but turned into a full-scale
highly authoritarian system in 1973. In 1957 Sukarno replaced
parliamentary democracy with guided democracy in Indonesia, and in 1965 the Indonesian military ended guided democracy and took over the government of their country. In 1972
President Ferdinand Marcos instituted a martial law regime
in the Philippines, and in 1975 Indira Gandhi suspended
democratic practices and declared emergency rule in India.
On Taiwan the nondemocratic KMT regime had tolerated liberal dissenters in the 1950s, but these were suppresed in the
"dark age" of the 1960s and "any sort of political discourse"
was silenced.[15]

In the Mediterranean area, Greek democracy went down
before a "royal" coup d'etat in 1965 and a military coup in
1967. The Turkish military overthrew the civilian government
of that country in 1960, returned authority to an elected government in 1961, intervened again in a "half coup" in 1971,
allowed a return to an elected government in 1973, and then
carried out a full-scale military takeover in 1980.

During the 1960s several non-African British colonies became independent and instituted democratic regimes that
lasted for significant periods of time. These included Jamaica
and Trinidad and Tobago in 1962, Malta in 1964, Barbados in
1966, and Mauritius in 1968. The vast bulk of the new countries that became independent in the 1960s, however, were
in Africa. The most important of these countries, Nigeria,
started out as a democracy but succumbed to a military coup
in 1966. The only African country consistently to maintain
democratic practices was Botswana. Thirty-three other African countries that became independent between 1956 and
1970 became authoritarian with independence or very shortly
after independence. The decolonization of Africa led to the

largest multiplication of independent authoritarian governments in history.

The global swing away from democracy in the 1960s and
early 1970s was impressive. In 1962, by one count, thirteen
governments in the world were the product of coups d'etat;
by 1975, thirty-eight were. By another estimate one-third of
32 working democracies in the world in 1958 had become
authoritarian by the mid-1970s.[16] In 1960 nine of ten South
American countries of Iberian heritage had democratically
elected governments; by 1973, only two, Venezuela and Colombia, did. This wave of transitions away from democracy
was even more striking because it involved several countries,
such as Chile, Uruguay ("the Switzerland of South America"), India, and the Philippines, that had sustained democratic regimes for a quarter century or more. These regime
transitions not only stimulated the theory of bureaucratic-
authoritarianism to explain the Latin American changes.
They also produced a much broader pessimism about the
applicability of democracy in developing countries and they
contributed to concern about the viability and workability of
democracy among the developed countries where it had existed for years.[17]

The third wave of democratization. Once again, however, the
dialectic of history upended the theories of social science. In
the fifteen years following the end of the Portuguese dictatorship in 1974, democratic regimes replaced authoritarian ones
in approximately thirty countries in Europe, Asia, and Latin
America. In other countries, considerable liberalization occurred in authoritarian regimes. In still others, movements
promoting democracy gained strength and legitimacy. Although obviously there were resistance and setbacks, as in
China in 1989, the movement toward democracy seemed to
take on the character of an almost irresistible global tide moving on from one triumph to the next.

This democratic tide manifested itself first in southern Europe. Three months after the Portuguese coup, the military

regime that had governed Greece since 1967 collapsed and a civilian government took over under the leadership of Constantine Karamanlis. In November 1974, the Greek people gave Karamanlis and his party a decisive majority in a hotly contested election and the following month they overwhelmingly voted not to restore the monarchy. On November 20, 1975, just five days before Eanes's defeat of the Marxist-Leninists in Portugal, the death of Gen. Francisco Franco ended his thirty-six-year rule of Spain. During the following eighteen months, the new king, Juan Carlos, assisted by his prime minister, Adolfo Suárez, secured parliamentary and popular approval of a political reform law that led to the election of a new assembly. The assembly drafted a new constitution, which was ratified by a referendum in December 1978 and under which parliamentary elections occurred in March 1979.

In the late 1970s the democratic wave moved on to Latin America. In 1977 the military leaders in Ecuador announced their desire to withdraw from politics; a new constitution was drafted in 1978; and elections in 1979 produced a civilian government. A similar process of military withdrawal in Peru led to the election of a constituent assembly in 1978, a new constitution in 1979, and the election of a civilian president in 1980. In Bolivia, military withdrawal produced four confusing years of coups and aborted elections beginning in 1978, but the eventual election of a civilian president in 1982. That same year defeat in the war with Great Britain undermined the Argentine military government and produced the election in 1983 of a civilian president and government. Negotiations between military and political leaders in Uruguay led to the election of a civilian president in November 1984. Two months later, the long process of *abertura*, or opening, that had begun in Brazil in 1974 reached a decisive point with the selection of that country's first civilian president since 1964. Meanwhile, the military was also withdrawing from office in Central America. Honduras installed a civilian president in

January 1982; Salvadoran voters chose José Napoleon Duarte as president in a hotly contested election in May 1984; and Guatemala elected a constituent assembly in 1984 and a civilian president in 1985.

The democratic movement also had its manifestations in Asia. Early in 1977, the premier democracy of the Third World, India, which for one and a half years had been under emergency rule, returned to the democratic path. In 1980 responding to violence and terrorism, the Turkish military for the third time took over the government of that country. In 1983, however, they withdrew and elections produced a civilian government. In the same year, the assassination of Benigno Aquino set in motion the train of events that led in February 1986 to the end of the Marcos dictatorship and the restoration of democracy in the Philippines. In 1987 the military government in Korea submitted its candidate for president to a highly contested electoral campaign and a relatively fair election, which he won. The following year the opposition secured control of the Korean parliament. In 1987 and 1988, the government on Taiwan significantly loosened the restrictions on political activity in that country and committed itself to the creation of a democratic political system. In 1988 military rule in Pakistan came to an end, and the opposition, led by a woman, won an electoral victory and took control of the government.

At the end of the decade, the democratic wave engulfed the communist world. In 1988 Hungary began the transition to a multiparty system. In 1989 elections for a national congress in the Soviet Union produced the defeat of several senior Communist party leaders and an increasingly assertive national parliament. In early 1990, multiparty systems were developing in the Baltic republics and the Communist Party of the Soviet Union (CPSU) abandoned its guiding role. In 1989, in Poland Solidarity swept the elections for a national parliament and a noncommunist government came into existence. In 1990 the leader of Solidarity, Lech Walesa, was elected president, replacing the Communist Gen. Wojciech Jaruzelski. In the last months of 1989, the communist regimes in East Germany, Czechoslovakia, and Romania collapsed, and competitive elections in these countries were held in 1990. In Bulgaria the communist regime also began to liberalize, and popular movements for democracy appeared in Mongolia. In 1990 what appear to be reasonably fair elections occurred in both these countries.

Meanwhile, back in the Western hemisphere, the Mexican ruling party, for the first time, only narrowly won a presidential election in 1988 and lost, for the first time, a state governorship in 1989. The Chilean public in 1988 voted in a referendum to end Gen. Augusto Pinochet's extended grip on power and the following year elected a civilian president. U.S. military intervention ended a Marxist-Leninist dictatorship in Grenada in 1983 and Gen. Manuel Noriega's military dictatorship in Panama in 1989. In February 1990 the Marxist-Leninist regime in Nicaragua went down to electoral defeat, and in December 1990 a democratic government was elected in Haiti.

The 1970s and early 1980s also witnessed the final phase of European decolonization. The end of the Portuguese empire produced five nondemocratic governments. In 1975, however, Papua New Guinea became independent with a democratic political system. The liquidation of the remnants, mostly islands, of the British empire produced a dozen minuscule new nations, almost all of which maintained democratic institutions, although in Grenada these institutions had to be restored by outside military intervention. In 1990 Namibia became independent with a government chosen in an internationally supervised election.

In Africa and the Middle East movement to democracy in the 1980s was limited. Nigeria shifted back from military rule to a democratically elected government in 1979 but this in turn was overthrown by a military coup at the beginning of 1984. By 1990 some liberalization had occurred in Senegal,

Tunisia, Algeria, Egypt, and Jordan. In 1978 the South African government began a slow process of reducing apartheid and expanding political participation for nonwhite minorities but not for the overwhelming black majority in that country. After a pause and then the election of F. W. de Klerk as president, the process was resumed in 1990 with negotiations between the government and the African National Congress. By 1990 democratic rumblings were occurring in Nepal, Albania, and other countries whose previous experience with democracy had been modest or nonexistent.

Overall, the movement toward democracy was a global one. In fifteen years the democratic wave moved across southern Europe, swept through Latin America, moved on to Asia, and decimated dictatorship in the Soviet bloc. In 1974 eight of ten South American countries had nondemocratic governments. In 1990 nine had democratically chosen governments. In 1973, according to Freedom House estimates, 32 percent of the world's population lived in free countries; in 1976, as a result of emergency rule in India, less than 20 percent of the world's population did. By 1990, in contrast, close to 39 percent of humankind lived in free societies.

In one sense, the democratization waves and the reverse waves suggest a two-step-forward, one-step-backward pattern. To date each reverse wave has eliminated some but not all of the transitions to democracy of the previous democratization wave. The final column in Table 1.1, however, suggests a less optimistic prognosis for democracy. States come in many shapes and sizes, and in the post–World War II decades the number of independent states doubled. Yet the proportions of democratic states in the world show a considerable regularity. At the troughs of the two reverse waves 19.7 percent and 24.6 percent of the countries in the world were democratic. At the peaks of the two democratization waves, 45.3 percent and 32.4 percent of the countries in the world were democratic. In 1990 roughly 45.4 percent of the independent countries of the world had democratic systems, the

TABLE 1.1
Democratization in the Modern World

Year	Demo-cratic States	Non-democratic States	Total States	Percentage Democratic of Total States
1922	29	35	64	45.3
1942	12	49	61	19.7
1962	36	75	111	32.4
1973	30	92	122	24.6
1990	59	71	130	45.4

Note: This estimate of regime numbers omits countries with a population of less than one million.

same percentage as in 1922. Obviously whether Grenada is democratic has less impact than whether China is democratic, and ratios of democratic to total states are not all that significant. In addition, between 1973 and 1990 the absolute number of authoritarian states decreased for the first time, yet as of 1990 the third wave of democratization still had not increased the proportion of democratic states in the world above its previous peak sixty-eight years earlier.

THE ISSUES OF DEMOCRATIZATION

The Supreme Court follows the election returns; social scientists forever try to catch up with history, elaborating theories explaining why what has happened had to happen. They attempted to explain the swing away from democracy in the 1960s and 1970s by pointing to the inappropriateness of democracy in poor countries, the advantages of authoritarianism for political order and economic growth, and the reasons why economic development itself tended to produce a new and more enduring form of bureaucratic-authoritarianism. The transition of countries back toward democracy began even as these theories were elaborated. Following hard on that change, social scientists shifted gears and began to produce a substantial literature on the preconditions for democratization, the processes by which it occurs, and, in due course, the consolidation problems of new democratic regimes. These studies greatly enlarged available knowledge of democratizing processes and general understanding of those processes.[18]

By the mid-1980s the democratic transitions also produced a wave of optimism about the prospects for democracy. Communism was, quite accurately, seen as "the grand failure," in Zbigniew Brzezinski's phrase. Others went further to argue that the "exhaustion of viable systematic alternatives" meant the "unabashed victory of economic and political liberalism." "Democracy's won!" was the claim of another. Optimism about democracy, said a third, is "better founded than the pessimism that reigned in 1975."[19] Certainly the contrasts in outlook between the mid-1970s and the late 1980s on the future of democracy could hardly have been more dramatic.

These swings in informed opinion once again raised basic issues concerning the relation between political democracy and historical development. The big issues concern democracy's extent and permanence. Is there a fundamentally irreversible, long-term, global trend, as Tocqueville and Bryce suggested, toward the extension of democratic political systems throughout the world? Or is political democracy a form of government limited, with a few exceptions, to that minority of the world's societies that are wealthy and/or Western? Or is political democracy for a substantial number of countries a sometime thing, a form of government that alternates with various forms of authoritarian rule?

Are these important issues?

Some may argue that they are not, on the grounds that it does not make much difference to a people or to its neighbors whether a country is governed democratically or nondemocratically. A substantial scholarly literature, for instance, suggests that much public policy is shaped more by a country's level of economic development than by the nature of its regime. Corruption, inefficiency, incompetence, domination by a few special interests are found in all societies no matter what their form of government. One widely read book on comparative politics even begins with the claim that "The most important political distinction among countries concerns not their form of government but their degree of government."[20]

There is truth in these arguments. Its form of government is not the only important thing about a country, nor even probably the most important thing. The distinction between order and anarchy is more fundamental than the distinction between democracy and dictatorship. Yet that distinction is also crucial for several reasons.

First, political democracy is closely associated with freedom of the individual. Democracies can and have abused individual rights and liberties, and a well-regulated authoritarian state may provide a high degree of security and order for its citizens. Overall, however, the correlation between the existence of democracy and the existence of individual liberty is extremely high. Indeed, some measure of the latter is an essential component of the former. Conversely, the long-term effect of the operation of democratic politics is probably to broaden and deepen individual liberty. Liberty is, in a sense, the peculiar virtue of democracy. If one is concerned with liberty as an ultimate social value, one should also be concerned with the fate of democracy.

Second, political stability and form of government are, as was pointed out, two different variables. Yet they are also interrelated. Democracies are often unruly, but they are not often politically violent. In the modern world democratic systems tend to be less subject to civil violence than are nondemocratic systems. Democratic governments use far less violence against their citizens than do authoritarian ones. Democracies also provide accepted channels for the expression of dissent and opposition within the system. Both government and opposition thus have fewer incentives to use violence against each other. Democracy also contributes to

stability by providing regular opportunities for changing political leaders and changing public policies. In democracies, change rarely occurs dramatically overnight; it is almost always moderate and incremental. Democratic systems are much more immune to major revolutionary upheaval than authoritarian ones. Revolution, as Che Guevara once said, cannot succeed against a government that "has come into power through some form of popular vote, fraudulent or not, and maintains at least an appearance of constitutional legality."[21]

Third, the spread of democracy has implications for international relations. Historically, democracies have fought wars as often as authoritarian countries. Authoritarian countries have fought democratic countries and have fought each other. From the early nineteenth century down to 1990, however, democracies did not, with only trivial or formal exceptions, fight other democracies.[22] So long as this phenomenon continues, the spread of democracy in the world means the expansion of a zone of peace in the world. On the basis of past experience, an overwhelmingly democratic world is likely to be a world relatively free of international violence. If, in particular, the Soviet Union and China become democracies like the other major powers, the probability of major interstate violence will be greatly reduced.

A permanently divided world, on the other hand, is likely to be a violent world. Developments in communications and economics are intensifying the interactions among countries. In 1858 Abraham Lincoln argued that "a house divided against itself cannot stand. This government cannot endure permanently half-slave and half-free." The world at the end of the twentieth century is not a single house, but it is becoming more and more closely integrated. Interdependence is the trend of the times. How long can an increasingly interdependent world survive part-democratic and part-authoritarian?

Finally, and more parochially, the future of democracy in the world is of special importance to Americans. The United

States is the premier democratic country of the modern world, and its identity as a nation is inseparable from its commitment to liberal and democratic values. Other nations may fundamentally change their political systems and continue their existence as nations. The United States does not have that option. Hence Americans have a special interest in the development of a global environment congenial to democracy.

The futures of liberty, stability, peace, and the United States thus depend, in some measure, on the future of democracy. This study does not attempt to predict that future. It does attempt to shed light on it by analyzing the wave of democratization that began in 1974. It attempts to explore the causes of this series of transitions (chapter 2), the processes by which the transitions occurred and the strategies of the supporters and opponents of democracy (chapters 3 and 4), and the problems confronting the new democracies (chapter 5). It ends with some speculations on the prospects for the further expansion of democratic regimes in the world (chapter 6).

In dealing with these topics, use is made of existing social science theories and generalizations in an effort to see which ones may help explain the recent transitions. This book, however, is not an effort to develop a general theory of the preconditions of democracy or the processes of democratization. It is not an attempt to explain why some countries have been democracies for over a century while others have been enduring dictatorships. Its purpose is the more modest one of attempting to explain why, how, and with what consequences a group of roughly contemporaneous transitions to democracy occurred in the 1970s and 1980s and to understand what these transitions may suggest about the future of democracy in the world.

CHAPTER 2

WHY?

EXPLAINING WAVES

DEMOCRATIZATION WAVES AND REVERSE WAVES are manifestations of a more general phenomenon in politics. At times in history, similar events happen more or less simultaneously within different countries or political systems. In 1848 revolutions occurred in several European countries. In 1968 student protests erupted in many countries on several continents. In Latin America and Africa military coups in different countries often have been bunched together in time. Elections in democratic countries produce a swing to the left in one decade and a swing to the right in the next. The long wave of democratization in the nineteenth century was spread over sufficient time to distinguish it significantly from later democratization and reverse waves. Each of the latter, however, occurred during a relatively brief period of time. The problem is to identify the possible causes of waves such as these in politics.

Let us assume a universe of six countries, numbered 1 through 6. Let us also assume that within a relatively short period of time a similar event, democratization, or x, happens in each country. What could have caused this outbreak of x's? Several explanations are possible.

Single cause. Conceivably all six x's could have a single cause, A, which occurred apart from events in any of the six countries. This might, for instance, be the rise of a new su-

perpower or some other major change in the international
distribution of power. It might be a major war or other important event that would have an impact on many other societies. Several Latin American nations, for instance, either
introduced democratic regimes or held new national elections
in 1945 and 1946. Evidence suggests that these x developments were in considerable measure a result of a single cause,
A, that is, Allied victory in World War II:

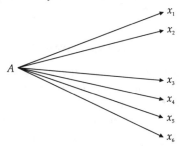

Parallel development. The x's could be caused by similar developments in the same independent variables (a_1, a_2, etc.)
manifesting themselves more or less simultaneously in all six
countries. Theorists have argued, for instance, that a country
is likely to develop democracy when it passes certain economic development thresholds, achieving a particular level
of per capita gross national product (GNP) or a particular
literacy rate. In this case, democratic progress within each
country is caused by something within and particular to that
country, but similar causes may also be at work more or less
simultaneously in other countries producing similar results:

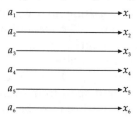

Snowballing. An important cause for x in one country may be the occurrence of x in another country. If the x's occurred absolutely simultaneously, this would be impossible. Perfect simultaneity, however, is very rare, and the possibility of isolated simultaneity is becoming rarer. Knowledge of significant political events is increasingly transmitted almost instantaneously around the world. Hence, event x in one country is increasingly capable of triggering a comparable event almost simultaneously in a different country. Demonstration effects are increasingly possible. Some unique and even idiosyncratic cause, a_1, in one country may cause x_1 in that country, but thereafter x_1 may cause comparable events in other countries that, in turn, may then have a snowballing effect on still other countries.

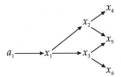

Prevailing nostrum. It is possible that the immediate causes of event x in different countries may differ significantly. These different causes, however, could prompt a common response if the elites in the different countries share a common belief in the efficacy of that response, the *zeitgeist*'s prevailing remedy or nostrum. Just as six individuals may more or less simultaneously take aspirin to cure six very different physical complaints, so six countries may simultaneously engage in similar regime transitions to cope with very different sets of problems: inflation in one, breakdown of law and order in another, deepening economic recession in a third, military defeat in a fourth, and so on. In this case, the specific individual causes (a_1, b_2, c_3, etc.) of political change act on a common set of political beliefs, z, to produce similar x responses:

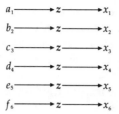

$$a_1 \longrightarrow z \longrightarrow x_1$$
$$b_2 \longrightarrow z \longrightarrow x_2$$
$$c_3 \longrightarrow z \longrightarrow x_3$$
$$d_4 \longrightarrow z \longrightarrow x_4$$
$$e_5 \longrightarrow z \longrightarrow x_5$$
$$f_6 \longrightarrow z \longrightarrow x_6$$

These four possible explanations of political waves are not exhaustive; nor are they mutually exclusive; nor are they necessarily contradictory. All four factors may be at work in any one situation. They are models of explanation to be kept in mind in attempting to explain political waves.

EXPLAINING DEMOCRATIZATION WAVES

The dependent variable of this study is not democracy but democratization. The purpose is to explain why some countries that were authoritarian became democratic in a particular period of time. The focus is on regime change, not regime existence.

This study thus differs from studies that deal primarily with the characteristics of societies with democratic and nondemocratic governments. A number of studies, for instance, have shown high correlations between various social and economic factors and the existence of democratic institutions. As Dankwart Rustow has emphasized, however, a genetic explanation differs from a functional one.[1] Almost all wealthy countries are democratic and almost all democracies are wealthy. That correlation alone says nothing about causation, and if the democracies were wealthy for a considerable length of time before they became democratic (as, relatively speaking, most northern European countries were), then wealth, by itself, is probably not a sufficient explanation of their transition from nondemocratic to democratic politics. Similarly, historically a high correlation has existed between Protestantism and democracy, yet many countries were Protestant and nondemocratic for two or more centuries before they became democratic. To explain change in a dependent variable normally requires some form of change in the independent variable.

The problem is complicated, however, by the fact that change in the independent variable may take the form of the persistence of the independent variable. Three years of economic stagnation under an authoritarian regime may not engender its downfall but five years of stagnation may do so. The cumulative effect of the independent variable over time eventually produces change in the dependent variable. Or, as Gabriel Almond has observed, "social and international change may continue for a long period and only begin to trigger change in the political system when a short-term kink or set of kinks occurs in the curve or curves."[2] Change in this sense is obviously much more likely to have political effects when it involves independent variables such as economic and social trends rather than others.

The dependent variable is not only dynamic; it is also complex. People sometimes assume that doing away with a dictatorship leads to the inauguration of a democracy. In fact, however, nondemocratic regimes are more likely to be replaced by other nondemocratic regimes than by democratic ones. In addition, the factors responsible for the end of a nondemocratic regime may differ significantly from those that lead to the creation of a democratic one. The economic failure of an authoritarian regime may undermine that regime but the economic success of an authoritarian regime may be more likely to create the basis for a democratic regime. Circumstances that contribute to the initial establishment of a democratic regime also may not contribute to its consolidation and long-term stability. At the simplest level, democratization involves: (1) the end of an authoritarian regime; (2) the installation of a democratic regime; and (3) the consolidation of the democratic regime. Different and contradictory causes may be responsible for each of these three developments.

Analyzing the independent variable, the possible causes of democratization, also poses problems. At one extreme is the danger of tautology. Political elites alter or overthrow authoritarian regimes and install and consolidate democratic ones. Why do political elites do this? They are, presumably, acting in terms of their interests, values, and goals as they see them. If they want democracy, they will produce and get democracy. Or as Rustow put it, the creation of democracy requires that elites arrive at a "procedural consensus on the rules of the game."[3] This focuses on what is probably the most immediate and significant explanatory variable: the beliefs and actions of political elites. It is a powerful explanatory variable but not a satisfying one. Democracy can be created even if people do not want it. So it is not perhaps tautological to say that democracy will be created if people want democracy, but it is close to that. An explanation, someone has observed, is the place at which the mind comes to rest. Why do the relevant political elites want democracy? Inevitably, the mind wants to move further along the causal chain.

The distinction between independent and dependent variables is clearest if they are of different orders, if, as is often the case, an economic variable is used to explain a political variable. The entire Marxist intellectual tradition tilts analysis in this direction. This is reinforced by the key-under-the-lamppost factor. Economic data, including a variety of statistics on many different subjects, are available for a large number of societies, especially since World War II but for Western societies back to the nineteenth century. Inevitably analysts are drawn to use this data and to see what correlational and causal connections may exist between economic factors and democratization. Sometimes such efforts are informed by theory; other times they are not.

Social scientists at times speak of the problem of over-determination. By this, they normally mean having a multiplicity of plausible theories to explain an event and the consequent problem of establishing the relative validity of those theories. This is a problem, however, only for those concerned with evaluating theories. The same problem does not exist for those concerned with explaining events. In politics, almost everything has many causes. Why did this candidate rather than that candidate win an election? Clearly a variety of variables and theories behind those variables are necessary to explain something as simple as an election outcome. To occur historically, an event almost has to be overdetermined theoretically. Such is clearly the case with democratization.

Numerous theories have been advanced and numerous independent variables identified to explain democratization. Among the variables that have been said to contribute to democracy and democratization are the following:

a high overall level of economic wealth;
relatively equal distribution of income and/or wealth;
a market economy;
economic development and social modernization;
a feudal aristocracy at some point in the history of society;
the absence of feudalism in the society;
a strong bourgeoisie ("no bourgeois, no democracy," in Barrington Moore's succinct formulation);
a strong middle class;
high levels of literacy and education;
an instrumental rather than consummatory culture;
Protestantism;
social pluralism and strong intermediate groups;
the development of political contestation before the expansion of political participation;
democratic authority structures within social groups, particularly those closely connected to politics;
low levels of civil violence;
low levels of political polarization and extremism;
political leaders committed to democracy;
experience as a British colony;
traditions of toleration and compromise;
occupation by a prodemocratic foreign power;
influence by a prodemocratic foreign power;
elite desire to emulate democratic nations;

traditions of respect for law and individual rights;
communal (ethnic, racial, religious) homogeneity;
communal (ethnic, racial, religious) heterogeneity;
consensus on political and social values;
absence of consensus on political and social values.

The theories relating these factors to democracy and democratization are almost always plausible. Each variable and
theory, however, is likely to have relevance to only a few
cases. In the half century after 1940, democratization occurred in India and Costa Rica, Venezuela and Turkey, Brazil
and Botswana, Greece and Japan. The search for a common,
universally present independent variable that might play a
significant role in explaining political development in such
different countries is almost certain to be unsuccessful if it is
not tautological. The causes of democratization differ substantially from one place to another and from one time to
another. The multiplicity of theories and the diversity of
experience suggest the probable validity of the following
propositions:

(1) No single factor is sufficient to explain the development of
democracy in all countries or in a single country.
(2) No single factor is necessary to the development of democracy in all countries.
(3) Democratization in each country is the result of a combination of causes.
(4) The combination of causes producing democracy varies
from country to country.
(5) The combination of causes generally responsible for one
wave of democratization differs from that responsible for other
waves.
(6) The causes responsible for the initial regime changes in a
democratization wave are likely to differ from those responsible
for later regime changes in that wave.

Reflecting on the diversity of societies that have democratic
governments, Myron Weiner concluded that to explain democratization one should look at the "strategies available to

those who seek a democratic revolution."[4] This advice appropriately highlights the crucial role of political leadership and political skill in bringing about democracy. It should not, however, lead to a total rejection of broader, contextual, social, economic, and cultural factors in explaining democratic development. A chain or funnel (choose your metaphor) of causation exists; and international, social, economic, cultural, and, most immediately, political factors all operate, often in conflicting ways, either to facilitate the creation of democracy or to sustain authoritarianism.

The causes of democratization are thus varied and their significance over time is likely to vary considerably. This is not the place for any detailed historical analysis of what produced democratization before 1974. A brief summary of what appear to be the principal causes of the first and second waves is, however, in order if only to set the context for a more extensive discussion of the causes of the third wave.

Economic development, industrialization, urbanization, the emergence of the bourgeoisie and of a middle class, the development of a working class and its early organization, and the gradual decrease in economic inequality all seem to have played some role in the movements toward democratization in northern European countries in the nineteenth century. These were also, generally, countries where the intellectual ethos was shaped, in some measure, by Locke, Bentham, Mill, Montesquieu, Rousseau, and the impact of the ideals of the French Revolution. In the British settler countries—the United States, Canada, Australia, New Zealand—many of these same factors were at work, enhanced by much greater economic opportunities, the weakness of existing status systems, and the more equal income distribution that was possible in frontier societies. Conceivably, Protestantism also encouraged democratization; three-quarters of the countries that developed democratic institutions before 1900 were overwhelmingly Protestant in religious composition.

The victory of the Western Allies in World War I and the

dismantling of empires that occurred after the war significantly affected democratization. The peripheral European countries—Finland, Iceland, Ireland—were relatively successful in sustaining democratic systems; the more centrally located successor states of the Romanov, Hapsburg, and Hohenzollern empires were not. In brief, the primary factors responsible for the first wave of democratization appear to be economic and social development, the economic and social environment of the British settler countries, and the victory of the Western Allies in World War I and the resulting breakup of the principal continental empires.

Political and military factors were clearly predominant in the second wave of democratization. Most of the countries that transited to democracy in this wave fall into one of three categories. First, the victorious Western Allies imposed democracy on a number of countries: West Germany, Italy, Japan, a major part of Austria, and South Korea. Second, many other countries moved in a democratic direction because the Western Allies had won the war. This category includes Greece, Turkey, Brazil, Argentina, Peru, Ecuador, Venezuela, Colombia.[5] Third, the weakening of the Western states by the war and the rising nationalism in their overseas colonies led them to initiate the process of decolonization. A significant number of the new states started off as democracies and a somewhat lesser number sustained democratic institutions for a respectable period of time. The victory of the established Western democracies in World War II and decolonization by those democracies after the war were thus largely responsible for the second wave. These were historically discrete events. The third wave had to result from a different mix of causes.

EXPLAINING THE THIRD WAVE

Explaining third wave democratizations requires answers to two questions. First, why did some thirty countries with authoritarian systems but not about one hundred other authoritarian countries shift to democratic political systems? Second, why did regime changes in these countries occur in the 1970s and 1980s and not at some other time?

With respect to the first question, whether or not countries transited from authoritarianism could depend on the nature of their authoritarian regimes. In fact, however, the regimes that moved toward democracy in the third wave were a diverse lot. They included one-party systems, military regimes, personal dictatorships, and the racial oligarchy in South Africa. Within each category of regime type, some countries did not democratize during the fifteen years after 1974: China and Vietnam among one-party systems; Burma and Indonesia among military regimes; Iraq and Cuba among personal dictatorships. The nature of the authoritarian regime, consequently, cannot explain why some regimes transited to democracy and others did not.

A different approach to answering this question could focus on the histories of regime changes in those countries that did democratize. In the *cyclical pattern*, countries alternated back and forth between democratic and authoritarian systems. This pattern was particularly prevalent in Latin America, including countries such as Argentina, Brazil, Peru, Bolivia, and Ecuador, but it characterized other countries such as Turkey and Nigeria. These countries tended to oscillate between more populistic democratic governments and more conservative military regimes. Under a democratic regime radicalism, corruption, and disorder reach unacceptable levels and the military overthrow it, to considerable popular relief and acclaim. In due course, however, the coalition supporting the military regime unravels, the military regime fails to deal effectively with the country's economic problems, professionally inclined military officers become alarmed at the politicization of the armed forces, and, again to great popular relief and acclaim, the military withdraw from or are pushed out

[handwritten margin note: not one specific regime type completely transsisted]

[handwritten bottom note: cyclical pattern — oscillation btwn democracy & military regime]

of office. In these countries, the change of regime thus performs the same function as the change of parties in a stable democratic system. The country does not alternate between democratic and authoritarian political systems; the alternation of democracy and authoritarianism *is* the country's political system.

A second pattern of regime change was the *second-try* pattern. A country with an authoritarian system shifts to a democratic one. Either the democratic system fails because the country lacks the social bases for democracy, or the leaders of the new democratic system pursue extremist policies that produce a drastic reaction, or some cataclysm (depression, war) undermines the regime. An authoritarian government then comes to power for a greater or shorter period of time. Eventually, however, a second and more successful effort is made to introduce democracy, with success increasing at least in part because democratic leaders learned from the previous unsuccessful experience with democracy. In varying ways, a number of countries—Germany, Italy, Austria, Japan, Venezuela, Colombia—established reasonably stable democratic systems in the second wave after suffering reversals in their earlier efforts. Spain, Portugal, Greece, Korea, Czechoslovakia, and Poland will fit into this second-try pattern if their third wave democratic regimes stabilize.

A third pattern was *interrupted democracy*. This involves countries that develop democratic regimes that exist for a relatively sustained period of time. At some point, however, instability, polarization, or other conditions develop and lead to the suspension of democratic processes. In the 1970s, democracy was suspended in India and the Philippines by democratically elected chief executives, in Uruguay by elected leaders in cooperation with the military, and in Chile by military leaders overthrowing an elected regime. These countries' lengthy experience with democracy, however, made it impossible for the political leaders who suspended democracy to do away entirely with democratic practices. In all four cases, they eventually felt compelled to submit to some form of popular vote, which they lost.

A fourth pattern of change involved the *direct transition* from a stable authoritarian system to a stable democratic system, either through gradual evolution over time or the abrupt replacement of the former by the latter. This pattern typified the transitions of the first wave. If their democracy is consolidated third wave efforts in Romania, Bulgaria, Taiwan, Mexico, Guatemala, El Salvador, Honduras, and Nicaragua would approximate this pattern.

Finally, there is the *decolonization pattern*. A democratic country imposes democratic institutions on its colonies. The colony becomes independent and, unlike most former colonies, successfully maintains its democratic institutions. Papua New Guinea was one third wave case. As Myron Weiner has pointed out, this pattern pertains primarily to former British colonies, most of which became independent in the second wave.[6] Those left to become independent and democratic in the third wave were mostly small and mostly insular. They included Antigua and Barbuda, Belize, Dominica, Kiribati, Saint Christopher–Nevis, Saint Lucia, Saint Vincent and the Grenadines, Solomon Islands, Tuvalu, and Vanuatu. With the possible exception of a very few remaining colonies (e.g., Hong Kong, Gibraltar, the Falklands), these countries are the last legacy of the British Empire to democratization. Because of their small size they are, unless stated to the contrary, excluded from analyses of third wave countries in this study.

If A and D are used to represent relatively stable and long-lasting authoritarian and democratic regimes and a and d are used to represent less stable and shorter-lived regimes, these five patterns of regime development may be portrayed as follows:

(1) cyclical: a—d—a—d—a—d
(2) second-try: A—d—a—D

(3) interrupted democracy: A—D—a—D
(4) direct transition: A—D
(5) decolonization: D/a—D.

The countries of the third wave encompass all five patterns of regime change. Twenty-three of twenty-nine countries that democratized between 1974 and 1990, however, had had previous experience with democracy. In some cases, this experience was distant in time; in some cases it was brief; in some cases it was both distant and brief. At some point, however, it occurred. Most of the countries with authoritarian systems in 1974 that did not democratize by 1990 had no previous experience with democracy. Thus an excellent predictor in 1974 of whether a country with an authoritarian government would become democratic was whether it had been democratic. By 1989, however, the third wave entered a second phase and began to affect countries without previous significant democratic experience, including Romania, Bulgaria, the Soviet Union, Taiwan, and Mexico. This posed a crucial question. To what extent would the third wave go beyond the first and second waves? Would countries that had not experienced democracy in the past become stable democracies in the future?

Plausible answers to the question why some countries but not others transited to democracy are not necessarily answers to the second question of why these transitions took place when they did and not at some other time. It does seem unlikely that the clustering of transitions within a decade and a half could be purely coincidental. It appears reasonable to assume that these transitions were produced in part by common causes affecting many countries, by parallel developments within several countries, and by the impact of early transitions on later ones. Previous democratic experience, however, does not explain why the shift to democracy in these countries came in the 1970s and 1980s. Similarly, some attributed the democratic transitions of the 1980s to a deeply felt and widespread "yearning for freedom" by people oppressed by authoritarian rulers. The presence of this yearning may distinguish countries that did democratize from those that did not, but it cannot explain why democratization occurred when it did. As the events of 1953, 1956, 1968, and 1980–81 show, East Europeans had been yearning for freedom for decades; they only got it, however, in 1989. Why then and not earlier? In other countries, people may not have had a yearning for freedom earlier in their history but developed it in the 1970s and 1980s. The problem is to explain why this desire emerged then. Analysis is forced to look for other developments that may have produced it.

The question to be answered is: What changes in plausible independent variables in, most probably, the 1960s and 1970s produced the dependent variable, democratizing regime changes in the 1970s and 1980s? Five such changes seem to have played significant roles in bringing about the third wave transitions in the countries where they occurred and when they occurred:

(1) the deepening legitimacy problems of authoritarian systems in a world where democratic values were widely accepted, the dependence of those regimes on performance legitimacy, and the undermining of that legitimacy by military defeats, economic failures, and the oil shocks of 1973–74 and 1978–79;

(2) the unprecedented global economic growth of the 1960s, which raised living standards, increased education, and greatly expanded the urban middle class in many countries;

(3) the striking changes in the doctrine and activities of the Catholic Church manifested in the Second Vatican Council in 1963–65 and the transformation of national churches from defenders of the status quo to opponents of authoritarianism and proponents of social, economic, and political reform;

(4) changes in the policies of external actors, including in the late 1960s the new attitude of the European Community toward expanding its membership, the major shift in U.S. policies beginning in 1974 toward the promotion of human rights and democracy in other countries, and Gorbachev's dramatic change in

the late 1980s in Soviet policy toward maintaining the Soviet empire; and

(5) "snowballing" or demonstration effects, enhanced by new means of international communication, of the first transitions to democracy in the third wave in stimulating and providing models for subsequent efforts at regime change in other countries.

DECLINING LEGITIMACY AND THE PERFORMANCE DILEMMA

Legitimacy is a mushy concept that political analysts do well to avoid. Yet it is essential to understanding the problems confronting authoritarian regimes in the late twentieth century. "The strongest is never strong enough to be always the master," observed Rousseau, "unless he transforms strength into right and obedience into duty." Whence springs the "right" of authoritarian leaders to rule and the "duty" of their people to obey?

In the past, tradition, religion, the divine right of kings, and social deference provided legitimation for nondemocratic rule. In an age of literate, mobilized populations, these traditional rationales for authoritarianism lose their efficacy. In modern times authoritarianism has been justified by nationalism and by ideology. The efficacy of the former as a basis for nondemocratic rule, however, depends in large part on the existence of a credible enemy to the national aspirations of a people. Nationalism is also a popular force and can equally well legitimate democratic as authoritarian rule. The principal ideological justification for authoritarianism in modern times has been Marxism-Leninism. It provides a rationale for one-party dictatorship and rule by a small self-perpetuating bureaucratic elite. Most authoritarian regimes in the late twentieth century, however, were not communist regimes. Together with the communist regimes they faced major problems in establishing and maintaining their legitimacy.

The victory of the Western Allies in World War II produced the second wave of democratization in practice. It also produced an even more pervasive and lasting change in the intellectual environment of politics. People in most countries came to accept—if not to implement—the rhetoric and ideas of democracy. A world democratic ethos came into being. Even those whose actions were clearly antidemocratic often justified their actions by democratic values. Explicit argument against democracy as a concept almost disappeared from public debate in most countries of the world. "For the first time in the history of the world," a UNESCO report noted in 1951, "no doctrines are advanced as antidemocratic. The accusation of antidemocratic action or attitude is frequently directed against others, but practical politicians and political theorists agree in stressing the democratic element in the institutions they defend and the theories they advocate."[7]

The pervasiveness of democratic norms rested in large part on the commitment to those norms of the most powerful country in the world. The principal alternative source of legitimacy, Marxism-Leninism, was espoused by the second strongest power. Communists, however, regularly paid tribute to the strength of democratic values by emphasizing the democratic elements in their ideology, by employing democratic phraseology, and by playing down the role of the vanguard Leninist party and the dictatorship of the proletariat.

Many authoritarian regimes in the 1970s also confronted legitimacy problems because of the previous experience of their country with democracy. In a sense, the body politic of their society had been infected with the democratic virus, and even if the previous democratic regime had not been terribly successful, the belief remained that a truly legitimate government had to be based on democratic practices. Authoritarian rulers were thus impelled to justify their own regimes by democratic rhetoric and claim that their regimes were truly democratic or would become so in the future once they had dealt with the immediate problems confronting their society.

The legitimacy problems of the authoritarian regimes varied with the nature of the regime. One-party systems that were a product of indigenous political development, such as in revolutionary communist states, Mexico, and the Republic of China, had a more secure basis of legitimacy. Ideology and nationalism could be jointly harnessed to buttress the regimes. In countries, as in Eastern Europe, where communism and the one-party system were imposed by external forces, regimes could benefit from the ideology but not from nationalism, which was always a potential source of instability. Over time, however, communist governments found it more difficult to invoke communist ideology to support their legitimacy. The appeal of the ideology declined as the state bureaucracy stagnated and socioeconomic inequalities ossified. Communist ideology also became the major obstacle to economic growth and frustrated the ability of the regime to legitimate itself on the basis of economic performance. In communist states, Marxism-Leninism thus initially provided ideological legitimacy but, when this weakened, Marxism-Leninism made it impossible to develop legitimacy based on economic performance.

Other things being equal, the legitimacy of most regimes declines over time, as choices are made, promises are unrealized, and frustrations develop. In most cases, the coalition supporting the regime also disintegrates over time. Democratic systems, however, renew themselves through elections, which make it possible for a new coalition to come to power with new policies and new promise for the future. In contrast, self-renewal is a major problem for authoritarian regimes, and the absence of mechanisms for self-renewal contributes significantly to the erosion of the legitimacy of those regimes. This problem is worst, of course, in personal dictatorships, where self-renewal (short of reincarnation) is impossible due to the nature of the regime.

In a few cases authoritarian regimes did develop mechanisms for regular replacement of their top leaders and thus for at least limited renewal. In Mexico and in Brazil the principle that no president could succeed himself was well-institutionalized. The benefits of such a system of routinized succession were at least twofold. First, it encouraged key figures within the authoritarian establishment to hope that next time around they might have a chance at the top office or a high office and hence reduced their incentives to become obstreperous or to overthrow the existing leadership. Second, regular succession in the top leadership position made possible and even probable changes in policy. In Mexico, for decades presidents more of the Right alternated with presidents more of the Left. Somewhat similarly in Brazil, two loosely structured coalitions—the Sorbonne group and the nationalists—competed for power within the military. The Sorbonne group came to power after the 1964 coup; it was displaced when Gen. Artur Costa e Silva assumed the presidency in 1967; it returned to power with Geisel in 1974. Mechanisms and processes such as these made it possible for these regimes to avoid some of the dysfunctional aspects of authoritarianism and also provided means for renewing their legitimacy in at least a limited way. Each new president offered new promise if only because he was different from the previous president. From 1929 to 1989 Mexico had a uniquely stable authoritarian regime requiring only a modest amount of repression because its legitimacy was enhanced both by its revolutionary ideology and by the regular change in its political leaders. Indigenous communist regimes had the former but not the latter; Brazil had the latter but not the former.

The legitimacy problem of the military regimes and personalistic dictatorships of the 1970s, particularly those created during the second reverse wave, typically evolved through three phases. The displacement of the democratic regime by an authoritarian regime was almost always greeted with a sense of great relief and overwhelming approval by the public. In this initial phase, the new regime benefitted from "negative legitimacy" deriving from the failures of the democratic regime and its apparent differences from the democratic regime. The new regimes typically justified themselves on the grounds that they were combatting communism and internal subversion, reducing social turmoil, reestablishing law and order, eliminating corruption and venal civilian politicians, and enhancing national values, purpose, and coherence. The Greek colonels in 1967, for instance, legitimated themselves through appeals to "the ideology of the anticommunist state"; and in its initial years the Brazilian military regime similarly sought legitimacy on the basis of "the 'anti' appeals: anticommunism, antisubversive, antichaos."[8]

Inevitably, negative legitimacy declined with time. The authoritarian regimes of the 1960s and 1970s were almost inescapably driven to look to performance as a principal if not the principal source of legitimacy. In some cases, as in Peru and the Philippines, the leaders of the authoritarian regimes promised economic and social reform. In most other cases they promised economic growth and development. The effort to base legitimacy on performance, however, gave rise to what can be termed the performance dilemma. In democracies the legitimacy of rulers usually depends on the extent to which they meet the expectations of key groups of voters, that is, on their performance. The legitimacy of the system, however, depends on procedures, on the ability of the voters to choose their rulers through elections. In office, the rulers, eventually, fail to perform, they lose legitimacy, they are defeated in elections, and a different set of rulers takes over. The loss of performance legitimacy by the rulers leads to the reaffirmation of the procedural legitimacy of the system. In authoritarian systems other than one-party systems, however, no distinction was possible between ruler legitimacy and regime legitimacy. Poor performance undermined the legitimacy of both the rulers and the legitimacy of the system.

In their analysis of eight major crises of political development ranging from the British Reform Act of 1832 to Cárdenas's economic reforms in the 1930s, Gabriel Almond, Scott C. Flanagan, and Robert J. Mundt found that every case was characterized by "declining economic performance components (depression, unemployment, food shortages, and famine)."[9] Unsatisfactory economic performance similarly played a key role in producing the crisis of authoritarian regimes in the 1970s. The drive for social and economic reform stagnated quickly in the Philippines and was eventually abandoned in Peru. The ability of many authoritarian governments to derive legitimacy from economic growth was undermined by the increases in oil prices in the 1970s and by the economic policies the authoritarian governments followed.

The oil price hike of 1973–74 triggered a global economic recession. It raised questions concerning the governability of democracy in the trilateral world of Europe, North America, and Japan, and it significantly undermined the efforts of Third World authoritarian regimes to use economic performance to bolster their legitimacy. Countries such as the Philippines, Spain, Portugal, Greece, Brazil, and Uruguay were particularly hard hit because of their overwhelming dependence on imported oil. The second oil price increase in 1979 aggravated the situation. In West Germany, Britain, France, Canada, and the United States, incumbent parties were turned out of office. In the Third World, the ability of the remaining authoritarian regimes to bolster their legitimacy through economic performance was further weakened. The oil price hikes and their economic consequences deserve a significant portion of the credit for the weakening of authoritarianism in the 1970s and early 1980s.

With rare exceptions, the policies adopted by authoritarian governments to deal with the oil and debt crises often made the economic situation worse, producing stagnation, depression, inflation, low or negative growth rates, expanded debt, or some combination of these conditions, and hence further undermining the regime's legitimacy. The Philippines provides an example:

> The New Society's *economic* foundation began to crack with the oil crisis of 1973–1974 and the global recession that followed. The Philippines, which imported 90 percent of its oil,

saw its energy costs quadruple, while the prices of commodity exports fell. With the second oil price squeeze of 1979, the economic slide accelerated. Marcos responded with more borrowing and spending, *doubling* Manila's foreign debt between 1979 and 1983. Almost half the debt was short-term, and . . . international lenders became nervous about the Philippines: During the last four months of 1982 alone some $700 million in credits were withdrawn.[10]

From 1980 on per capita income in the Philippines declined steadily.

In Argentina the economic policies of Martínez de Hoz between 1978 and 1980 created an artificial boom

> that could not last. Imports became so cheap that local industry was collapsing under the competition. Exports became so expensive that agriculture was priced out of the world market. . . . In 1981, the balloon burst. . . . The economy plunged into recession almost overnight.
>
> In nine months, both inflation and unemployment exploded upwards. The peso, under tremendous speculative pressure, fell in value more than 400 percent. Argentines holding dollar debts suddenly found that it took five times more pesos to pay them back. They could not meet their payments. . . . Panicked savers, meanwhile, started a long-term run on the banks. The country's reserves fell precipitously.[11]

In Uruguay the military regime in the early 1980s ran up the second largest per capita foreign debt in Latin America and produced a four-year recession that cut real salaries to half what they had been a decade earlier. In Portugal, the huge costs of its colonial war combined with the oil price increases and economic mismanagement to produce similarly unhappy economic results.

> One of the other casualties [of the war] was Portugal's economy. By the time of the coup, the country's inflation rate had reached 30 percent (the highest in Western Europe), its trade deficit was the worst ever, and unemployment was ris-

ing—despite a steady exodus of emigrants seeking work or avoiding conscription.

With nearly half of government spending going to the military, Portugal's rate of "fixed" investment—the kind that creates jobs and exports—was the lowest in Western Europe. . . . Portugal, which imports 80 percent of its energy and more than half its food, was hit especially hard by the global bout of recession and inflation that followed the 1973 Organization of Petroleum Exporting Countries (OPEC) oil embargo. As Portugal's export markets went soft, the cost of everything from codfish to bullfight tickets raced ahead of wages. Though both unions and strikes were illegal in the New State, Communist-led workers started some 40 major walkouts in 1973. Plants owned by International Telephone and Telegraph, Grundig, British Leyland, and other firms closed down.[12]

Greece experienced significant if unbalanced economic growth under the military regime that took over in 1967. The new military group that assumed power at the end of 1973, however, "showed itself quite incapable of dealing with the pressing problems confronting the country. . . . Inflation continued unchecked, and Greece, with few indigenous sources of energy, was particularly severely affected by the oil crisis that followed the Yom Kippur War."[13] In Peru, the "military regime's efforts to spur the country's economic growth . . . misfired badly. Productivity declined in both agriculture and industry, real wages fell, open unemployment rose, inflation climbed, and Peru's public debt skyrocketed." Even Brazil had problems with economic performance. As the regime began gradually to democratize in the later 1970s, economic problems increased, and "there was a marked deterioration in the ability of government to deliver economic growth and to promise a better future for all Brazilians." By 1982 large proportions of the Brazilian public were attributing these deficiencies to the policy failures of the government.[14]

Communist regimes were relatively insulated from oil price hikes and other developments in the world economy, al-

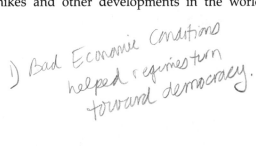

) Bad Economic Conditions
   helped regimes turn
      forward democracy.

though Poland and Hungary did run up substantial debts. Their poor economic performance was primarily a result of the command economies that the Soviet Union imposed on them after World War II. During the 1950s these economies grew at very rapid rates. Growth slowed in the 1960s and stagnated in the 1970s and 1980s. Economic failure engendered tremendous disaffection from and some opposition to the existing political-economic system. By itself, however, this economic stagnation was not enough to produce movement in a democratic direction. It did not become a factor promoting democratization in those countries until the Soviet Union allowed that to happen. In Eastern Europe politics was in command, and Soviet support inured the communist regimes to the consequences of their poor economic performance.

Military failure contributed to the downfall or weakening of at least five authoritarian regimes between 1974 and 1989. The military forces of two personal dictatorships became disaffected because they were fighting insurgencies that they saw little chance of defeating. The obvious inability of the Portuguese government and military forces to win their colonial wars was the underlying cause behind the formation of the MFA and the April coup. In the Philippines, a somewhat similar Reform of the Armed Forces Movement (RAM) attacked the cronyism, inefficiency, and corruption Marcos had caused in the Philippine military. The perception of the growing strength of the communist guerrillas of the New People's Army (NPA) during the last years of the Marcos regime contributed generally to the weakening of the regime. The large costs of the Afghan War and the inability of the Soviet military to bring it to a successful conclusion contributed to the political liberalization Gorbachev brought to the Soviet Union. In Greece and Argentina conflicts provoked by military regimes produced defeat and the downfall of those regimes.

The legitimacy of an authoritarian regime was also under-

2) military Failure -
   cause for democratization
3) legitimacy of authoritarian-
   purpose is to achieve purpose -
   once achieved, then done.

mined if it did deliver on its promises. By achieving its purpose, it lost its purpose. This reduced the reasons why the public should support the regime, given the other costs (e.g., lack of freedom) connected with the regime. It promoted uncertainty and conflict within the regime about what new purposes it should pursue. In Argentina in 1980 and 1981, for instance, the economy was in a tailspin. At the same time, the regime had eliminated the Montonero guerrillas and restored order (if not law) to the country. This removed a major reason for support of the regime, and the military government "showed signs of ennui, precisely because it had achieved one of its main objectives: the defeat of the armed guerrilla groups." Somewhat similarly, in Brazil in 1974, "given the unequivocal establishment of order, the regime was forced to begin either the long-term institutionalization of its power or, conversely, the beginning of the liberalization process."[15] A similar situation existed in Uruguay after the military government eliminated the Tupamaros. Because their legitimacy was based on performance criteria, authoritarian regimes lost legitimacy if they did not perform and also lost it if they did perform.

Confronted with this erosion of legitimacy, authoritarian leaders could and did respond in one or more of five ways. First, they could simply refuse to acknowledge their increasing weakness with the hope or the conviction they would somehow survive in power. The weakness of feedback mechanisms in most authoritarian regimes and the delusions of many personal dictators reinforced these tendencies. Neither the hope nor the belief, however, was likely to be warranted. Second, the regime could attempt to survive by becoming increasingly repressive, by, in effect, replacing evaporating duty with coerced obedience. This often required a shift in regime leadership, such as happened in Greece in 1973, Argentina in 1981, and China in 1989. If the leaders of the regime substantially agree on such a course, they may be able to delay significantly the consequence of their declining legitimacy.

A third option was to provoke foreign conflict and attempt to restore legitimacy by an appeal to nationalism. In the spring of 1974 the Ioannidis regime organized a coup which overthrew Archbishop Makarios on Cyprus and installed a government favorable to *enosis* (union) with Greece. The Turks invaded Cyprus and Ioannidis attempted to rally the Greek army and people to fight the Turks. The Greeks were, however, militarily incapable of taking on the Turks, and their military commanders refused to do so. The colonels' regime thus fell in humiliating fashion as a result, in effect, of a strike by its own officer corps. In Argentina, the legitimacy of the military regime reached a low point in 1982 as a result of its economic failure, and Gen. Leopoldo Galtieri attempted to reestablish support for his government by his invasion of the Falklands. If he had been militarily successful, he would have become a major hero in Argentine history. His failure and the British recovery of the island precipitated the transition to democracy in the following year.

The efforts by authoritarian leaders to bolster fading legitimacy by foreign war face an inherent obstacle. The military forces of a military regime are involved in politics, may lack an effective command structure (as was the case in Argentina), and tend to become more politicized the older the regime gets (which is one reason why professionally inclined military leaders often wish to end military regimes). In a personal dictatorship, like that of the shah of Iran or Marcos in the Philippines, on the other hand, the military may not be in politics but politics pervades the military because the dictator's major fear is a coup d'etat. Hence incompetents and cronies get preference in appointments. Both military regimes and personal dictatorships are thus likely to have armed forces low in military professionalism and military effectiveness. As the Greek and Argentine cases suggest, provoking a war is, consequently, a high-risk strategy.

A fourth option was to attempt to establish some semblance of democratic legitimacy for their regime. Most authoritarian regimes—apart from the ideologically based one-party systems—in existence in the early 1970s claimed that in due course they would restore democracy. As their performance legitimacy declined, they came under increasing pressure to deliver on that promise and they had increasing incentives to attempt to relegitimize themselves through elections. In some cases the leaders apparently believed they could fairly win elections. That, however, was almost never the case, particularly if the opposition achieved a minimum degree of unity. The performance dilemma thus gave way to the election dilemma. Should they sponsor an election? If they did, should they rig the election? If they did that, would they gain in legitimacy? If they did not rig the election, would they lose it?

Fifth, the authoritarian leaders could seize the bull by the horns and take the lead in ending authoritarian rule and introducing a democratic system. This happened often but it almost always first required a change of leadership within the authoritarian system.

Declining legitimacy usually provoked doubt in the minds of authoritarian leaders and divisions within the leadership over which response to choose. The resulting hesitation, disagreement, and fluctuations in action then further decreased the legitimacy of the regimes and encouraged political groups to think about successors to them.

The successor regime did not need to be democratic. In 1978 and 1979, Iran and Nicaragua shifted from modernizing personal dictatorships to Islamic fundamentalism and Marxism-Leninism respectively. As the third democratic wave got underway in the mid-1970s, a number of transitions also occurred to Marxist-Leninist regimes in Africa and elsewhere in the Third World. After a struggle, Portugal went democratic; after independence, its former colonies went Marxist-Leninist. Between the mid-1960s and the early 1980s the total number of ostensibly Marxist-Leninist Third World regimes increased from six to seventeen. These regimes were, for the most part, relatively narrowly based, and they did not meet with economic success or sustained political stability. In the early 1960s, both Latin American politicians and U.S. leaders had seen the political choices for Latin America as reform or revolution, John F. Kennedy or Fidel Castro. With a few exceptions, however, Latin America got neither reform nor revolution but instead repression in the form of the military and bureaucratic-authoritarian regimes. The economic failures of these regimes then eliminated this form of government as an alternative for the immediate future.

Right-wing dictatorships, as in the Philippines and El Salvador, often stimulate the growth of left-wing revolutionary movements. In South America, however, the ruthless and successful repression by the military regimes physically eliminated many revolutionary extremists and also kindled new appreciation among Marxist and socialist groups of the virtues of democracy. In the 1980s, as Juan Linz and Alfred Stepan noted, the Latin American left came to view "procedural democracy" as "a valuable norm in itself and as a political arrangement that offers both protection against state terrorism and some hope of electoral progress toward social and economic democracy." In a comparable vein, one of the fathers of liberation theology, Father Gustavo Gutiérrez of Peru, observed in 1988 that "Experience with dictatorship has made liberation theologians appreciative of political rights." [16] The collapse of the communist regimes in Eastern Europe further weakened the possibility of Marxism-Leninism as an alternative to other authoritarian regimes. Thus, while authoritarian regimes came in many forms—military government, one-party system, personal tyranny, absolute monarchy, racial oligarchy, Islamic dictatorship—by the 1980s, they were not, by and large, perceived as alternatives to each other. Outside of Africa and a few countries elsewhere, democracy had come to be seen as the only legitimate and viable alternative to an authoritarian regime of any type.

ECONOMIC DEVELOPMENT AND ECONOMIC CRISES

The relation between economic development, on the one hand, and democracy and democratization, on the other, is complex and probably varies in time and space. Economic factors have significant impact on democratization but they are not determinative. An overall correlation exists between the level of economic development and democracy yet no level or pattern of economic development is in itself either necessary or sufficient to bring about democratization.

Economic factors affected third wave democratizations in three ways. First, as was pointed out above, the oil price hikes in some countries and Marxist-Leninist constraints in others created economic downturns that weakened the authoritarian regimes. Second, by the early 1970s many countries had achieved overall levels of economic development that provided an economic basis for democracy and that facilitated transition to democracy. Third, in a few countries extremely rapid economic growth destabilized authoritarian regimes, forcing them either to liberalize or to intensify repression. Economic development, in short, provided the basis for democracy; crises produced by either rapid growth or economic recession weakened authoritarianism. All three factors did not appear in every country, but virtually no third wave country escaped all of them. They provided the economic impetus and context for democratization in the 1970s and 1980s.

Economic development. Eighteenth-century political theorists argued that wealthy countries were likely to be monarchies, while poor countries would be republics or democracies. This was a plausible hypothesis for agrarian societies. Industrialization, however, reversed the relation between level of wealth and form of government, and a positive correlation between wealth and democracy emerged in the nineteenth century. It has remained strong. Most wealthy countries are democratic and most democratic countries—India is the most dramatic exception—are wealthy. This relationship was highlighted by Seymour Martin Lipset in 1959 and has been strongly reinforced by a large number of subsequent studies.[17] In 1985, for instance, Kenneth A. Bollen and Robert W. Jackman found that in the 1960s "level of economic development has a pronounced effect on political democracy, even when other noneconomic factors are considered. . . . GNP is the dominant explanatory variable."[18] In 1989 the World Bank classified as "high income" twenty-four countries with per capita incomes ranging from $6,010 (Spain) to $21,330 (Switzerland). Three of these (Saudi Arabia, Kuwait, and United Arab Emirates) were oil exporters and nondemocratic. Of the remaining twenty-one high-income countries, all except Singapore were democratic. At the other extreme, the World Bank categorized as "poor" forty-two countries with per capita incomes ranging from $130 (Ethiopia) to $450 (Liberia). Only two of these countries (India, Sri Lanka) had had any extensive experience with democracy. Among the fifty-three "middle-income" countries, ranging from Senegal (per capita GNP of $520) to Oman (per capita GNP of $5,810), there were twenty-three democracies, twenty-five nondemocracies, and five countries that could, in 1989, be plausibly classified as in transition from nondemocracy to democracy.

The correlation between wealth and democracy implies that transitions to democracy should occur primarily in countries at the middle levels of economic development. In poor countries democratization is unlikely; in rich countries it has already occurred. In between there is a political transition zone; countries in that particular economic stratum are most likely to transit to democracy and most countries that transit to democracy will be in that stratum. As countries develop economically and move into this zone, they become prospects for democratization. During the first wave of democratization in the nineteenth and early twentieth centuries democracy generally emerged in northern European countries when their per capita GNPs, in 1960 dollars, were between $300 and $500. In the 1920s and 1930s, a variety of factors, including economic crises, produced the first reverse wave to authoritarianism. Overall, however, economic development continued and hence the income level of the transition zone separating democracies and nondemocracies moved upward.[19]

The 1950s and 1960s were years of impressive global economic growth, particularly among less developed countries. Between 1950 and 1975 per capita GNP of the developing countries grew at an average rate of 3.4 percent per year, a rate that "exceeded both official goals and private expectations."[20] This rate was historically unprecedented for both the developing countries and for the developed countries. In the 1960s, the "decade of development," the annual GNP growth rates of the developing countries averaged well over 5 percent, generally more than twice the rates of European countries during their comparable phases of economic development. The rates for individual countries, of course, varied considerably—higher in southern Europe, East Asia, the Middle East, and Latin America; lower in South Asia and Africa. Overall, however, the post–World War II surge of economic growth that lasted until the oil shocks of 1973–74 moved many countries into the transition zone, creating within them the economic conditions favorable to the development of democracy. In considerable measure, the wave of democratizations that began in 1974 was the product of the economic growth of the previous two decades.

By the 1970s the center of the economic transition zone had moved upward from the prewar level of $300–$500 (1960 dollars) to the $500–$1,000 range. Nine, or almost half, of twenty-one third wave democratizations occurred in countries within these limits; four occurred in countries in the $300–$500 range; two (Greece, Spain) in countries with per capita GNPs slightly over $1,000 (1960 dollars); and six (India, Pakistan, El Salvador, Honduras, Bolivia, Philippines) in countries with 1960 per capita GNPs of less than $300. The

range in the level of economic development, from India ($87)
to Greece ($1,291) was substantial, but about two-thirds of
the transitions were in countries between roughly $300 and
$1,300 in per capita GNP (1960 dollars) at the time of transi-
tion. Transitions clearly were most likely to occur in countries
at the middle and upper-middle levels of economic development and, as expected, were concentrated in the income zone
just above that where Sunshine had found them concentrated
before World War II.

The third wave transition zone also appears in the data presented in Table 2.1. Countries are classified according to their
per capita GNPs in 1976, as reported by the World Bank, and
as to whether they had democratic political systems in 1974,
whether they democratized or liberalized between 1974 and

TABLE 2.1
Economic Development and Third Wave Democratization

(1)	(2)	(3)	(4)	(5)	(6)
1976 per Capita GNP (in dollars)	Demo-cratic 1974	Democ-ratized/ Liberal-ized 1974–89	Non-demo-cratic	Total	Percentage of Countries that Democ-ratized/ Liberal-ized[a]
<250	1	2[b]	31	34	6
250–1,000	3	11	27[c]	41	29
1,000–3,000	5	16	5	26	76
>3,000	18	2	3	23	40
Total	27	31	66	124	32

Source: Economic data are from World Bank, *World Development Report
1978* (Washington: The World Bank, 1978), pp. 76–77.

[a]During the period from 1974 to 1989, and excluding countries that
were already democratic in 1974.

[b]Includes India, which became nondemocratic in 1975 and then democratized in 1977.

[c]Includes Nigeria, which transited to democracy in 1980 and back to
military rule in 1984, and the Sudan, which traversed a similar course in
1986 and 1989.

1989, or whether they had nondemocratic regimes throughout these years.[21] These figures again indicate that third wave countries varied greatly in their level of economic development, India and Pakistan having 1976 per capita GNPs less than $250 and Czechoslovakia and East Germany having ones over $3,000. Twenty-seven out of thirty-one countries that liberalized or democratized, however, were in the middle-income range, neither poor nor wealthy, and half of the third wave countries had 1976 per capita GNPs between $1,000 and $3,000. Three-quarters of the countries that were at this level of economic development in 1976 and that had nondemocratic governments in 1974 democratized or liberalized significantly by 1989. A social scientist in the mid-1970s who wished to predict future democratizations, in short, would have done reasonably well if he had simply fingered the nondemocratic countries in the $1,000–$3,000 transition zone.

This is not to argue that democratization is determined simply by economic development. Clearly it is not. In 1976 Czechoslovakia and East Germany were well up in the wealthy economic zone where they "should" have been democratic already, and the Soviet Union, Bulgaria, Poland, and Hungary were high in the transition zone with per capita GNP over $2,000. Politics and external forces, however, held back their movement toward democracy until the end of the 1980s. Interesting to note, in an early 1960s study, Phillips Cutright established a strong correlation between level of communications development and democracy, and used this to highlight anomalous cases off his regression line. The principal European countries that were much less democratic then than they "should" have been were Spain, Portugal, Poland, and Czechoslovakia.[22] In the less constrained Iberian environment, political development caught up with economic development in the mid-1970s; in Eastern Europe that did not happen until Soviet controls were removed fifteen years later.

Five countries with 1976 per capita GNPs between $1,000 and $3,000 did not democratize by 1990. Iraq and Iran were large-population oil producers. Lebanon had had a limited form of consociational democracy but disintegrated into civil war after the mid-1970s. Yugoslavia, which in some respects had been more liberal than other East European communist countries, was overtaken by the democratization surge of its neighbors in 1989, although its wealthiest states, Slovenia and Croatia, did begin to move in a democratic direction. The city-state of Singapore, the wealthiest non-oil-producing Third World country, remained throughout the 1980s under the generally benign but ruthlessly firm rule of its philosopher-king. There, as in the Soviet bloc, politics dominated economics.

An economic transition zone can also be seen in a parallel analysis by Mitchell Seligson arguing that in Latin America the thresholds that made democracy possible although not necessary were per capita GNP (1957 dollars) of $250 and 50 percent literacy. Of eleven Latin American countries, only three, Argentina, Chile, and Costa Rica, were above these thresholds in 1957. By the 1980s, however, seven more nations—Brazil, Peru, Ecuador, El Salvador, Nicaragua, Guatemala, and, marginally, Honduras—had reached or passed them. Only Bolivia, among the eleven nations covered in this study, remained significantly below the thresholds. The economic basis for democracy was thus emerging in Latin America. That did not, of course, guarantee the emergence of democracy, yet by 1990 transitions to democracy had occurred or were occurring in all these countries. In a similar vein, Enrique Baloyra pointed out that in Latin America old-style personalistic dictatorships (Paraguay) tended to survive longer than new-style bureaucratic authoritarian regimes (Brazil).[23] The viability of an authoritarian regime appears to be a function more of the nature of its society than of the nature of the regime.

Why did economic development and the movement of countries into the upper-middle income levels promote democratization? The evidence suggests that sheer wealth itself may not have been a crucial factor. Iran and Iraq were in the transition zone but did not democratize. Three small-population oil producers (Saudi Arabia, Libya, Kuwait) were undemocratic, although they had 1976 per capita GNPs over $4,000, ranking well up among the wealthy countries. The implication is that broad-based economic development involving significant industrialization may contribute to democratization but wealth resulting from the sale of oil (and, probably, other natural resources) does not. Oil revenues accrue to the state: they therefore increase the power of the state bureaucracy and, because they reduce or eliminate the need for taxation, they also reduce the need for the government to solicit the acquiescence of its subjects to taxation. The lower the level of taxation, the less reason for publics to demand representation.[24] "No taxation without representation" was a political demand; "no representation without taxation" is a political reality.

In contrast to patterns in the oil states, processes of economic development involving significant industrialization lead to a new, much more diverse, complex, and interrelated economy, which becomes increasingly difficult for authoritarian regimes to control. Economic development created new sources of wealth and power outside the state and a functional need to devolve decision making. More directly, economic development appears to have promoted changes in social structure and values that, in turn, encouraged democratization. First, the level of economic well-being within a society itself, it has been argued, shapes "the values and attitudes of its citizens," fostering the development of feelings of interpersonal trust, life satisfaction, and competence, which, in turn, correlate strongly with the existence of democratic institutions.[25] Second, economic development increases the levels of education in society. Between 1960 and 1981 the proportion of the relevant age group attending secondary school in developing countries increased dramatically.[26] More highly educated people tend to develop the characteristics of trust,

Social Structural Changes caused by economic development, thus encouraging democratization.

satisfaction, and competence that go with democracy. Third, economic development makes greater resources available for distribution among social groups and hence facilitates accommodation and compromise. Fourth, economic development in the 1960s and 1970s both required and promoted the opening of societies to foreign trade, investment, technology, tourism, and communications. Involvement of a country in the world economy created nongovernmental sources of wealth and influence and opened the society to the impact of the democratic ideas prevailing in the industrialized world. Governments, such as that in China, that wished to open their economies to the world in order to promote economic development and yet also to maintain a closed political system confronted an apparently irresoluble conflict. Autarky and development were an impossible combination, development and liberalizing foreign influences an unavoidable one.

Finally, economic development promotes the expansion of the middle class: a larger and larger proportion of society consists of businesspeople, professionals, shopkeepers, teachers, civil servants, managers, technicians, clerical and sales workers. Democracy is premised, in some measure, on majority rule, and democracy is difficult in a situation of concentrated inequalities in which a large, impoverished majority confronts a small, wealthy oligarchy. Democracy may be possible in a relatively poor agricultural society, such as early nineteenth-century United States or twentieth-century Costa Rica, where land ownership is relatively equal. A substantial middle class is normally, however, the product of industrialization and economic growth. In its early phases, the middle class is not necessarily a force for democracy. At times in Latin America and elsewhere, middle-class groups acquiesced in or actively supported military coups designed to overthrow radical governments and to reduce the political influence of labor and peasant organizations. As the process of modernization continued, however, rural radical movements had decreasing leverage on the political process, and the urban middle class increased in size compared to the industrial working class. The potential threats democracy posed to middle-class groups thus declined, and those groups became increasingly confident of their ability to advance their interests through electoral politics.

Third wave movements for democratization were not led by landlords, peasants, or (apart from Poland) industrial workers. In virtually every country the most active supporters of democratization came from the urban middle class. In Argentina, for instance, the choice in the 1960s and 1970s had been between an elected Peronista government based on the working class or a coup-originated military regime with middle-class support. By the 1980s, however, the middle class had become sufficiently numerous so as to provide the core element in the victory of the Radical party under Raúl Alfonsín and to induce the Peronista candidates to be sensitive to its interests. In Brazil the middle class overwhelmingly supported the 1964 coup. By the mid-1970s, however, "it was precisely those sectors which benefitted most from the years of the 'economic miracle' which were the most vocal in demanding a return to democratic rule: the population of the large and developed cities, and the middle class."[27]

In the Philippines, middle-class professionals and businesspeople filled the ranks of the demonstrations against Marcos in 1984. The following year the core groups in the Aquino campaign were "middle class, non-politician doctors and lawyers, who had volunteered their services to the opposition candidates or to the citizen watchdog groups NAMFREL [National Movement for Free Elections], rather than to any party."[28] In Spain economic development had created "a nation of the modern middle classes," which made possible the rapid and peaceful process of bringing the political system into line with society.[29] On Taiwan the "main actors for political change" were "the newly emerged middle class-intellectuals who came to age during the period of rapid economic growth."[30] In Korea the movement for democracy in the 1980s only became a serious threat to the authoritarian regime after the emergence by the 1980s of "a flourishing urban middle class," and middle-class professionals joined the students in demanding the end of authoritarianism. The mobilization of the "managerial and professional classes of Seoul . . . was perhaps of greater moment than any other" factor in forcing the transition to democracy in 1987. Reporting the 1987 demonstrations against the authoritarian Chun regime, the *Economist* asked, "What happens when tear gas meets the middle class in Seoul?"[31] The answer was soon clear: tear gas loses. In several countries, including Spain, Brazil, Peru, Ecuador, and the Philippines, the business community, which had previously supported the creation of authoritarian regimes, played crucial roles in promoting the transitions to democracy.[32] In contrast, where the urban middle class was smaller or weaker, as in China, Burma, the Sudan, Bulgaria, and Romania, either democratization was unsuccessful or democracy was unstable.

The processes of economic development, which, if O'Donnell is correct, produced bureaucratic-authoritarianism in the 1960s, thus also provided the impetus for democratization in the 1980s. A plausible approximation of the causal connections that led to this outcome is depicted in Figure 2.1.

Rapid growth. The movement of countries into the middle-income ranges of the economic transition zone thus led to changes in social structures, beliefs, and culture that were conducive to the emergence of democracy. Extremely high rates of economic growth in some countries also generated dissatisfaction with the existing authoritarian government. In the two decades before their transitions in the mid-1970s, Spain, Portugal, and Greece experienced explosive economic growth. Between 1913 and 1950 the average annual compound rate of growth of real output per capita had been negative in Spain and less than 1 percent in Greece and Portugal. Between 1950 and 1973, the rates were 5.2 percent in Spain, 5.3 percent in Portugal, and 6.2 percent in Greece. GNP

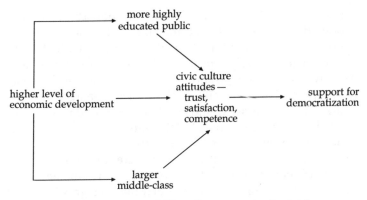

Figure 2.1. Economic Development as a Factor in
Democratization

growth rates in these three countries between 1960 and 1973
were 6–8 percent compared to 4–5 percent in other Western
European countries; and GNP per capita grew faster between
1960 and 1980 than in all other countries of the Organization
for Economic Co-operation and Development (OECD) except
Japan.[33]

Rapid economic growth creates rapidly the economic base
for democracy that slower economic growth creates more
slowly. It also, however, raises expectations, exacerbates inequalities, and creates stresses and strains in the social fabric
that stimulate political mobilization and demands for political
participation. In Greece, for instance, in the 1950s and 1960s,
rapid, unequal economic growth produced "increased aware-
ness, politicization, frustration, and resentment" leading to
"social unrest and political mobilization."[34] These pressures
were a significant cause of the 1967 coup, one purpose of
which was to stifle them. Economic growth, however, continued under the military regime until 1973. The regime simultaneously pursued two conflicting policies. It "attempted to
halt and reverse the process of democratization. But at the
same time it was committed to rapid economic growth and

modernization."[35] Social frustration and political discontent
mounted. At the end of 1973, the oil price hike added an additional source of discontent and the regime either had to liberalize or to intensify repression. Papadopoulos moved ten-
tatively toward liberalization; the students at the National
Technical University (Polytechnic) protested and demanded
more. They were shot, and the hardliners under Ioannidis
ousted Papadapolous, only to fall themselves a half year later
when they provoked a military confrontation in Cyprus.

In Spain similar contradictions were produced by the
"unprecedented period of economic growth" in the 1960s.
Leaders of the Franco regime hoped that this growth would
lead to a happy, contented populace uninterested in politics.
"In practice, however, rapid economic change exacerbated or
catalyzed major conflicts in Spanish society and promoted
cultural, social, and political changes that placed the regime's
viability in doubt. Political arrangements, originally con-
structed in a primarily agrarian society in the aftermath of a
debilitating Civil War, appeared anachronistic when confronted with the tensions of a rapidly changing industrialized
society."[36] The political demands generated by rapid growth
were superimposed on an economy that had fully established
the economic and social base of democracy. In the 1960s, Lau-
reano Lopez Rodo, Franco's minister of planning, prophesied
that Spain would become democratic when its per capita GNP
reached $2,000. It did. The transition was also furthered by
the timely death of Franco in 1975. If he had not died then or
if Juan Carlos had not been committed to creating a parliamentary democracy, polarization could have led to social violence and could have seriously diluted the prospects for democracy in Spain. As it was, however, the economic and
social prerequisites for democracy existed in Spain in 1975
and hence skilled and committed leadership could bring democratization about relatively quickly and smoothly.

In the late 1960s and early 1970s, Brazil experienced its
"economic miracle." From 1968 to 1973, its GNP grew at an

average rate of close to 10 percent a year. This intensified its already highly unequal distribution of income and led some to portray Brazil as the epitome of capitalist development in which multinational corporations and their local partners benefited and local workers and peasants suffered. It also led Ernesto Geisel, when he became president of Brazil in 1974, to comment that "Brazil has done very well, but Brazilians have done very poorly." The pressures of rapid economic growth that had led to the demise of the military regime in Greece and to the transformation of the dictatorship in Spain were equally manifest in Brazil. The military leaders of Brazil, however, were aware of these pressures and determined to accommodate them. In the last year of his regime President Médici began to consider ways of bringing about *distensão* (decompression). President Geisel and his top advisor, General Golbery do Couto e Silva, started this process and carried it forward to 1978. President João Figueiredo continued and broadened it into a process of *abertura*, or opening. The actions of the two presidents averted intensified social conflict and paved the way for democracy.

From the 1960s to the 1980s the growth rates achieved by South Korea and Taiwan were among the highest in the world. The two societies were transformed economically and socially. The pressures in these countries for democratization developed more slowly than in European and Latin American societies for two reasons. First, Confucian cultural traditions emphasizing hierarchy, authority, community, and loyalty delayed the articulation by social groups of intense demands on the polity. Second, in contrast to other societies, rapid economic growth in Korea and Taiwan took place in the context of relatively equal patterns of income distribution. The latter resulted from a variety of causes including land reform programs in the late 1940s and early 1950s and early attainment of high levels of literacy and education. The inequalities associated with rapid growth in Brazil were notably absent from these two East Asian countries. By the 1980s, nonetheless, economic development had proceeded to the point where pressures for expanded political participation compelled governments in both countries to begin processes of democratization. Very rapid economic growth inevitably produced challenges for authoritarian leaders. It did not necessarily lead them to introduce democracy. Between 1960 and 1975 Brazil's GNP grew at an average annual rate of 8 percent. During these same years, Iran's GNP grew at a rate of 10 percent. Between 1980 and 1987, China's GNP also grew at an annual rate of 10 percent. These rates of growth generated highly destabilizing stresses and strains in these three authoritarian systems, intensified inequities and frustrations, and stimulated social groups to make demands on their governments. The leaders of the three countries responded in three different ways. Geisel opened up; Deng cracked down; the shah shilly-shallied. Democracy, repression, and revolution were the respective results of their choices.

Summary. Over the long-term, economic development creates the basis for democratic regimes. In the short-term, very rapid economic growth and economic crises may undermine authoritarian regimes. If economic growth occurs without economic crisis democracy evolves slowly, as it did in nineteenth-century Europe. If the destabilizing growth or economic crisis occurs without achievement of transition zone wealth, the authoritarian regimes may fall but their replacement with long-lived democratic regimes is highly problematical. In the third wave, the combination of substantial levels of economic development and short-term economic crisis or failure was the economic formula most favorable to the transition from authoritarian to democratic government. [37]

RELIGIOUS CHANGES

Two developments in religion promoted democratization in the 1970s and 1980s.

A strong correlation exists between Western Christianity

and democracy. Modern democracy developed first and most vigorously in Christian countries. As of 1988 Catholicism and/or Protestantism were the dominant religions in thirty-nine of forty-six democratic countries. These thirty-nine democratic countries made up 57 percent of a total of sixty-eight countries that were predominantly Western Christian. In contrast, only seven, or 12 percent of fifty-eight countries with other predominant religions were democratic. Democracy was especially scarce among countries that were predominantly Muslim, Buddhist, or Confucian.[38]

This correlation does not prove causation. Western Christianity emphasizes, however, the dignity of the individual and the separate spheres of church and state. In many countries, Protestant and Catholic church leaders have been central in the struggles against repressive countries. It seems plausible to hypothesize that the expansion of Christianity encourages democratic development.

Where did Christianity expand significantly in the 1960s and 1970s? The answer is, in very few places. The most prominent case was South Korea. With only a brief break between them, Korea had first a semidemocratic civilian regime under Syngman Rhee in the 1950s, a semidemocratic military regime under Park Chung Hee in the 1960s, and military dictatorships under Park and Gen. Chun Doo Hwan in the 1970s and 1980s, with the transition to democracy coming in 1987. At the end of World War II Korea was primarily a Buddhist country with a Confucian overlay. Perhaps 1 percent of the population was Christian. By the mid-1980s, roughly 25 percent of the population was Christian—four-fifths Protestant, largely Presbyterian, and one-fifth Catholic. The Christian converts were primarily young, urban, and middle class. Their reasons for espousing Christianity stemmed from the profound social and economic change taking place in Korea. "For the millions who poured into the cities," as one account described it, "and for many who stayed behind in the altered countryside, the quiescent Buddhism of Korea's agrarian age lost its appeal. Christianity with its message of personal salvation and individual destiny offered a surer comfort in a time of confusion and change."[39]

Christianity also offered a surer doctrinal and institutional basis for opposing political repression. Christianity, as one South Korean put it, "made a difference, because it promotes the idea of equality and respect for some authority independent of the state."[40] Confucian authoritarianism and Buddhist passivity were replaced by Christian militancy. In 1974 five bishops led 5,000 Roman Catholics in the first major demonstration against President Park's martial law regime. Many of the principal leaders of the opposition movements, such as Kim Dae Jung and Kim Young Sam, were Christian, and Protestant and Catholic clergy, such as the Rev. Moon Ik Hwan and Cardinal Kim Sou Hwan, were leaders in attacking the repression of the military government. By the early 1980s the churches had become "the principal forum for opposition to the regime." In 1986 and 1987 Cardinal Kim, other Catholic leaders, and the principal Protestant organization, the National Council of Churches, all strongly supported the opposition campaign for direct election of the president. In the conflict with the government, "Churches and cathedrals provided an institutional basis for the activities of human rights and justice, and a public space to share dissenting opinions and faiths. Catholic priests, Roman Catholic Association of Young Catholic Workers, and Urban Industrial Mission and Protestant ministers were politicized and began to represent an important part of the antigovernment movement. Myongdong Cathedral in Seoul had been a symbolic site for political dissidents."[41] Korea thus, in a sense, reversed the Weber connection: economic development promoted the expansion of Christianity, and the Christian churches, their leaders and communicants, were a major force bringing about the transition to democracy in 1987 and 1988.

The second and more important religious development encouraging democratization involved the far-reaching changes that occurred in the doctrine, leadership, popular involvement, and political alignment of the Roman Catholic Church globally and in many countries. Historically Protestantism and democracy were linked with each other. The first democratic impulse in the Western world came with the Puritan revolution in the seventeenth century. The overwhelming majority of the countries that became democratic in the first wave of democratization in the nineteenth century were Protestant. The second wave countries after World War II were religiously diverse. Nonetheless, in the 1960s a significant relation existed between these two variables. For ninety-nine countries, one study showed, "the greater the proportion of the population that is Protestant, the higher the level of democracy." In contrast, Catholicism was associated with the absence of democracy or with limited or late democratic development. Catholicism, Lipset had noted, "appeared antithetical to democracy in pre World War II Europe and in Latin America."[42]

Three plausible reasons were advanced to explain these relationships. Doctrinally, Protestantism stressed the individual conscience, the access of the individual to the Holy Writ in the Bible, and the direct relation of the individual to God. Catholicism emphasized the intermediary role of the priesthood epitomized in the Latin mass. Second, Protestant churches were themselves more democratically organized, stressing the supremacy of the congregation and with no or only a limited bishopric. The Catholic Church, in contrast, was an authoritarian organization with its ranks of priests, bishops, archbishops, and cardinals, culminating in the Pope and the doctrine of papal infallibility. Catholic countries, as Pierre Elliot Trudeau noted, "are authoritarian in spiritual matters; and since the dividing line between the spiritual and the temporal may be very fine or even confused, they are often disinclined to seek solutions in temporal affairs through the mere counting of heads."[43] Finally, there is the Weber thesis: Protestantism encourages economic enterprise, the development of a bourgeoisie, capitalism, and economic wealth, which facilitate the emergence of democratic institutions.

Until the 1960s these arguments and the association they explained between religion and democracy seemed unchallengeable. That is no longer the case. The third wave of the 1970s and 1980s was overwhelmingly a Catholic wave. Two (Portugal and Spain) of the first three third wave countries to democratize were Catholic. Democratization then swept through six South American and three Central American countries. It moved on to the Philippines, the first East Asian country to democratize, doubled back to Chile and affected Mexico, and then burst through in Catholic Poland and Hungary, the first East European countries to democratize. Catholic countries were in the lead in every region of the world, and the most Catholic region, Latin America, was the region that democratized most fully. Overall, roughly three-quarters of the countries that transited to democracy between 1974 and 1989 were Catholic countries.

How can this be explained? One partial answer, of course, is that by the early 1970s, most of the major Protestant countries in the world had become democratic. The principal exceptions were East Germany and South Africa, and Protestant church leaders promoted democratization in those countries as well as in Korea. If, however, many more countries were to become democratic they would have to be Catholic, Orthodox, or non-Christian. The question remains: Why Catholic? One partial explanation may lie in the reversal of another previously existing unfavorable Catholic correlation. Historically Protestant countries developed economically more rapidly than Catholic countries and achieved higher levels of economic well-being. Catholic countries were poor countries. Beginning in the 1950s, however, Catholic countries began to have higher rates of economic growth than Protestant countries. In large part, of course, this was because they were generally at lower levels of economic development. Economic growth, nonetheless, undoubtedly facilitated transitions to democracy in several Catholic countries.[44]

A more pervasive cause of the surge to democracy in Catholic countries was change in the Catholic Church. Historically in Iberia, Latin America, and elsewhere the Church had been associated with the local establishment, the landowning oligarchy, and authoritarian government. In the 1960s, the Church changed. The changes within the Church brought a powerful social institution into opposition to dictatorial regimes, deprived those regimes of whatever legitimacy they might claim from religion, and provided protection, support, resources, and leadership to prodemocratic opposition movements. Before the mid-1960s, the Catholic Church usually accommodated itself to authoritarian regimes and frequently legitimated them. After the mid-1960s, the Church almost invariably opposed authoritarian regimes; and in some countries, such as Brazil, Chile, the Philippines, Poland, and Central American countries, it played a central role in the efforts to change such regimes. This repositioning of the Catholic Church from a bulwark of the status quo, usually authoritarian, to a force for change, usually democratic, was a major political phenomenon. The social scientists of the 1950s were right: Catholicism then was an obstacle to democracy. After 1970, however, Catholicism was a force for democracy because of changes within the Catholic Church.*

These changes occurred at two levels. At the global level

---

*Why and how these momentous changes occurred in the Catholic Church are beyond the scope of this study. George Weigel identifies several factors reaching back to the late nineteenth century as responsible for the shift in the Church's position concerning the liberal democratic state. "Particularly important" among them, he argues, were the United States and the American bishops. Their influence, he says, culminated in Vatican II and its Declaration on Religious Freedom (*Dignitatis Humanae Personae*), which was "a child of the American experience and experiment" and especially of the American theologian John Courtney Murray. See George Weigel, "Catholicism and Democracy: The Other Twentieth-Century Revolution," in *The New Democracies: Global Change and U.S. Policy*, ed. Brad Roberts (Cambridge: MIT change was introduced by Pope John XXIII. The changes stemmed from his own style and commitment and from the doctrines he articulated in his encyclicals. Most important, however, the changes flowed from the Second Vatican Council, which he called and which met from 1962 to 1965. Vatican II stressed the legitimacy and need for social change, the importance of collegial action by bishops, priests, and laity, dedication to helping the poor, the contingent character of social and political structures, and the rights of individuals. Church leaders, Vatican II asserted, have responsibility to "pass moral judgments, even on matters of the political order whenever basic personal rights . . . make such judgment necessary."[45] These views were reaffirmed and elaborated in the Latin American bishops' conferences in Medellin in 1968 and in Puebla in 1979 and in gatherings of bishops elsewhere.

Equally significant changes were occurring simultaneously in popular involvement and priestly activity at the base of the Church. In Spain in the 1960s, for instance, as Juan Linz pointed out,

> New generations of priests, some of them late vocations, perhaps a less rural recruitment of the clergy, a greater awareness of social injustice and contact with the de-Christianized working class, sociological studies of religious practice, the identification of the clergy with the cultural, linguistic minorities in the Basque country and Catalonia, and above all, the impact of the Second Vatican Council, produced a ferment of criticism

---

Press, 1990), pp. 20–25. To the extent that Weigel's argument is valid, the United States played two roles in bringing about the third wave: directly through its new policies in the 1970s and 1980s (see below, pp. 91–98) and at one remove through its impact over time on the Catholic Church.

With rare exceptions, social scientists ignored the significance for democratic development of the changes in the Catholic Church as they also initially ignored the comparably important, if totally different, developments in Islam in the 1960s and 1970s. One prescient exception on the Church was George C. Lodge's 1970 book *Engines of Change: United States Interests and Revolution in Latin America* (New York: Alfred A. Knopf).

and unrest among younger catholic intellectuals, laymen, and clergy and conflicts with authority.[46]

In Brazil the 1960s and 1970s saw the rapid spread throughout the country of popular ecclesiastical base communities (CEBs), which by 1974 numbered 40,000 and gave an entirely new character to the Brazilian church. Simultaneously in the Philippines a "Christian left" developed that included priests and grass-roots activists, some of whom were Marxist and others of whom supported a social democracy that was both anti-imperialist and anticommunist. In the late 1970s in Argentina, the Church shifted dramatically away from its previous conservative coloration, with priests mobilizing a massive youth movement leading to "an extraordinary evangelical revival." Similarly, in both Poland and Chile, a "grass-roots politicization of the church" occurred: "the foundation of the church's position in each country can be traced to movements of aggressive, young priests who have strongly identified themselves with the aspirations of local society and sought to organize or protect authentically representative and nonviolent social movements."[47] These new streams of grass-roots mobilization combined with the new stream of doctrine coming from the Vatican created a new church that almost invariably came into opposition to authoritarian governments.

In non-communist countries, the relations between the Church and authoritarian governments tended to move through three phases: acceptance, ambivalence, and opposition. Initially, conservative elements within the hierarchy were usually dominant, embodying the historical position of the Church as establishment partner and defender of social peace. Church leaders usually welcomed the establishment of the authoritarian regime. In Spain the Church helped Franco to victory and long bolstered his government. Brazilian bishops adopted an "enthusiastically pro-military government stance" immediately after the 1964 coup. In Argentina,

Chile, and elsewhere the Church similarly legitimated military takeovers.[48]

As the authoritarian regime sustained itself in power and usually intensified its repression, and as the converging trends from the grass-roots and the Vatican were felt in the national hierarchy, the position of the Church typically shifted. In Brazil, the Philippines, Chile, Central American countries, and elsewhere, two strands of opposition thought and activity tended to develop within the Church. A socialist or "red" strand preached social justice, the evils of capitalism, the overwhelming need to help the poor, and frequently incorporated into its thinking substantial Marxist elements of "liberation theology." The latter influence did not lead the Church in the direction of democracy, but in countries other than Nicaragua it did help mobilize Catholics in opposition to the existing dictatorship. In most countries also, a moderate or "yellow" strand (as it was known in the Philippines) of opposition also developed that typically included the major segment of the episcopacy and emphasized human rights and democracy. As a result of these developments, the overall position of churches usually shifted from accommodation to ambivalence.

At some time, in most countries, a breaking point came in church-state relations when the national bishops' conference or a top church leader explicitly placed the Church in opposition to the regime. In Chile the brutal abuses of human rights by the military regime shortly after coming to power led to an early break and the formation of the Vicariate of Solidarity in January 1976. In Brazil, the break also came early in the life of the military government, when the National Conference of Brazilian Bishops issued a paper denouncing the government's national security doctrine as "fascist" and paved the way for active Church opposition by reminding Brazilians of Nazi Germany, where Christians "accepted government doctrines without recognizing that they contradicted the true demands of Christianity." Shortly thereafter the cardinal of São Paulo dramatically confirmed the break when, in a calculated insult, he refused to celebrate a birthday mass for the military president of Brazil.[49] In Spain, the break came much later in the history of the regime with the convening of a unique Assembly of Bishops and Priests in Madrid in September 1971. For the Spanish Church, this was an extraordinarily democratic gathering; its proceedings were widely reported; it "provided a lesson in democracy" to the Spanish people and passed resolutions endorsing "the right to freedom of expression, free association and free union meetings, in effect all the rights whose exercise has always been very limited during the Franco regime." As a result of the assembly "the Church clearly separated itself from the state and abandoned the role of legitimizer of the regime."[50] These changes were fully supported by the Vatican. In the Philippines the break came in 1979 when Cardinal Jaime Sin demanded the end of martial law and new elections in which Marcos would not run. In Argentina it came in 1981 with the issuance by the Church of a document on "Church and National Community." In Guatemala, the Church ceased to be a defender of the existing order and became an advocate of social justice, reform, and democracy when the bishops issued "a series of more than fifteen pastoral letters and public denunciations between 1983 and 1986, all calling for respect of human rights and social, economic, and land reform."[51] In El Salvador the Church under Archbishop Romero similarly broke with the government after 1977.

In virtually all the cases where Church leaders denounced the regime, the regime retaliated with intensified attacks on Catholic clergy, activists, publications, organizations, and property. Priests and Church workers were often seized, tortured, and, on occasion, killed. Martyrs were created. The result was often political, ideological, and economic warfare between church and state, with the Church becoming, as in Brazil, "the most conspicuous opponent" to the authoritarian state and, in Chile, "the center of moral opposition to the regime."[52] In the Philippines and other countries the Church became the principal institution denouncing repression, defending human rights, and pushing for the transition to democracy. The one interesting exception in a deeply Catholic country was Poland, where beginning in 1980 Solidarity monopolized the role of principal opposition and the Polish Church, under the cautious Cardinal Józef Glemp, played for several years a mediating role between government and opposition.

The national churches brought many resources to their war against authoritarianism. Church organizations and church buildings provided refuge and support for regime opponents. Church radio stations, newspapers, and periodicals articulated the opposition cause. As a countrywide and popular institution, the Church had, as in Brazil, a "national network of members who could be mobilized."[53] It was, in a sense, a latent national political machine with hundreds or thousands of priests, nuns, and lay activists who could provide people power for opposition protests. The Church often had leaders, such as Cardinals Arns in Brazil, Sin in the Philippines, Romero in El Salvador, and Kim in Korea, who were highly skilled politically. The Church created organizations such as the Vicariate of Solidarity in Chile to provide support to the opposition and the second National Movement for Free Elections (NAMFREL, or "Nunfrel" as it was often called) in the Philippines to promote return to the electoral process and to ensure honest elections.[54] (The first NAMFREL had been created for similar purposes by the U.S. Central Intelligence Agency in 1953.)

In addition, of course, the Church was a transnational organization. On occasion Vatican influence could be brought to bear, as well as that of other national churches and Catholics in other countries. The Brazilian Church, for instance, mobilized support abroad "through the Vatican, sympathetic clergy and laymen in Europe and the U.S., and other human rights activists outside Brazil, thereby generating protests in the U.S. and European press. Criticism from those quarters made the Brazilian military especially uneasy."[55]

With the accession of John Paul II, the Pope and the Vatican moved to central stage in the Church's struggle against authoritarianism. In March 1979 in his first encyclical John Paul II denounced violations of human rights and explicitly identified the Church as "the guardian" of freedom "which is the condition and basis for the human person's true dignity." Papal visits came to play a key role. John Paul II seemed to have a way of showing up in full pontifical majesty at critical points in democratization processes: Poland, June 1979, June 1983, and June 1987; Brazil, June–July 1980; the Philippines, February 1981; Argentina, June 1982; Guatemala, Nicaragua, El Salvador, Haiti, March 1983; Korea, May 1984; Chile, April 1987; Paraguay, May 1988.

The purpose of these visits, like that of his many visits elsewhere, was always said to be pastoral. Their effects were almost invariably political. In a few cases, as in Korea and the Philippines, local supporters of democratization expressed regret that the Pope had not been more outspoken in backing their cause. More generally, however, he was quite explicit in supporting local churches in their struggles with authoritarian governments, and in Poland, Guatemala, Nicaragua, Chile, Paraguay, and elsewhere he clearly identified himself with the opposition to the regime.[56] His greatest impact, of course, was in Poland, where his dramatic 1979 visit, as one Polish bishop said, altered "the mentality of fear, the fear of police and tanks, of losing your job, of not getting promoted, of being thrown out of school, of failing to get a passport. People learned that if they ceased to fear the system, the system was helpless." This "first great pilgrimage," Timothy Garton Ash observed, was the "beginning of the end" of communism in Eastern Europe. "Here, for the first time, we saw that large-scale, sustained, yet supremely peaceful and self-disciplined manifestation of social unity, the gentle crowd against the Party-state, which was both the hallmark and the essential domestic catalyst of change in 1989, in every country except Romania (and even in Romania, the crowds did not start the violence)."[57] Confronting Pinochet in Chile in 1987, the Pope spelled out the relation of democracy to his mission: "I am not the evangelizer of democracy; I am the evangelizer of the Gospel. To the Gospel message, of course, belong all the problems of human rights; and, if democracy means human rights, it also belongs to the message of the Church."[58]

Finally, Church leaders and organizations at times intervened politically at critical moments in the democratization process. In 1978 in the Dominican Republic the Church denounced the effort to stop the vote counting and prolong the tenure of President Belaguer. In 1989 in Panama Church leaders similarly denounced Noriega's theft of the election and invited Panamanian troops to disobey orders that they act against opposition demonstrators. In Nicaragua Cardinal Obando y Bravo organized opposition to the Sandinista government. In Chile Cardinal Juan Francisco Fresno, like his predecessor, Cardinal Raúl Silva Enríquez, was in the forefront of the struggle against the Pinochet regime and in August 1985 played an active role in bringing together the leaders of eleven political parties to sign the National Accord demanding constitutional reform and elections. At a crucial moment in 1986 in the campaign for democracy in Korea, Cardinal Kim in an open political move explicitly endorsed the need for "constitutional revision" and stated "We have to bring democracy to Korea urgently."[59]

The most extreme political involvement of a Church leader was undoubtedly in the Philippines. Cardinal Sin negotiated the arrangements between Aquino and Salvador Laurel to join together on a united opposition ticket. A month before the election, the cardinal sent a letter to all 2,000 parishes in the Philippines instructing Catholics to vote for "persons who embody the Gospel values of humility, truth, honesty, respect for human rights and life." This was unlikely to leave any doubt in people's minds as to whom the cardinal was supporting, but he followed it up anyway with a virtually explicit endorsement of Aquino. After Marcos attempted to steal the election and the military revolt occurred at Camp Craeme, he used the Church organization and the Church radio station to mobilize the populace on the military's behalf. "The religious overtone of the three-day revolt could not be mistaken as nuns and priests occupied the front lines of the human barricades, and rebel generals hoisted up the statue of the Virgin Mary before the crowd. After Marcos had finally gone to Hawaii, Cardinal Sin presided over a triumphal thanksgiving mass at the Luneta, chanting 'Cory' and flashing the Laban sign."[60] Cardinal Sin may have played a more active and more powerful role in bringing about the end of a regime and a change in national political leadership than any Catholic prelate since the seventeenth century.

All in all, if it were not for the changes within the Catholic Church and the resulting actions of the Church against authoritarianism, fewer third wave transitions to democracy would have occurred and many that did occur would have occurred later. In country after country the choice between democracy and authoritarianism became personified in the conflict between the cardinal and the dictator. Catholicism was second only to economic development as a pervasive force making for democratization in the 1970s and 1980s. The logo of the third wave could well be a crucifix superimposed on a dollar sign.

NEW POLICIES OF EXTERNAL ACTORS

Democratization in a country may be influenced, perhaps decisively, by the actions of governments and institutions external to that country. In fifteen of the twenty-nine democratic countries in 1970, as Robert Dahl pointed out, democratic regimes were instituted either during periods of foreign rule or as the country became independent from foreign rule.[61] Obviously foreign actors may also overthrow democratic regimes or prevent countries that might otherwise become democratic from doing so. Foreign actors can perhaps best be thought of as hastening or retarding the effects of economic and social development on democratization. As has been pointed out, when countries reach a certain social and economic level, they enter a transition zone where the probability of their moving in a democratic direction increases markedly. Foreign influences may lead to democratization efforts before countries reach that zone or they may retard or prevent democratization by countries which have reached that level of development. Jonathan Sunshine, for instance, argues that external influences in Europe before 1830 were fundamentally antidemocratic and hence held up democratization. Between 1830 and 1930, however, the external environment was neutral with respect to democratization; hence democraticization proceeded in different countries more or less at the pace set by economic and social development.[62] Somewhat similarly, the Allied victory in World War I produced democratic institutions in central and eastern European countries that socially and economically (except for Czechoslovakia) were not ready for them and hence they did not last long. After World War II, the Soviet intervention prevented the creation of democratic institutions in East Germany, Czechoslovakia, Hungary, and Poland, which by then were more economically and socially prepared for democratization. Similarly, decolonization produced many new countries with democratic institutions modeled on those of the colonial power, but with social and economic conditions that were extremely hostile (as in Africa) or posed major obstacles to democratic development.

External actors significantly helped third wave democratizations. Indeed, by the late 1980s the major sources of power and influence in the world—the Vatican, the European Community, the United States, and the Soviet Union—were actively promoting liberalization and democratization. Rome delegitimated authoritarian regimes in Catholic countries; Brussels provided incentives for democratization in southern and eastern Europe; Washington pushed democratization in Latin America and Asia; Moscow removed the principal obstacle to democratization in Eastern Europe. In each case, the actions of these external institutions reflected significant changes in their policies. In the absence of those policy changes and the influence of these external actors, the third wave would have been much more circumscribed than it was.

European institutions. The European Community had its origins in the 1951 treaty among France, West Germany, Italy, and the three low countries that created the European Coal and Steel Community. In 1957 the Treaties of Rome created the European Atomic Energy Community (Euratom) and the European Economic Community with these same six members. In 1969 these three bodies were brought together in the European Community. As a result of de Gaulle's veto of British entry in 1963, the membership of the combined communities remained the six original signatories of the Treaty of Paris. In 1970, however, the Community shifted course and negotiations were inaugurated with Norway, Denmark, Ireland, and Great Britain. In 1973 the latter three countries became members in the "first enlargement" of the Community. By the mid-1970s the issue of further expansion in southern Europe became a central one.

This shift in direction on the part of the Community coincided with and reinforced the processes of democratization taking place in Mediterranean Europe. For Greece, Portugal, and Spain, democratization and entry into the European Community went hand in hand. Membership in the Community was desirable and even necessary on economic grounds; to be a member a country had to be democratic; hence democracy was an essential step to economic growth and prosperity. At the same time, membership in the Community would reinforce the commitment to democracy and provide an external anchor against retrogression to authoritarianism. When the new democratic governments applied for membership, the existing members "could do little else but accept them. A general consensus in favor of enlargement emerged fairly easily."[63]

Greece had been an associate of the Community since 1962. With the end of the military dictatorship in 1974, the new leadership of Greece rapidly moved to develop this relationship and in June 1975 applied for full membership. The Karamanlis government and Greeks who supported this move wanted to promote economic development, to ensure access to Western European markets for Greek products— particularly agricultural products, to decrease dependence on the United States, and to strengthen relations with Western European countries in order to counterbalance Turkey and the Slavic states. Crucial also, however, was the recognition by the dominant centrist and conservative groups in Greek politics that joining the Community would provide "the best safeguard for Greece's fledgling democratic institutions."[64]

In Spain and Portugal in the mid-1970s there was a pervasive desire to identify their countries with Europe. Tourism, trade, and investment had made the Spanish economy a part of Europe. Almost half of Portugal's foreign trade was with the Community. The Spanish vocation, Juan Carlos emphasized, is with Europe and in Europe. "The future of Portugal," said General Spinola, "lies unequivocally with Europe."[65] These sentiments were particularly strong among the middle classes in both countries, which also provided the social basis for the movement to democracy. Portugal applied for membership in the Community in March 1977, Spain in June 1977. In both countries, as in Greece, the establishment of democracy was seen as necessary to secure the economic benefits of Community membership, and Community membership was seen as a guarantee of the stability of democracy. In January 1981 Greece became a full member of the Community and five years later Portugal and Spain did also.

In Portugal the impact of the Community on democratization was not limited to passively providing an economic incentive and a political anchor. The West German government and the Social Democratic Party (SPD) took the initiative in actively intervening in the struggle with the communists and provided substantial resources to the Portuguese government and the Portuguese socialists.[66] By so doing they also provided a model, an incentive, and a means for the United States to become similarly engaged and to funnel substantial sums to the forces fighting for democracy. Given the immense financial resources that the Soviet Union was providing the communists (estimated at $45–$100 million) in 1975, the Western intervention led by the Germans was crucial to Portuguese democratization.

The beginning of the third wave more or less coincided with the Conference on Security and Cooperation in Europe (CSCE), the Helsinki Final Act, and the beginning of what came to be known as the Helsinki Process. Three elements of this process affected the development of human rights and democracy in Eastern Europe. First, the initial and subsequent conferences adopted a variety of documents giving international legitimacy to human rights and freedoms and to the international monitoring of these rights in individual countries. The Final Act, signed by the heads of government of thirty-five European and North American countries in August 1975, set forth as one of ten principles "respect for human rights and fundamental freedoms, including the freedom of thought, conscience, religion or belief." Basket III of the agreement elaborated the responsibilities of governments to promote the free flow of information, minority rights, freedom of travel, and the reunion of families. In January 1989 the concluding document of the Vienna CSCE meeting included more detailed provisions concerning human rights and basic freedoms. It also created a Conference on the Human Dimension, which met in Paris in May–June 1989 and in Copenhagen in June 1990. The latter meeting approved a comprehensive document endorsing the rule of law, democracy, political pluralism, the right to form political parties, and free and fair elections. Over the course of fifteen years, the CSCE nations thus moved from commitments to a limited number of human rights to endorsement of the full range of democratic liberties and institutions.

Second, the Helsinki Final Act was attacked by many in the United States as legitimating the Soviet-delineated borders in Eastern Europe in return for relatively meaningless promises by the Soviets to observe certain human rights. The subsequent CSCE conferences in Belgrade (1977–78), Madrid (1980–83), and Vienna (1986–89), however, provided the United States and Western European nations with the opportunity to press the Soviet Union and Eastern European countries on their Helsinki commitments and to call attention to and demand correction of particular violations of those commitments.

Finally, the Helsinki Process also involved the creation within countries of commissions or watch groups to monitor compliance with the agreement. Yuri Orlov and other Soviet dissidents formed the first such group in May 1976, which was followed by the Czechoslovak Charter '77 group and comparable committees in other countries. These groups, often persecuted and suppressed by their governments, nonetheless constituted domestic lobbies for liberalization.

The impact of the Helsinki Process in all three dimensions on democratization in Eastern Europe was limited but real. Communist governments endorsed Western principles concerning standards for human rights and hence laid themselves open to international and domestic criticism when they violated those rights. Helsinki was an incentive and a weapon for reformers to use in attempting to open up their societies. In at least two cases, the impact was very direct. In September 1989 the reform-minded government of Hungary used its commitment to the right of an individual to emigrate (spelled out in the concluding document of the Vienna meeting) to justify violating its agreement with the East German government and letting East Germans exit through Hungary to West Germany. This process set in motion the series of events leading to the collapse of East German communism. In October 1989 the meeting of a CSCE conference on the environment in Bulgaria stimulated demonstrations in Sofia that were brutally suppressed by the government and started the series of events that led to the ouster of the standpatter dictator, Todor Zhivkov, the following month.

The European Community actively promoted democratization, and prospective Community membership was an incentive to countries to democratize. CSCE was a process that committed communist governments to liberalize and that legitimated the efforts of internal dissidents and foreign governments to induce them to do so. It did not create democracies but it helped foster political openings in Eastern Europe and the Soviet Union.

The United States. American policy toward the promotion of human rights and democracy in other countries began to change in the early 1970s and evolved through four phases between 1973 and 1989. During the late 1960s and early 1970s these goals occupied a subordinate position in American foreign policy. The activist approach of the Alliance for Progress was sidelined; the government and the country were preoccupied with the Vietnam War; President Nixon and Henry Kissinger espoused a realpolitik approach to foreign policy. In 1973, however, the tide began to move in the other direction. The initiative for change came from Congress and began with the fifteen-session hearings conducted by Representative Donald Fraser's Subcommittee on International Organizations and Movements in the last half of 1973. The subcommittee's report in early 1974 urged that the United States make the promotion of human rights a major foreign policy goal and recommended a variety of actions to promote that goal. In 1974 Congress added human rights amendments to the Foreign Assistance Act, the Mutual Assistance Act, and the Trade Reform Act. Three years later it similarly amended the International Financial Institutions Act. These amendments generally provided that no assistance could be given to countries guilty of gross violations of human rights unless the President found that there were compelling reasons to do so. During 1974, 1975, and 1976, Congress's concern with human rights and its desire to apply economic sanctions to human rights violators became dramatically evident.

A second phase in U.S. policy came with the Carter administration in 1977. Carter had made human rights a major theme in his election campaign and it became a prominent aspect of his foreign policy during his first year in office. Presidential actions (such as, immediately after taking office, his letter to Andrei Sakharov and his reception of Vladimir Bukovsky at the White House); speeches and statements by the president, the secretary of state, and other members of the administration, the suspension of economic assistance to several countries, the organizational upgrading of human rights in the governmental bureaucracy—all served to emphasize the central role of human rights in American foreign policy and to place human rights on "the world agenda," as President Carter put it.

The Reagan administration came into office determined to distinguish its foreign policy from that of its predecessor. One element of this was to criticize the Carter human rights approach because it focused on individual human rights abuses rather than on the political systems that denied human rights. Initially, the Reagan administration thus downplayed the human rights problems in "authoritarian" regimes in Latin America and Asia and emphasized the need to challenge communist regimes. By the end of 1981, however, under pressure from Congress and the democratic transitions in Latin America, the administration began to shift its position, a change manifested in President Reagan's address to Parliament in June 1982. By 1983 and 1984 U.S. policy had entered its fourth phase with the administration moving actively to promote democratic change in both communist and noncommunist dictatorships, symbolizing its commitment with the creation of the National Endowment for Democracy. In the end, the Carter and Reagan administrations both followed similar "moralistic" approaches to promoting human rights and democracy abroad.[67] In the third wave, the United States government used a variety of means—political, economic, diplomatic, and military—to promote democratization. They included the following:

(1) statements by presidents, secretaries of state, and other officials endorsing democratization in general and in particular countries; the annual ratings by the State Department of human rights in other countries; advocacy of democracy by the U.S. Information Agency, Voice of America, Radio Free Europe, and Radio Liberty;

(2) economic pressures and sanctions, including congressional limitations on or prohibitions of U.S. assistance, trade, and investment in fifteen countries; executive suspensions of aid in other cases; and negative votes or abstentions with respect to loans by multilateral financial institutions;

(3) diplomatic action, including promotion of democratization by a new activist breed of "freedom-pusher" U.S. ambassadors (the prototype of which was Frank Carlucci in Portugal in 1975 *), such as Lawrence Pezzullo in Uruguay and Nicaragua, Stephen Bosworth in the Philippines, Deane R. Hinton in El Salvador,

---

* "Carlucci, with strong West German backing, proposed a policy of subtle support for the Socialists. He also remained at arm's length from the old right-wing hard-liners who had previously had Washington's ear; he helped to strengthen the moderate Left within the military, and he worked mightily to provide substantial economic aid to the coalition of Socialists and moderate army officers who routed the Communists and radical soldiers in November 1975." Kenneth Maxwell, "Regime Overthrow and the Prospects for Democratic Transition in Portugal," in *Transitions from Authoritarian Rule: Southern Europe*, eds. Guillermo O'Donnell, Philippe C. Schmitter, and Laurence Whitehead (Baltimore: Johns Hopkins University Press, 1986), p. 131.

The idea that it was the responsibility of the American ambassador to promote democracy in the country to which he was accredited, rather than simply to maintain good relations with its government however horrendous it might be, signaled a revolutionary change in the ethos of the Department of State. Serious study is needed of why and how this shift in bureaucratic mentality from cookie pusher to freedom pusher came about.

Pakistan, and Panama, Edwin Corr in Peru, Bolivia, and El Salvador, Clyde Taylor in Paraguay, Harry Barnes in Chile, and
Mark Palmer in Hungary; and also including lobbying by the
commander in chief of the U.S. Southern Command in Ecuador
and Chile;

(4) material support for democratic forces, including what
were probably tens of millions of dollars from the Central Intelligence Agency (CIA) to the Socialist party in Portugal in 1975,
substantial financial support to Solidarity in Poland, several millions of dollars from the Agency for International Development
(AID) and the National Endowment for Democracy to ensure a
fair referendum on General Pinochet in Chile in 1988, and fund-
ing to promote a democratic outcome in Nicaragua in 1990;

(5) military action, including the Carter administration's deployment of American warships off the Dominican Republic to
ensure a fair count in the 1978 election, the Reagan administration's invasion of Grenada in 1983, and the Bush Administration's overflights in support of Aquino and invasion of Panama
in 1989; military aid to democratically elected governments in
the Philippines and El Salvador in their wars with Marxist-
Leninist insurgencies; and financial support to insurgencies
against nondemocratic governments in Afghanistan, Angola,
Cambodia, and Nicaragua;

(6) multilateral diplomacy, including the pressuring of the
Soviet Union by Carter-Reagan appointee Max Kampelman on
Basket III of the Helsinki Accords at the CSCE talks in Belgrade
and Madrid, and efforts to mobilize opposition by United
Nations (UN) agencies against notorious human rights violators.

To what extent did these actions help democratization? Undoubtedly the most significant effect was to make human
rights and democracy major issues in international relations.
In 1977, the International League for Human Rights noted,
human rights "had for the first time become a subject of
national policy in many countries" and "the focus of discussion in international organizations and of greater attention
in the world media. A most significant factor in this has been
President Carter and the U.S. human rights policy." Carter's
campaign, as Arthur Schlesinger wrote, "altered the international environment" and "placed human rights on the

world's agenda—and on the world's conscience."[68] President
Reagan's endorsement of "Project Democracy" in the first
year of his administration, his 1982 speech to Parliament, the
creation of the National Endowment for Democracy in 1984,
his message to Congress in March 1986, plus the activities of
American diplomats in a range of countries helped to keep
democratization a central focus of international affairs in the
1980s and to strengthen the overall global intellectual environment favorable to democracy.

In some countries, the American role was direct and crucial. Like cardinals and papal nuncios, American ambassadors at times promoted agreement among opposition groups
and served as mediators between those groups and the authoritarian government. In 1980, 1983, and 1984, the United
States intervened to prevent planned military coups in El Salvador, Honduras, and Bolivia. In 1987 President Reagan and
Secretary George Shultz urged President Chun of Korea to
enter into a dialogue with the opposition and the State Department delivered "hard warnings" to the Korean military
not to attempt a coup d'etat. In Peru in January 1989 a
military coup appeared imminent; the American ambassador
forcefully announced U.S. opposition to such a coup; the
coup did not occur.[69] On several occasions the United States
acted to sustain Philippine democracy against military coups.
American actions in these and other cases may or may not
have been decisive, but they clearly were significant in
bolstering movement toward democracy. In effect, under
Carter, Reagan, and Bush the United States adopted a democratic version of the Brezhnev doctrine: within its area of influence it would not permit democratic governments to be
overthrown.

The impact of the Carter-Reagan efforts obviously varied
greatly from country to country and it would require extraordinary effort to evaluate that impact in even a single country.
Two measures are, perhaps, relevant. One is the judgments
of those whom the policies were designed to benefit. In 1986,

for instance, Osvaldo Hurtado, democratic president of Ecuador 1981–84, said, "The United States has committed itself to democratic institutions as never in the past; without the prodemocratic policies espoused by Presidents Carter and Reagan, some Latin American democratic processes would never have been launched or been met with such success." In December 1984, one week after becoming the first democratically elected president of Uruguay since 1971, Julio Sanguinetti expressed similar sentiments: "The vigorous policies of the Carter Administration were the most important outside influence on Uruguay's democratization process. In those years of dictatorship, those of us in the opposition had to struggle practically in the dark. One of the few significant sources of support we had was the policy of the U.S. government, which was constantly looking for human-rights violations." Commenting on the successful struggle against Marcos in the Philippines, Cardinal Sin observed, "No one wins here without the help of America." Even the Soviet Union felt the effects. "I don't know if President Carter will enter American history," commented the head of the Moscow chapter of Amnesty International in 1980, "but he has already entered Russian history with this policy."[70]

A second measure of U.S. impact on democratization comes from those who wanted to maintain dictatorships. During the Carter and Reagan administrations, the top leaders of authoritarian governments in Brazil, Argentina, Chile, Uruguay, the Philippines, China, the Soviet Union, Poland, and other countries complained bitterly and in some cases frequently about American "interference" in their domestic politics. The evidence strongly suggests that in most cases the complaints were justified.

These judgments by participants are reinforced for many countries by those of expert observers. In Peru in 1977, according to Luis Abugattas,

> The redemocratization thus was reinforced by the human
> rights policies of the Carter Administration and the need to

develop external legitimacy in view of the foreign debt negotiations. Negotiations with the IMF had been suspended since
mid-1976, and the military government was unable to resume
them because of its unwillingness to adopt the "shock policies" demanded by the Fund. The democratic opening caught
the attention of the U.S. State Department, and every step in
that direction received a positive response, such as an increase
in foreign aid to the regime. Moreover, the U.S. embassy received orders to oppose rightist military officers and factions
of local capital who sought military *continuismo* along the lines
of Southern Cone countries, and let it be known that this option would not be accepted by the Carter Administration. If
redemocratization was a possibility after July 1976, after July
1977 it was a fact.

In Ecuador U.S. pressure was one of three factors that "appear to have prevented an authoritarian relapse" in 1978, and
when President Febres-Cordero wanted to suspend the 1985
midterm elections he "ultimately scheduled them only under
heavy pressure from the United States embassy." In 1984
when the president of Bolivia was kidnapped by the security
forces he was released due to "severe opposition from workers, loyal military sectors, and the United States embassy."
Democratization in the Dominican Republic has been labeled
"the transition 'from without,'" with involvement by the U.S.
culminating in its third wave intervention to ensure an honest
account of the ballots in the 1978 election. In Chile, "con-
tinual United States pressure" helped make possible the free
and honest referendum on the Pinochet regime in 1988. The
Reagan administration was particularly influential in encouraging democratization in countries such as Chile, El Salvador,
Guatemala, and Honduras because their military establishments perceived the administration as basically friendly.[71]

The most publicized and controversial effort of the United
States to promote democratization in another country was the
passage by Congress over President Reagan's veto of the
Comprehensive Anti-Apartheid Act of 1986 imposing sanctions on South Africa. In the debates over this measure, its

supporters argued that sanctions would have significant impact on the South African economy and compel the South African regime to move quickly to end apartheid. Its opponents also argued that sanctions would seriously affect the economy, eliminating jobs for blacks and worsening black living standards and prospects for advancement. Both claims were overstated. U.S. sanctions and the less stringent European Community sanctions had some economic impact on South Africa in the 1980s. It is unclear whether or not they significantly affected movement away from apartheid. That movement had begun in 1979 as a direct result of economic development in South Africa and the need to open up skilled jobs to blacks, to establish legal black trade unions, to improve black education, to permit the free movement of labor, and to expand black purchasing power. Apartheid was compatible with a relatively poor rural economy; it was not compatible with a complex, wealthy, urban commercial and industrial economy. As in other countries, economic development generated political liberalization. American and European sanctions in the mid-1980s undoubtedly affected the psychology and sense of isolation of South African whites and added extra incentives for movement away from apartheid. They probably affected the speed and nature of that movement, but their effect was second to the impact of economic and social change within South Africa.

No definitive evaluation of the U.S. role in third wave democratizations is possible here. Overall, however, it would appear that U.S. support was critical to democratization in the Dominican Republic, Grenada, El Salvador, Guatemala, Honduras, Uruguay, Peru, Ecuador, Panama, and the Philippines and that it was a contributing factor to democratization in Portugal, Chile, Poland, Korea, Bolivia, and Taiwan. As with the Catholic Church, the absence of the United States from the process would have meant fewer and later transitions to democracy.

The Soviet Union. Democratization in the late 1980s in Eastern Europe was the result of changes in Soviet policy even more far-reaching and dramatic than those that Congress and President Carter made in American policy in the 1970s. President Mikhail Gorbachev revoked the Brezhnev doctrine and conveyed to Eastern European governments as well as opposition groups the clear message that the Soviet government would not act to maintain the existing communist dictatorships and instead favored economic liberalization and political reform. Just how much political reform Gorbachev supported and anticipated is uncertain. He undoubtedly favored the removal of old-guard leaders like Erich Honecker in East Germany, Todor Zhivkov in Bulgaria, and Milos Jakes in Czechoslovakia and their replacement by reform communists who would be his natural allies. It is not clear that he also favored the full democratization of Eastern European countries and the virtually total collapse of Soviet influence in those societies. Yet that is what his actions produced.

The new Soviet approach opened the way for the ouster of established communist leaders, the participation in power of noncommunist groups, the selection of governmental officials through competitive elections, the opening of frontiers with Western Europe, and intensified efforts to move toward more market-oriented economies. The Polish transition of 1988–89 apparently derived primarily from internal developments. In August 1989, however, Gorbachev reportedly intervened to urge Communist party leaders to join in a Solidarity-led government. In September the Soviets did not object to the Hungarians opening their border with the West. In early October Gorbachev's visit to East Berlin and his declaration that "he who comes late gets punished by life" triggered the removal of Honecker. The Kremlin made clear that Soviet troops would not be used to put down the protests in Leipzig and other cities. In November the Soviets collaborated in the removal of Zhivkov as party chief in Bulgaria and the creation of a reformist government under Petar Mladenov. With respect to Czechoslovakia, Gorbachev reportedly urged change on Jakes and Ladislav Adamec in the summer of 1989. In November the Soviets indicated they would repudiate the 1968 invasion, thereby delegitimating the Czechoslovak party leadership, and strenuously warned the Czechs against using force to prevent change.[72]

In Latin America and East Asia the exercise of American power contributed to democratization; in Eastern Europe the withdrawal of Soviet power had similar effects. The Soviet shift led to highly nationalistic prodemocracy demonstrators chanting, "Gorby! Gorby!" in the streets of Leipzig, Budapest, and Prague, and to Mikhail Gorbachev joining John Paul II, Jimmy Carter, and Ronald Reagan as a major transnational promoter of democratic change in the late twentieth century.

DEMONSTRATION EFFECTS OR SNOWBALLING

A fifth factor contributing to the third wave may be variously termed demonstration effect, contagion, diffusion, emulation, snowballing, or perhaps even the domino effect. Successful democratization occurs in one country and this encourages democratization in other countries, either because they seem to face similar problems, or because successful democratization elsewhere suggests that democratization might be a cure for their problems whatever those problems are, or because the country that has democratized is powerful and/ or is viewed as a political and cultural model. In their study of *Crisis, Choice, and Change*, Almond and Mundt found demonstration effects to be moderately important among the five environmental causes they analyzed. Statistical studies of coups and other political phenomena have shown the existence, in at least some circumstances, of a contagion pattern.[73] Analyzing the effects of demonstration effects in individual cases is difficult and would require more intensive study than is possible here, but it may be possible to set forth some plausible hypotheses about the general role of demonstration effects in the third wave.

In practice, what did demonstration effects demonstrate? First, they demonstrated to leaders and groups in one society the ability of leaders and groups in another society to bring about the end of an authoritarian system and to install a democratic system. They showed that it could be done, and hence presumably stimulated those in the second society to attempt to emulate those in the first. Second, demonstration effects showed how it could be done. People in the follow-on society learned from and attempted to imitate the techniques and the methods used to bring about the earlier democratizations. Korean groups consciously emulated the "people-power" approach that had brought down the Marcos dictatorship. At times the learning was the result of direct consultation between democratizers and of a conscious education process, as occurred between Hungarian democratizers and their Spanish predecessors. Third, the later democratizers also learned about dangers to be avoided and difficulties to be overcome. The upheavals and social conflict in Portugal in 1974 and 1975, for instance, stimulated democratization leaders in Spain and Brazil to attempt "a process of managed political change to avoid precisely the discontinuity that Portugal suffered." Similarly, Spanish democratic leaders considered the Turkish military coup d'etat of September 1980 "as a dangerous example" of what had to be avoided in Spain.[74]

The general role of demonstration effects in the third wave can be summed up in three propositions.

First, demonstration effects were much more important in the third wave than in the first two waves of democratization or, very probably, in any other political waves in the twentieth century. The reason is the tremendous expansion in global communications and transportation that occurred in the decades after World War II and particularly the blanketing of the world by television and communications satellites in the 1970s. Governments could still control the local media and, at times, virtually eliminate the ability of their peoples to receive messages they did not wish them to receive. The difficulties and costs of doing this, however, increased markedly. It could lead to an extensive underground media network as happened in Poland and other countries. Shortwave radio, satellite television, computers, and facsimile (FAX) machines made it increasingly difficult for authoritarian governments to keep from their elites and even their publics information on the struggles against and the overthrow of authoritarian regimes in other countries. Thanks in large part to the impact of global communications, by the mid-1980s the image of a "worldwide democratic revolution" undoubtedly had become a reality in the minds of political and intellectual leaders in most countries of the world. Because people believed it to be real, it was real in its consequences. People could and did ask about the relevance for themselves of political events in far-off countries. Solidarity's struggle in Poland and Marcos's downfall in the Philippines had a resonance in Chile that would have been most unlikely in earlier decades.[75]

Second, while intensified communications made distant events seem relevant, demonstration effects still were strongest among countries that were geographically proximate and culturally similar. The downfall of authoritarianism in Portugal had an immediate impact in southern Europe and in Brazil. "What we need is a Greek Gen. Spinola to oust the junta and return constitutional government," as one Athenian said in June 1974, two months after the coup in Portugal and one month before the collapse of the Greek military regime. The end of forty-five years of Portuguese dictatorship also "came as a profound shock to the Spanish bunker and as a great morale booster to the opposition. The fact that the poor relation could manage democracy could only intensify demands for change in Spain."[76] In the nature of things, Greek democratization had little effect elsewhere. Spanish democratization, however, was immensely relevant to and influential in Latin America. As one Argentine observed, "to replicate the United States is something we could never reasonably be expected to do, but to resemble Spain is quite another matter." The transitions in Spain and Portugal demonstrated most convincingly that Iberian cultures were not inherently and immutably antidemocratic. If Spain and Portugal could do it, "Latin America could free itself from tyranny." Alfonsín made extensive use of the Spanish "metaphor" to legitimate his activities in Argentina.[77] The Argentine democratization, in turn, in the words of Bolivia's president, "shored up democracy in all Latin America" and had particular impact on its neighbors. The effect on Uruguay was both positive and negative. Democracy in its large neighbor made democracy in Uruguay virtually inevitable; yet the early actions of the Alfonsín regime in prosecuting the former military rulers stimulated some Uruguayan military to back away from their commitment to relinquish power. "The Argentines have done us such horrible damage," lamented Julio Sanguinetti. The Argentine democratization encouraged democratizers in Chile and in Brazil and reportedly discouraged military coups against the new democratic regimes in Peru and Bolivia. Alfonsín personally met with and supported leaders of democratic opposition groups in other Latin American countries.[78]

The downfall of Marcos in February 1986 stimulated anxiety and hope among authoritarian leaders and opposition democrats elsewhere in Asia. Its most significant impact was on South Korea. A month after Cardinal Sin played a central role in the regime change in the Philippines, Cardinal Kim for the first time called for constitutional change and democracy in Korea. "You have many dictatorships in Asia," said opposition leader Kim Dae Jung. "But only in South Korea and the Philippines do you have people actively seeking democracy. They succeeded in the Philippines, and maybe we will succeed here. . . . This is the time of people's power in the developing countries of Asia. We have never been so sure before."[79] It seems probable, although little evidence is avail-

able, that events in the Philippines and Korea helped stimulate the demonstrations for democracy in Burma in the summer of 1988 and those in China in the fall of 1986 and the
spring of 1989, as well as having some impact on the liberalization that occurred in Taiwan.

The most dramatic snowballing occurred in Eastern Europe. Once the Soviet Union acquiesced in and even perhaps encouraged the coming to power of noncommunists in
Poland in August 1989, the tide of democratization swept
through Eastern Europe successively to Hungary in September, East Germany in October, Czechoslovakia and Bulgaria
in November, and Romania in December. As one East German remarked, "We saw what Poland and Hungary were doing; we heard Gorbachev. Everyone felt, Why are we being
left behind?" In Czechoslovakia, as Timothy Garton Ash put
it, "Everyone knew from their neighbors' experience, that it
could be done."[80] The democratization of some countries also
aroused the pride of their neighbors. Was sophisticated, industrialized, middle-class Spain to trail behind small, poor
Portugal? Were Uruguay and Chile, with their long experiences of democratic government, to be outshone by Argentina and Brazil? Was Czechoslovakia, the one Eastern European country with a truly democratic tradition, to lag behind
the others?

The East European and East Asian democratization processes illustrate a third important aspect of demonstration effects: the change over time in the relative importance of the
causes of a democratization wave. The demonstration effect
obviously cannot affect the first democratization. The early
democratizations of the third wave were the result of triggers,
not snowballs. An unwinnable colonial war, a military defeat
in Cyprus, and the death of Franco triggered the democratizations in Portugal, Greece, and Spain. The Falklands defeat,
the murder of Benigno Aquino, and the visit of the Pope had
similar effects in Argentina, the Philippines, and Poland.
These processes were, in considerable measure, autochtho-

nous. Once they occurred, however, the changes in these lead countries—Spain, Portugal, Argentina, the Philippines, Poland—helped stimulate demands for comparable changes in neighboring and culturally similar countries. The impact of the demonstration effects did not depend significantly on the existence of economic and social conditions favorable to democracy in the recipient country. As the snowballing process went on, indeed, that process itself tended to become a substitute for those conditions. This was reflected in its acceleration. In Poland, as the phrase went, democratization took ten years, in Hungary ten months, in East Germany ten weeks, in Czechoslovakia ten days, and in Romania ten hours.[81]

At the end of 1989 an Egyptian commented on the future politics of the Arab world: "There is no escaping from democracy now."[82] His prediction epitomized the assumption of snowballing as cause: because democratization happened there, it will happen here. Snowballs rolling downhill, however, not only accelerate and grow; they also melt in unsympathetic environments. At the close of the 1980s, demonstration effects produced efforts at democratization in countries where other conditions conducive to democratization and democracy were weak or absent. After the movements toward democracy in the Philippines and in Poland and Hungary, the Koreans, East Germans, and Czechoslovaks appropriately asked, "Why not us?" After these peoples moved toward democracy, the Chinese and Romanians then also asked, "Why not us?" In their cases, however, there may have been compelling answers to that question. Chinese per capita GNP was half that of the Philippines and one-tenth that of Korea; economically China was far from the political transition zone. China lacked a powerful bourgeoisie. It had never been occupied by or colonized by the United States. Christianity was weak and the Catholic Church almost nonexistent. China had no previous democratic experience and its traditional culture had many authoritarian elements. Romania was, next to Albania, the poorest country in Eastern Europe; it had no experience with democracy; Western Christianity was almost totally absent; it was isolated from the external influences of the European Community, the Vatican, the United States, and even the Soviet Union. Yet demonstration effects were a powerful force promoting efforts at democratization in both Romania and China. They moved the third wave from the carnations of Lisbon to the carnage of Beijing and Bucharest.

FROM CAUSES TO CAUSERS

Factors contributing to the breakdown or weakening of authoritarian regimes in the 1970s and 1980s included: the prevalence of democratic norms globally and in many individual countries; the resulting general absence of ideology-based legitimacy for authoritarian regimes other than one-party systems; military defeats; economic problems and failures stemming from OPEC oil shocks, Marxist-Leninist ideology, and unwise and ineffective economic policies; success in achieving some goals that either (as with the suppression of guerrilla insurgencies) reduced the need for the regime or (as with very rapid economic growth) intensified social stresses and demands for political participation; the development of divisions within the ruling coalitions in authoritarian regimes, particularly in military regimes over the politicization of the armed forces; and the snowballing effects of the downfall of some authoritarian regimes on the confidence of rulers and oppositions in other authoritarian countries.

Factors contributing to the emergence in the 1970s and 1980s of democratic regimes in previously authoritarian countries included: most important, higher levels of economic well-being, which led to more widespread literacy, education, and urbanization, a larger middle class, and the development of values and attitudes supportive of democracy; changes at both the popular and the leadership levels in the Catholic Church leading the Church to oppose authoritarian regimes and support democracy; the changed policies supporting democratic development of the European Community, the

United States, and, in the mid-1980s, the Soviet Union; and the snowballing effects that the emergence of democratic regimes in lead countries such as Spain, Argentina, the Philippines, and Poland had in strengthening movements toward democracy in other countries.

These were the general causes of the third wave of democratization. They differ significantly from the principal causes of the second wave and, less significantly, from the principal causes of the first wave. The relative significance of these general causes varied from region to region and from one type of authoritarian system to another, as well as from one country to another. Their relative significance also varied over time during the third wave. Military defeat, economic development, and economic crises induced by the oil shocks were prominent among the causes of the earlier democratizations. External actors and, most notably, snowballing were more significant in the later democratizations. In any particular country, democratization was the result of a combination of some general causes plus other factors unique to that country.

General factors create conditions favorable to democratization. They do not make democratization necessary, and they are at one remove from the factors immediately responsible for democratization. A democratic regime is installed not by trends but by people. Democracies are created not by causes but by causers. Political leaders and publics have to act. Why did Eanes and Soares, Karamanlis, Juan Carlos and Suárez, Evren and Ozal, Geisel and Figueiredo, Alfonsín, Duarte, Aquino and Ramos, Roh and two Kims, Chiang and Lee, Walesa and Jaruzelski, de Klerk and Mandela, as well as comparable leaders elsewhere, lead their countries toward democracy? The motives of political leaders are varied and variable, mixed and mysterious, and often unclear to themselves. Leaders may produce democracy because they believe democracy is an end in itself, because they see it as a means to other goals, or because democracy is the by-product of their pursuit of other goals. In many cases, democracy may not be the outcome leaders desire most but it may be the outcome that is least unacceptable.[83]

The emergence of social, economic, and external conditions favorable to democracy is never enough to produce democracy. Whatever their motives, some political leaders have to want it to happen or be willing to take steps, such as partial liberalization, that may lead to it happening. Political leaders cannot through will and skill create democracy where preconditions are absent. In the late 1980s, the obstacles to democracy in Haiti were such as to confound even the most skilled and committed democratic leader. If he had wanted to, however, a political leader far less skilled than Lee Kwan Yew could have produced democracy in Singapore. In the third wave, the conditions for creating democracy had to exist, but only political leaders willing to take the risk of democracy made it happen.

CHAPTER 3

HOW? PROCESSES OF DEMOCRATIZATION

HOW DID THIRD WAVE DEMOCRATIZATIONS HAPPEN? The why and how of democratization are intertwined, but at this point in the analysis the emphasis shifts from the former to the latter, from causes to processes: the ways in which political leaders and publics in the 1970s and 1980s ended authoritarian systems and created democratic ones. The routes of change were diverse, as were the people primarily responsible for bringing about change. Moreover, the starting and ending points of the processes were asymmetric. Obvious differences exist among democratic regimes: some are presidential, some are parliamentary, some embody the Gaullist mixture of the two; so also some are two-party, some are multiparty, and major differences exist in the nature and strength of the parties. These differences have significance for the stability of the democratic systems that are created, but relatively little for the processes leading to them.[1] Of greater importance is that in all democratic regimes the principal officers of government are chosen through competitive elections in which the bulk of the population can participate. Democratic systems thus have a common institutional core that establishes their identity. Authoritarian regimes—as the term is used in this study—are defined simply by the absence of this institutional core. Apart from not being democratic they may have little else in common. It will, consequently, be necessary to start the discussion of change in authoritarian regimes by identifying the differences among those regimes and the significance of those differences for democratization processes. The analysis then turns to the nature of those processes and the strategies employed by democratizers and antidemocrats. The following chapter concludes the consideration of "how" with a discussion of some common features of third wave democratizations.

AUTHORITARIAN REGIMES

Historically, nondemocratic regimes have taken a wide variety of forms. The regimes democratized in the first wave were generally absolute monarchies, lingering feudal aristocracies, and the successor states to continental empires. Those democratized in the second wave had been fascist states, colonies, and personalistic military dictatorships and often had had some previous democratic experience. The regimes that moved to and toward democracy in the third wave generally fell into three groups: one-party systems, military regimes, and personal dictatorships.

The one-party systems were created by revolution or Soviet imposition and included the communist countries plus Taiwan and Mexico (with Turkey also fitting this model before its second wave democratization in the 1940s). In these systems, the party effectively monopolized power, access to power was through the party organization, and the party legitimated its rule through ideology. These systems often achieved a relatively high level of political institutionalization.

The military regimes were created by coups d'etat replacing democratic or civilian governments. In them, the military exercised power on an institutional basis, with the military leaders typically either governing collegially as a junta or circulating the top governmental position among top generals. Military regimes existed in large numbers in Latin America (where some approximated the bureaucratic-authoritarian model) and also in Greece, Turkey, Pakistan, Nigeria, and South Korea. Personal dictatorships were a third, more diverse group of nondemocratic systems. The distinguishing characteristic of a personal dictatorship is that the individual leader is the source of authority and that power depends on access to, closeness to, dependence on, and support from the leader. This category included Portugal under Salazar and Caetano, Spain under Franco, the Philippines under Marcos, India under Indira Ghandi, and Romania under Nicolae Ceausescu. Personal dictatorships had varied origins. Those in the Philippines and India were the result of executive coups. Those in Portugal and Spain began with military coups (which in the latter case led to civil war) with the dictators subsequently establishing bases of power independent of the military. In Romania, a personal dictatorship evolved out of a one-party system. Chile under Pinochet originated as a military regime but in effect became a personal dictatorship due to his prolonged tenure and his differences with and dominance over the leaders of the military services. Some personal dictatorships, such as those of Marcos and Ceausescu, like those of Somoza, Duvalier, Mobutu, and the shah, exemplified Weber's model of sultanistic regimes characterized by patronage, nepotism, cronyism, and corruption.

One-party systems, military regimes, and personal dictatorships suppressed both competition and participation. The South African system differed from these in that it was basically a racial oligarchy with more than 70 percent of the population excluded from politics but with fairly intense political competition occurring within the governing white community. Historical experience suggests that democratization proceeds more easily if competition expands before participation.[2] If this is the case, the prospects for successful democratization were greater in South Africa than in countries with the other types of authoritarian systems. The process in South Africa would, in some measure, resemble the nineteenth-century democratizations in Europe in which the central feature was the expansion of the suffrage and the establishment of a more inclusive polity. In those cases, however, exclusion had been based on economic, not racial, grounds. Hierarchical communal systems, however, historically have been highly resistant to peaceful change.[3] Competition within the oligarchy thus favored successful South African democratization; the racial definition of that oligarchy created problems for democratization.

Particular regimes did not always fit neatly into particular categories. In the early 1980s, for instance, Poland combined elements of a decaying one-party system and of a military-based martial law system led by a military officer who was also secretary general of the Communist party. The communist system in Romania (like its counterpart in North Korea) started out as a one-party system but by the 1980s had evolved into a sultanistic personal dictatorship. The Chilean regime between 1973 and 1989 was in part a military regime but also, in contrast to other South American military regimes, during its entire existence had only one leader who developed other sources of power. Hence it had many of the characteristics of a personal dictatorship. The Noriega dictatorship in Panama, on the other hand, was highly personalized but dependent almost entirely on military power. The categorizations in Table 3.1, consequently, should be viewed as rough approximations. Where a regime combined elements of two types it is categorized in terms of what seemed to be its dominant type as the transition got underway.

In the second wave, democratization occurred in large measure through foreign imposition and decolonization. In the third wave, as we have seen, those two processes were less significant, limited before 1990 to Grenada, Panama, and several relatively small former British colonies also mostly in the Caribbean area. While external influences often were significant causes of third wave democratizations, the processes themselves were overwhelmingly indigenous. These pro-

TABLE 3.1
Authoritarian Regimes and Liberalization/Democratization
Processes, 1974–90

	Regimes			
Processes	One-Party	Personal	Military	Racial Oligarchy
Trans-formation	(Taiwan)[a] Hungary (Mexico) (USSR) Bulgaria	Spain India Chile	Turkey Brazil Peru Ecuador Guatemala Nigeria* Pakistan Sudan*	
16	5	3	8	
Trans-placement	Poland Czechoslovakia Nicaragua Mongolia	(Nepal)	Uruguay Bolivia Honduras El Salvador Korea	(South Africa)
11	4	1	5	1
Replace-ment	East Germany	Portugal Philippines Romania	Greece Argentina	
6	1	3	2	
Inter-vention	Grenada		(Panama)	
2	1		1	
Totals				
35	11	7	16	1

Note: The principal criterion of democratization is selection of a government through an open, competitive, fully participatory, fairly administered election.

[a]Parentheses indicate a country that significantly liberalized but did not democratize by 1990.

*Indicates a country that reverted to authoritarianism.

cesses can be located along a continuum in terms of the relative importance of governing and opposition groups as the sources of democratization. For analytical purposes it is useful to group the cases into three broad types of processes. Transformation (or, in Linz's phrase, *reforma*) occurred when the elites in power took the lead in bringing about democracy. Replacement (Linz's *ruptura*) occurred when opposition groups took the lead in bringing about democracy, and the authoritarian regime collapsed or was overthrown. What might be termed transplacement or *"ruptforma"* occurred when democratization resulted largely from joint action by government and opposition groups.* In virtually all cases groups both in power and out of power played some roles, and these categories simply distinguish the relative importance of government and opposition.

As with regime types, historical cases of regime change did not necessarily fit neatly into theoretical categories. Almost all transitions, not just transplacements, involved some negotiation—explicit or implicit, overt or covert—between government and opposition groups. At times transitions began as one type and then became another. In the early 1980s, for instance, P. W. Botha appeared to be initiating a process of

---

*For reasons that are undoubtedly deeply rooted in human nature, scholars often have the same ideas but prefer to use different words for those ideas. My tripartite division of transition processes coincides with that of Donald Share and Scott Mainwaring, but we have our own names for those processes:

Huntington		Linz		Share/Mainwaring
(1) transformation	=	*reforma*	=	transaction
(2) replacement	=	*ruptura*	=	breakdown/collapse
(3) transplacement	=	—	=	extrication

See Juan J. Linz, Crisis, Breakdown, and Reequilibration, in *The Breakdown of Democratic Regimes*, ed. Juan J. Linz and Alfred Stepan (Baltimore: Johns Hopkins University Press, 1978), p. 35; Donald Share and Scott Mainwaring, "Transitions Through Transaction: Democratization in Brazil and Spain," in *Political Liberalization in Brazil: Dynamics, Dilemmas, and Future Prospects*, ed. Wayne A. Selcher (Boulder, Colo.: Westview Press, 1986), pp. 177–79.

transformation in the South African political system but he stopped short of democratizing it. Confronting a different political environment, his successor, F.W. de Klerk, shifted to a transplacement process of negotiation with the principal opposition group. Similarly, scholars agree that the Brazilian government initiated and controlled the transition process for many years. Some argue that it lost control over that process as a result of popular mobilization and strikes in 1979–80; others, however, point to the government's success in resisting strong opposition demands for direct election of the president in the mid-1980s. Every historical case combined elements of two or more transition processes. Virtually every historical case, however, more clearly approximated one type of process than others.

How did the nature of the authoritarian regime relate to the nature of the transition process? As Table 3.1 suggests, there was no one-to-one relation. Yet the former did have consequences for the latter. With three exceptions, all the transitions from military regimes involved transformation or transplacement. In the three exceptions—Argentina, Greece, and Panama—military regimes suffered military defeats and collapsed as a result. Elsewhere military rulers took the lead, at times in response to opposition and popular pressure, in bringing about the change in regime. Military rulers were better placed to terminate their regimes than were leaders of other regimes. The military leaders virtually never defined themselves as the permanent rulers of their country. They held out the expectation that once they had corrected the evils that had led them to seize power they would exit from power and return to their normal military functions. The military had a permanent institutional role other than politics and governorship. At some point, consequently, the military leaders (other than those in Argentina, Greece, and Panama) decided that the time had come to initiate a return to civilian democratic rule or to negotiate their withdrawal from power with opposition groups. Almost always this occurred after there had been at least one change in the top leadership of the military regime.[4]

Military leaders almost invariably posited two conditions or "exit guarantees" for their withdrawal from power. First, there would be no prosecution, punishment, or other retaliation against military officers for any acts they may have committed when they were in power. Second, the institutional roles and autonomy of the military establishment would be respected, including its overall responsibility for national security, its leadership of the government ministries concerned with security, and often its control of arms industries and other economic enterprises traditionally under military aegis. The ability of the withdrawing military to secure agreement of civilian political leaders to these conditions depended on their relative power. In Brazil, Peru, and other instances of transformation, the military leaders dominated the process and civilian political leaders had little choice but to acquiesce to the demands of the military. Where relative power was more equal, as in Uruguay, negotiations led to some modifications in the military demands. Greek and Argentinean military leaders asked for the same assurances other leaders did. Their requests, however, were rejected out of hand by civilian leaders and they had to agree to a virtual unconditional surrender of power.[5]

It was thus relatively easy for military rulers to withdraw from power and to resume professional military roles. The other side of the coin, however, is that it could also be relatively easy for them to return to power when exigencies and their own interests warranted. One successful military coup in a country makes it impossible for political and military leaders to overlook the possibility of a second. The third wave democracies that succeeded military regimes started life under this shadow.

Transformation and transplacement also characterized the transitions from one-party systems to democracy through

1989, except for those in East Germany and Grenada. One-party regimes had an institutional framework and ideological legitimacy that differentiated them from both democratic and military regimes. They also had an assumption of permanence that distinguished them from military regimes. The distinctive characteristic of one-party systems was the close interweaving of party and state. This created two sets of problems, institutional and ideological, in the transition to democracy.

The institutional problems were most severe with Leninist party states. In Taiwan as in communist countries the "separation of the party from the state" was "the biggest challenge of a Leninist party" in the process of democratization.[6] In Hungary, Czechoslovakia, Poland, and East Germany constitutional provisions for "the leading role" of the communist party had to be abrogated. In Taiwan comparable "temporary provisions" added to the constitution in 1950 were similarly challenged. In all Leninist party systems major issues arose concerning ownership of physical and financial assets—did they belong to the party or the state? The proper disposition of those assets was also in question—should they be retained by the party, nationalized by the government, sold by the party to the highest bidder, or distributed in some equitable manner among social and political groups? In Nicaragua, for instance, after losing the election in February 1990, the Sandinista government apparently moved quickly "to transfer large amounts of Government property to Sandinista hands." "They are selling houses to themselves, selling vehicles to themselves," alleged one anti-Sandinista businessman.[7] Similar allegations were made about the disposal of government property to the Communist party as Solidarity was about to take over the government in Poland. (In a parallel move in Chile, the Pinochet government as it went out of power transferred to the military establishment property and records that had belonged to other government agencies.)

In some countries party militias had to be disbanded or

brought under government control, and in almost all one-party states the regular armed forces had to be depoliticized. In Poland, as in most communist countries, for instance, all army officers had to be members of the Communist party; in 1989, however, Polish army officers lobbied parliament to prohibit officers from being members of any political party.[8] In Nicaragua the Sandinista People's Army had been the army of the movement, became also the army of the state, and then had to be converted into being only the latter. The question of whether party cells within economic enterprises should continue was also a highly controversial issue. Finally, where the single party remained in power, there was the question of the relation between its leaders in government and the top party bodies such as the Politburo and the central committee. In the Leninist state the latter dictated policy to the former. Yet this relationship was hardly compatible with the supremacy of elected parliamentary bodies and responsible cabinets in a democratic state.

The other distinctive set of problems was ideological. In one-party systems, the ideology of the party defined the identity of the state. Hence opposition to the party amounted to treason to the state. To legitimize opposition to the party it was necessary to establish some other identity for the state. This problem manifested itself in three contexts. First, in Poland, Hungary, Czechoslovakia, Romania, and Bulgaria, communist ideology and rule had been imposed by the Soviet Union. The ideology was not essential to defining the identity of the country. In fact, in at least three of these countries nationalism opposed communism. When the communist parties in these countries gave up their claim to undisputed rule based on that ideology, the countries redefined themselves from "people's republics" to "republics" and reestablished nationalism rather than ideology as the basis of the state. These changes hence occurred relatively easily.

Second, several one-party systems where democratization became an issue had been created by national revolutions.

In these cases—China, Mexico, Nicaragua, and Turkey—the nature and purpose of the state were defined by the ideology of the party. In China the regime staunchly adhered to its ideology and identified democratic opposition to communism with treason to the state. In Turkey, the government followed an uncertain and ambivalent policy toward Islamic groups challenging the secular basis of the Kemalist state. In Mexico the leadership of the Partido Revolucionario Institucional (PRI) held somewhat comparable views concerning the liberal challenge of the opposition Partido Acción Nacional (PAN) to the revolutionary, socialist, corporatist character of the PRI state. In Nicaragua Sandinista ideology was the basis of not just the program of a party but also of the legitimacy of the state created by the Nicaraguan revolution.

Third, in some instances the ideology of the single party defined both the nature of the state and its geographical scope. In Yugoslavia and the Soviet Union communist ideology provided the ideological legitimacy for multinational states. If the ideology were rejected, the basis for the state would disappear and each nationality could legitimately claim its own state. In East Germany communism provided the ideological basis for a separate state; when the ideology was abandoned, the rationale for an East German state disappeared. The ideology of the Kuomintang (KMT) defined the government on Taiwan as the government of China, and the regime saw opposition elements supporting an independent Taiwan as subversive. The problem here was less serious than in the other three cases because the ideology legitimated an aspiration rather than a reality. The KMT government functioned in fact as the highly successful government of Taiwan even though in its own eyes its legitimacy depended on the myth that it was the rightful government of all China.

When the military give up their control of government, they do not also give up their control of the instruments of violence with which they could resume control of government. Democratization of a one-party system, however, means that the monopolistic party places at risk its control of government and becomes one more party competing in a multiparty system. In this sense its separation from power is less complete than it is for the military when they withdraw. The party remains a political actor. Defeated in the 1990 election, the Sandinistas could hope "to fight again another day" and come back to power through electoral means.[9] In Bulgaria and Romania former communist parties won elections; in other East European countries they had less sanguine expectations of participating in a coalition government sometime in the future.

After democratization a former monopolistic party is in no better position than any other political group to reinstate an authoritarian system. The party gives up its monopoly of power but not the opportunity to compete for power by democratic means. When they return to the barracks, the military give up both, but they also retain the capacity to reacquire power by nondemocratic means. The transition from a one-party system to democracy, consequently, is likely to be more difficult than the transition from a military regime to democracy, but it is also likely to be more permanent.[10] The difficulties of transforming one-party systems are perhaps reflected in the fact that as of 1990 the leaders of such regimes in Taiwan, Mexico, and the Soviet Union had initiated the liberalization of their regimes but were moving only slowly toward full democratization.

The leaders of personal dictatorships were less likely than those of military and one-party regimes to give up power voluntarily. Personal dictators in countries that transited to democracy as well as those that did not usually tried to remain in office as long as they could. This often created tensions between a narrowly based political system and an increasingly complex and modern economy and society.[11] It also led on occasion to the violent overthrow of the dictator, as happened in Cuba, Nicaragua, Haiti, and Iran, and the dictator's replacement by another authoritarian regime. In the third wave of democratization, uprisings similarly overthrew personal dictatorships in Portugal, the Philippines, and Romania. In Spain, the dictator died and his successors led a classic case of democratic transformation from above. In India and in Chile, the leaders in power submitted themselves to elections in the apparent but mistaken belief that the voters would confirm them in office. When this did not happen, they, unlike Marcos and Noriega, accepted the electoral verdict. In the cases of sultanistic regimes, the transitions to democracy were complicated by the weakness of political parties and other institutions. Transitions to democracy from personal dictatorship thus occurred when the founding dictator died and his successors decided on democratization, when the dictator was overthrown, and when he or she miscalculated the support that the dictator could win in an election.

TRANSITION PROCESSES

The third wave transitions were complex political processes involving a variety of groups struggling for power and for and against democracy and other goals. In terms of their attitudes toward democratization, the crucial participants in the processes were the standpatters, liberal reformers, and democratic reformers in the governing coalition, and democratic moderates and revolutionary extremists in the opposition. In noncommunist authoritarian systems, the standpatters within the government were normally perceived as right-wing, fascist, and nationalist. The opponents of democratization in the opposition were normally left-wing, revolutionary, and Marxist-Leninist. Supporters of democracy in both government and opposition could be conceived as occupying middle positions on the left-right continuum. In communist systems left and right were less clear. Standpatters were normally thought of as Stalinist or Brezhnevite. Within the

Attitudes Toward Democracy

	Against	For		Against
		Reformers		
Government		Democratizers	Liberals	Standpatters
	Radical	Democratic		
Opposition	Extremists	Moderates		

Figure 3.1. Political Groups Involved in Democratization

opposition, the extremist opponents of democracy were not revolutionary left-wingers but often nationalist groups thought of as right-wing.

Within the governing coalition some groups often came to favor democratization, while others opposed it, and others supported limited reform or liberalization (see Figure 3.1). Opposition attitudes toward democracy were also usually divided. Supporters of the existing dictatorship always opposed democracy; opponents of the existing dictatorship often opposed democracy. Almost invariably, however, they used the rhetoric of democracy in their efforts to replace the existing authoritarian regime with one of their own. The groups involved in the politics of democratization thus had both conflicting and common objectives. Reformers and standpatters divided over liberalization and democratization but presumably had a common interest in constraining the power of opposition groups. Moderates and radicals had a common interest in bringing down the existing regime and getting into power but disagreed about what sort of new regime should be created. Reformers and moderates had a common interest in creating democracy but often divided over how the costs of creating it should be borne and how power within it should be apportioned. Standpatters and radicals were totally opposed on the issue of who should rule but had a common interest in weakening the democratic groups in the center and in polarizing politics in the society.

The attitudes and goals of particular individuals and

groups at times changed in the democratization process. If democratization did not produce the dangers they feared, people who had been liberal reformers or even standpatters might come to accept democracy. Similarly, participation in the processes of democratization could lead members of extremist opposition groups to moderate their revolutionary propensities and accept the constraints and opportunities democracy offered.

The relative power of the groups shaped the nature of the democratization process and often changed during that process. If standpatters dominated the government and extremists the opposition, democratization was impossible, as, for example, where a right-wing personal dictator determined to hang on to power confronted an opposition dominated by Marxist-Leninists. Transition to democracy was, of course, facilitated if prodemocratic groups were dominant in both the government and opposition. The differences in power between reformers and moderates, however, shaped how the process occurred. In 1976, for instance, the Spanish opposition urged a complete "democratic break" or *ruptura* with the Franco legacy and creation of a provisional government and a constituent assembly to formulate a new constitutional order. Adolfo Suárez was powerful enough, however, to fend this off and produce democratization working through the Franco constitutional mechanism.[12] If democratic groups were strong in the opposition but not in the government, democratization depended on events undermining the government and bringing the opposition to power. If democratic groups were dominant in the governing coalition, but not in the opposition, the effort at democratization could be threatened by insurgent violence and by a backlash increase in power of standpatter groups possibly leading to a coup d'etat.

The three crucial interactions in democratization processes were those between government and opposition, between reformers and standpatters in the governing coalition, and between moderates and extremists in the opposition. In all transitions these three central interactions played some role. The relative importance and the conflictual or cooperative character of these interactions, however, varied with the overall nature of the transition process. In transformations, the interaction between reformers and standpatters within the governing coalition was of central importance; and the transformation only occurred if reformers were stronger than standpatters, if the government was stronger than the opposition, and if the moderates were stronger than the extremists. As the transformation went on, opposition moderates were often coopted into the governing coalition while standpatter groups opposing democratization defected from it. In replacements, the interactions between government and opposition and between moderates and extremists were important; the opposition eventually had to be stronger than the government, and the moderates had to be stronger than the extremists. A successive defection of groups often led to the downfall of the regime and inauguration of the democratic system. In transplacements, the central interaction was between reformers and moderates not widely unequal in power, with each being able to dominate the antidemocratic groups on its side of the line between the government and the opposition. In some transplacements, government and former opposition groups agreed on at least a temporary sharing of power.

TRANSFORMATIONS

In transformations those in power in the authoritarian regime take the lead and play the decisive role in ending that regime and changing it into a democratic system. The line between transformations and transplacements is fuzzy, and some cases might be legitimately classified in either category. Overall, however, transformations accounted for approximately sixteen out of thirty-five third wave transitions that had occurred or that appeared to be underway by the end of the 1980s. These sixteen cases of liberalization or democratization included changes from five one-party systems, three personal dictatorships, and eight military regimes. Transformation requires the government to be stronger than the opposition. Consequently, it occurred in well-established military regimes where governments clearly controlled the ultimate means of coercion vis-à-vis the opposition and/or vis-à-vis authoritarian systems that had been successful economically, such as Spain, Brazil, Taiwan, Mexico, and, compared to other communist states, Hungary. The leaders of these countries had the power to move their countries toward democracy if they wanted to. In every case the opposition was, at least at the beginning of the process, markedly weaker than the government. In Brazil, for example, as Stepan points out, when "liberalization began, there was no significant political opposition, no economic crisis, and no collapse of the coercive apparatus due to defeat in war."[13] In Brazil and elsewhere the people best situated to end the authoritarian regime were the leaders of the regime—and they did.

The prototypical cases of transformation were Spain, Brazil, and, among communist regimes, Hungary. The most important case, if it materializes, will be the Soviet Union. The Brazilian transition was "liberation from above" or "regime-initiated liberalization." In Spain "it was a question of reformist elements associated with the incumbent dictatorship, initiating processes of political change from within the established regime."[14] The two transitions differed significantly, however, in their duration. In Spain in less than three and a half years after the death of Franco, a democratizing prime minister had replaced a liberalizing one, the Franco legislature had voted the end of the regime, political reform had been endorsed in a referendum, political parties (including the Communist party) were legalized, a new assembly was elected, a democratic constitution was drafted and approved in a referendum, the major political actors reached agreement on economic policy, and parliamentary elections were held under the new constitution. Suárez reportedly told his cabinet that "his strategy would be based on speed. He would keep ahead of the game by introducing specific measures faster than the *continuistas* of the Francoist establishment could respond to them." While the reforms were compressed within a short period of time, however, they were also undertaken sequentially. Hence, it has also been argued that "By staggering the reforms, Suárez avoided antagonizing too many sectors of the franquist regime simultaneously. The last set of democratic reforms provoked open hostility from the military and other franquist hardliners, but the President [Suárez] had greatly gained considerable momentum and support." In effect, then, Suárez followed a highly compressed version of the Kemalist "Fabian strategy, blitzkrieg tactics" pattern of reform.[15]

In Brazil, in contrast, President Geisel determined that political change was to be "gradual, slow, and sure." The process began at the end of the Médici administration in 1973, continued through the Geisel and Figueiredo administrations, jumped forward with the installation of a civilian president in 1985, and culminated in the adoption of a new constitution in 1988 and the popular election of a president in 1989. The regime-decreed movements toward democratization were interspersed with actions taken to reassure hardliners in the military and elsewhere. In effect, Presidents Geisel and Figueiredo followed a two-step forward, one-step backward policy. The result was a creeping democratization in which the control of the government over the process was never seriously challenged. In 1973 Brazil had a repressive military dictatorship; in 1989 it was a full-scale democracy. It is customary to date the arrival of democracy in Brazil in January 1985, when the electoral college chose a civilian president. In fact, however, there was no clear break; the genius of the Brazilian transformation is that it is virtually impossible to say at what point Brazil stopped being a dictatorship and became a democracy.

Spain and Brazil were the prototypical cases of change from

above, and the Spanish case in particular became the model for subsequent democratizations in Latin America and Eastern Europe. In 1988 and 1989, for instance, Hungarian leaders consulted extensively with Spanish leaders on how to introduce democracy and in April 1989 a Spanish delegation went to Budapest to offer advice. Six months later one commentator pointed to the similarities in the two transitions:

> The last years of the Kadar era did bear some resemblance to the benign authoritarianism of Franco's decaying dictatorship. Imre Pozsgay plays the part of Prince Juan Carlos in this comparison. He is a reassuring symbol of continuity in the midst of radical change. Liberal-minded economic experts with links to the old establishment and the new entrepreneurial class provide a technocratic elite for the transition, much as the new bourgeois elites associated with Opus Dei did in Spain. The opposition parties also figure in this analogy, emerging from underground in much the same way the Spanish exiles did once it was safe to come out. And as in Spain, the Hungarian oppositionists—moderate in style, radically democratic in substance—are playing a vital role in the reinvention of democracy.[16]

Third wave transformations usually evolved through five major phases, four of which occurred within the authoritarian system.

Emergence of reformers. The first step was the emergence of a group of leaders or potential leaders within the authoritarian regime who believed that movement in the direction of democracy was desirable or necessary. Why did they conclude this? The reasons why people became democratic reformers varied greatly from country to country and seldom were clear. They can, however, be grouped into five categories. First, reformers often concluded that the costs of staying in power—such as politicizing their armed forces, dividing the coalition that had supported them, grappling with seemingly unsolvable problems (usually economic), and increasing repression—had reached the point where a graceful exit from power was desirable. The leaders of military regimes were particularly sensitive to the corrosive effects of political involvement on the integrity, professionalism, coherence, and command structure of the military. "We all directly or indirectly," Gen. Morales Bermudez observed as he led Peru toward democracy, "had been witnesses to what was happening to this institution fundamental to our fatherland, and in the same vein, to the other institutions. And we don't want that." In a similar vein, Gen. Fernando Matthei, head of the Chilean air force, warned, "If the transition toward democracy is not initiated promptly, we shall ruin the armed forces in a way no Marxist infiltration could."[17]

Second, in some cases reformers wished to reduce the risks they faced if they held on to power and then eventually lost it. If the opposition seemed to be gaining strength, arranging for a democratic transition was one way of achieving this. It is, after all, preferable to risk losing office than to risk losing life.

Third, in some cases, including India, Chile, and Turkey, authoritarian leaders believed that they or their associates would not lose office. Having made commitments to restore democratic institutions and being faced with declining legitimacy and support these rulers could see the desirability of attempting to renew their legitimacy by organizing elections in anticipation that the voters would continue them in power. This anticipation was usually wrong. (See the discussion of "stunning elections," below, pp. 174ff.).

Fourth, reformers often believed that democratizing would produce benefits for their country: increase its international legitimacy, reduce U.S. or other sanctions against their regime, and open the door to economic and military assistance, International Monetary Fund (IMF) loans, invitations to Washington, and inclusion in international gatherings dominated by the leaders of the Western alliance.

Finally, in many cases, including Spain, Brazil, Hungary, and Turkey and some other military regimes, reformers believed that democracy was the "right" form of government and that their country had evolved to the point where, like other developed and respected countries, it too should have a democratic political system.

Liberal reformers tended to see liberalization as a way of defusing opposition to their regime without fully democratizing the regime. They would ease up on repression, restore some civil liberties, reduce censorship, permit broader discussion of public issues, and allow civil society—associations, churches, unions, business organizations—greater scope to conduct their affairs. Liberalizers did not, however, wish to introduce fully participatory competitive elections that could cause current leaders to lose power. They wanted to create a kinder, gentler, more secure and stable authoritarianism without altering fundamentally the nature of their system. Some reformers were undoubtedly unsure themselves how far they wished to go in opening up the politics of their country. They also at times undoubtedly felt the need to veil their intentions: democratizers tended to reassure standpatters by giving the impression that they were only liberalizing; liberalizers attempted to win broader popular support by creating the impression they were democratizing. Debates consequently raged over how far Geisel, Botha, Gorbachev, and others "really" wanted to go.

The emergence of liberalizers and democratizers within an authoritarian system creates a first-order force for political change. It also, however, can have a second-order effect. In military regimes in particular it divides the ruling group, further politicizes the military, and hence leads more officers to believe that "the military as government" must be ended in order to preserve "the military as institution." The debate over whether or not to withdraw from government in itself becomes an argument to withdraw from government.

Acquiring power. Democratic reformers not only had to exist within the authoritarian regime, they also had to be in power in that regime. How did this come about? In three cases leaders who created the authoritarian regime presided over its transition to democracy. In India and Turkey, authoritarian regimes were defined from the start as interruptions in the formal pattern of democracy. The regimes were short-lived, ending with elections organized by the authoritarian leaders in the false anticipation that they or the candidates they supported would win those elections. In Chile General Pinochet created the regime, remained in power for seventeen years, established a lengthy schedule for the transition to democracy, implemented that schedule in anticipation that the voters would extend him in office for eight more years, and exited grudgingly from power when they did not. Otherwise those who created authoritarian regimes or who led such regimes for prolonged periods of time did not take the lead in ending those regimes. In all these cases, transformation occurred because reformers replaced standpatters in power.

Reformers came to power in authoritarian regimes in three ways. First, in Spain and Taiwan, the founding and long-ruling authoritarian leaders, Franco and Chiang Kai-shek died. Their designated successors, Juan Carlos and Chiang Ching-kuo, succeeded to the mantle, responded to the momentous social and economic changes that had occurred in their countries, and began the process of democratization. In the Soviet Union, the deaths in the course of three years of Brezhnev, Andropov, and Chernenko allowed Gorbachev to come to power. In a sense, Franco, Chiang, and Brezhnev died in time; Deng Xiao-ping did not.

In Brazil and in Mexico, the authoritarian system itself provided for regular change in leadership. This made the acquisition of power by reformers possible but not necessary. In Brazil, as was pointed out previously, two factions existed in the military. Repression reached its peak between 1969 and 1972 during the presidency of General Médici, a hard-liner. In a major struggle within the military establishment at the end of his term, the soft-line Sorbonne group was able to secure the nomination of General Ernesto Geisel for president, in part because his brother was minister of war. Guided by his chief associate, General Golbery do Couto e Silva, Geisel began the process of democratization and acted decisively to ensure that he would, in turn, be succeeded in 1978 by another member of the Sorbonne group, General João Batista Figueiredo. In Mexico, outgoing President José Lopez Portillo in 1981 followed standard practice in selecting his minister of planning and budgets, Miguel de la Madrid, as his successor. De la Madrid was an economic and political liberalizer and, rejecting more traditional and old-guard candidates, chose a young reforming technocrat, Carlos Salinas, to continue the opening up process.

Where authoritarian leaders did not die and were not regularly changed, democratic reformers had to oust the ruler and install prodemocratic leadership. In military governments, other than Brazil, this meant the replacement by coup d'etat of one military leader by another: Morales Bermudez replaced Velasco in Peru; Poveda replaced Rodríguez Lara in Ecuador; Mejía replaced Rios Montt in Guatemala; Murtala Muhammed replaced Gowon in Nigeria.[18] In the one-party system in Hungary, reformers mobilized their strength and deposed the long-ruling Janos Kadar at a special party conference in May 1988, replacing him as secretary general with Karoly Grosz. Grosz, however, was only a semireformer, and a year later the Central Committee replaced him with a four-person presidium dominated by reformers. In October 1989 one of them, Rezso Nyers, became party president. In Bulgaria in the fall of 1989, reform-minded Communist party leaders ousted Todor Zhivkov from the dominant position he had occupied for thirty-five years. The leadership changes associated with some liberalizing and democratizing reforms are summarized in Table 3.2.

The failure of liberalization. A critical issue in the third wave concerned the role of liberal reformers and the stability of a liberalized authoritarian polity. Liberal reformers who succeeded standpatter leaders usually turned out to be transition

TABLE 3.2

Country	Standpat Leader	Change	Reform Leader I
Nigeria	Gowon	July 1975 coup	Murtala Mohammed
Ecuador	Rodriguez Lara	January 1976 coup	Poveda
Peru	Velasco	August 1975 coup	Morales Bermudez
Brazil	Medici	March 1974 succession	Geisel
Guatemala	Rios Montt	August 1983 coup	Mejia
Spain	Franco	November 1975 death	Juan Carlos
	Carrero Blanco	December 1973 death	Arias
Taiwan	Chiang Kai-shek	April 1975 death	Chiang Ching-kuo
Hungary	Kadar	May 1988 ouster	Grosz
Mexico	Portillo	December 1982 succession	De la Madrid
South Africa	Vorster	September 1978 ouster	Botha
USSR	Chernenko	March 1985 death	Gorbachev
Bulgaria	Zhivkov	November 1989 ouster	Mladenov

Leadership Change and Reform, 1973–90

Change	Reform Leader II	First Democratic Election
February 1976 death	Obasanjo	August 1979
—	—	April 1979
—	—	May 1980
March 1979 succession	Figueiredo	January 1985
—	—	December 1985
—	Juan Carlos	March 1979
July 1976 ouster	Suárez	
January 1988 death	Lee Teng-hui	
May–October 1989 ouster	Nyers-Pozsgay	March 1990
December 1988 succession	Salinas	
September 1989 ouster	de Klerk	
—	—	June 1990

figures with brief stays in power. In Taiwan, Hungary, and Mexico, liberalizers were quickly succeeded by more democratically oriented reformers. In Brazil, although some analysts are dubious, it seems reasonably clear that Geisel and Golbery were committed to meaningful democratization from the start.[19] Even if they did just intend to liberalize the authoritarian system rather than replace it, Figueiredo extended the process to democratization. "I have to make this country into a democracy," he said in 1978 before taking office, and he did.[20]

In Spain the hard-line prime minister, Admiral Luis Carrero Blanco, was assassinated in December 1973, and Franco appointed Carlos Arias Navarro to succeed him. Arias was the classic liberal reformer. He wished to modify the Franco regime in order to preserve it. In a famous speech on February 12, 1974, he proposed an opening (*apertura*) and recommended a number of modest reforms including, for instance, permitting political associations to function but not political parties. He "was too much of a conservative and Francoist at heart to carry out a true democratization of the regime." His reform proposals were torpedoed by the standpatters of the "bunker," including Franco; at the same time the proposals stimulated the opposition to demand a more extensive opening. In the end, Arias "discredited *aperturismo* just as Carrero had discredited immobilism."[21] In November 1975 Franco died and Juan Carlos succeeded him as chief of state. Juan Carlos was committed to transforming Spain into a true, European-style parliamentary democracy, Arias resisted this change, and in July 1976 Juan Carlos replaced him with Adolfo Suárez, who moved quickly to introduce democracy.

The transition from liberalized authoritarianism, however, could move backward as well as forward. A limited opening could raise expectations of further change that could lead to instability, upheaval, and even violence; these, in turn, could provoke an antidemocratic reaction and replacement of the liberalizing leadership with standpatter leaders. In Greece,

Papadopoulos attempted to shift from a standpatter to a liberalizing stance; this led to the Polytechnic student demonstration and its bloody suppression; a reaction followed and the liberalizing Papadopoulos was replaced by the hard-line Ioannidis. In Argentina General Roberto Viola succeeded the hard-line General Jorge Videla as president and began to liberalize. This produced a reaction in the military, Viola's ouster, and his replacement by hard-line General Leopoldo Galtieri. In China ultimate power presumably rested with Deng Xiao-ping. In 1987, however Zhao Ziyang became general secretary of the Communist party and began to open up the political system. This led to the massive student demonstrations in Tiananmen Square in the spring of 1989, which, in turn, provoked a hard-line reaction, the crushing of the student movement, the ouster of Zhao, and his replacement by Li Peng. In Burma, Gen. Ne Win, who had ruled Burma for twenty-six years, ostensibly retired from office in July 1988 and was replaced by Gen. Sein Lwin, another hard-liner. Mounting protests and violence forced Sein Lwin out within three weeks. He was succeeded by a civilian and presumed moderate, Maung Maung, who proposed elections and attempted to negotiate with opposition groups. Protests continued, however, and in September the army deposed Maung Maung, took control of the government, bloodily suppressed the demonstrations, and ended the movement toward liberalization.

The dilemmas of the liberalizer were reflected in the experiences of P. W. Botha and Mikhail Gorbachev. Both leaders introduced major liberalizing reforms in their societies. Botha came to power in 1978 with the slogan "Adapt or die" and legalized black trade unions, repealed the marriage laws, established mixed trading zones, granted citizenship to urban blacks, permitted blacks to acquire freehold title, substantially reduced petty apartheid, increased significantly investment in black education, abolished the pass laws, provided for elected black township councils, and created houses of parliament representing coloureds and Asians, although not blacks. Gorbachev opened up public discussion, greatly reduced censorship, dramatically challenged the power of the Communist party apparat, and introduced at least modest forms of government responsibility to an elected legislature. Both leaders gave their societies new constitutions incorporating many reforms and also creating new and very powerful posts of president, which they then assumed. It seems probable that neither Botha nor Gorbachev, however, wanted fundamental change in their political systems. Their reforms were designed to improve and to moderate, but also to bolster the existing system and make it more acceptable to their societies. They themselves said as much repeatedly. Botha did not intend to end white power; Gorbachev did not intend to end communist power. As liberal reformers they wanted to change but also to preserve the systems that they led and in whose bureaucracies they had spent their careers.

Botha's liberalizing but not democratizing reforms stimulated intensified demands from South African blacks for their full incorporation into the political system. In September 1984 black townships erupted with protests that led to violence, repression, and the deployment of military forces into the townships. The efforts at reform simultaneously ended, and Botha the reformer was widely viewed as having become Botha the repressor. The reform process only got underway again in 1989 when Botha was replaced by F. W. de Klerk, whose more extensive reforms led to criticisms from Botha and his resignation from the National party. In 1989 and 1990 Gorbachev's liberalizing but not democratizing reforms appeared to be stimulating comparable upheaval, protests, and violence in the Soviet Union. As in South Africa, communal groups fought each other and the central authorities. The dilemma for Gorbachev was clear. Moving forward toward full-scale democratization would mean not only the end of communist power in the Soviet Union but very probably the end of the Soviet Union. Leading a hard-line reaction to the up-

heavals would mean the end of his efforts at economic reform, his greatly improved relations with the West, and his
global image as a creative and humane leader. Andrei Sakharov put the choices squarely to Gorbachev in 1989: "A
middle course in situations like these is almost impossible.
The country and you personally are at a crossroads—either
increase the process of change maximally or try to retain the
administrative command system with all its qualities."[22]

Where it was tried, liberalization stimulated the desire for
democratization in some groups and the desire for repression
in others. The experience of the third wave strongly suggests
that liberalized authoritarianism is not a stable equilibrium;
the halfway house does not stand.

Backward legitimacy: Subduing the standpatters. The achievement of power enabled the reformers to start democratizing
but it did not eliminate the ability of the standpatters to
challenge the reformers. The standpatter elements of what
had been the governing coalition—the Francoist "bunker"
in Spain, the military hard-liners in Brazil and other Latin
American countries, the Stalinists in Hungary, the mainlander old guard in the KMT, the party bosses and bureaucracy in the PRI, the *Verkrampte* wing of the National party—
did not give up easily. In the government, military, and party
bureaucracies standpatters worked to stop or slow down the
processes of change. In the non-one-party systems—Brazil,
Ecuador, Peru, Guatemala, Nigeria, and Spain—standpatter
groups in the military attempted coups d'etat and made other
efforts to dislodge the reformers from power. In South Africa
and in Hungary, standpatter factions broke away from the
dominant parties, charging them with betraying the basic
principles on which the parties were based.

Reform governments attempted to neutralize standpatter
opposition by weakening, reassuring, and converting the
standpatters. Countering standpatter resistance often required a concentration of power in the reform chief executive.
Geisel asserted himself as "dictator of the *abertura*" in order

to force the Brazilian military out of politics.[23] Juan Carlos exercised his power and prerogatives to the full in moving Spain toward democracy, not least in the surprise selection of Suárez as prime minister. Botha and Gorbachev, as we have seen, created powerful new presidential offices for themselves. Salinas dramatically asserted his powers during his first years as Mexico's president.

The first requirement for reform leaders was to purge the governmental, military, and, where appropriate, party bureaucracies, replacing standpatters in top offices with supporters of reform. This was typically done in selective fashion so as not to provoke a strong reaction and so as to promote fissions within the standpatter ranks. In addition to weakening standpatters, reform leaders also tried to reassure and convert them. In military regimes, the reformers argued that it was time to go back, after a necessary but limited authoritarian interlude, to the democratic principles that were the basis of their country's political system. In this sense, they appealed for a "return to legitimacy." In the nonmilitary authoritarian systems, reformers invoked "backward legitimacy" and stressed elements of continuity with the past.[24] In Spain, for instance, the monarchy was reestablished and Suarez adhered to the provisions of the Franco constitution in abolishing that constitution: no Francoist could claim that there were procedural irregularities. In Mexico and South Africa the reformers in the PRI and National party cast themselves in the traditions of those parties. On Taiwan the KMT reformers appealed to Sun Yat-Sen's three principles.

Backward legitimacy had two appeals and two effects: it legitimated the new order because it was a product of the old, and it retrospectively legitimated the old order because it had produced the new. It elicited consensus from all except opposition extremists who had no use for either the old authoritarian regime or the new democratic one. Reformers also appealed to standpatters on the grounds that they were preempting the radical opposition and hence minimizing instability and violence. Suárez, for instance, asked the Spanish army to support him for these reasons and the dominant elements in the army accepted the transition because there "was no illegitimacy, no disorder in the streets, no significant threat of breakdown and subversion." Inevitably, the reformers also found that, as Geisel put it, they could "not advance without some retreats" and that hence, on occasion, as in the 1977 "April package" in Brazil, they had to make concessions to the standpatters.[25]

Coopting the opposition. Once in power the democratic reformers usually moved quickly to begin the process of democratization. This normally involved consultations with leaders of the opposition, the political parties, and major social groups and institutions. In some instances relatively formal negotiations occurred and quite explicit agreements or pacts were reached. In other cases, the consultations and negotiations were more informal. In Ecuador and Nigeria the government appointed commissions to develop plans and policies for the new system. In Spain, Peru, Nigeria, and eventually in Brazil elected assemblies drafted new constitutions. In several instances referenda were held to approve the new constitutional arrangements.

As the reformers alienated standpatters within the governing coalition, they had to reinforce themselves by developing support within the opposition and by expanding the political arena and appealing to the new groups that were becoming politically active as a result of the opening. Skillful reformers used the increased pressure from these groups for democratization to weaken the standpatters, and used the threat of a standpatter coup as well as the attractions of a share in power to strengthen moderate groups in the opposition.

To these ends, reformers in government negotiated with the principal opposition groups and arrived at explicit or tacit agreements with them. In Spain, for instance, the Communist party recognized that it was too weak to follow a "radical *rupturista* policy" and instead went along with a "*ruptura pac-*

tada" even though the pact was "purely tacit." In October 1977 Suarez won the agreement of the Communist and Socialist parties to the *Pactos de la Moncloa* comprising a mixture of fairly severe economic austerity measures and some social reforms. Secret negotiations with Santiago Carrillo, the principal Communist leader, "played on the PCE [Partido Comunista de España] leader's anxiety to be near the levers of power and secured his backing for an austerity package."[26] In Hungary explicit negotiations occurred in the fall of 1989 between the Communist party and the Opposition Round Table representing the principal other parties and groups. In Brazil informal understandings developed between the government and the opposition parties, the Movimento Democrático Brasileiro (MDB) and the Partido Movimento Democrático Brasileiro (PMDB). On Taiwan in 1986 the government and the opposition arrived at an understanding on the parameters within which political change would take place and, in a week-long conference in July 1990, agreed on a full schedule of democratization.

Moderation and cooperation by the democratic opposition—their involvement in the process as junior partners—were essential to successful transformation. In almost all countries, the principal opposition parties—the MDB-PMDB in Brazil, the Socialists and Communists in Spain, the Democratic Progressive Party (DPP) on Taiwan, the Civic Forum in Hungary, the Alianza Popular Revolucionaria Americana (APRA) in Peru, the Christian Democrats in Chile—were led by moderates and followed moderate policies, at times in the face of considerable provocation by standpatter groups in the government.

Skidmore's summary of what occurred in Brazil neatly catches the central relationships involved in transformation processes:

> In the end, liberalization was the product of an intense dialectical relationship between the government and the op-

position. The military who favored *abertura* had to proceed cautiously, for fear of arousing the hardliners. Their overtures to the opposition were designed to draw out the "responsible" elements, thereby showing there were moderates ready to co-operate with the government. At the same time, the opposition constantly pressed the government to end its arbitrary excesses, thereby reminding the military that their rule lacked legitimacy. Meanwhile, the opposition moderates had to remind the radicals that they would play into the hands of the hardliners if they pushed too hard. This intricate political relationship functioned successfully because there was a consensus among both military and civilians in favor of a return to an (almost) open political system.[27]

Guidelines for Democratizers 1:
Reforming Authoritarian Systems

The principal lessons of the Spanish, Brazilian, and other transformations for democratic reformers in authoritarian governments include the following:

(1) Secure your political base. As quickly as possible place supporters of democratization in key power positions in the government, the party, and the military.

(2) Maintain backward legitimacy, that is, make changes through the established procedures of the nondemocratic regime and reassure standpatter groups with symbolic concessions, following a course of two steps forward, one step backward.

(3) Gradually shift your own constituency so as to reduce your dependence on government groups opposing change and to broaden your constituency in the direction of opposition groups supporting democracy.

(4) Be prepared for the standpatters to take some extreme action to stop change (e.g., a coup attempt)—possibly even stimulate them to do so—and then crack down on them ruthlessly, isolating and discrediting the more extreme opponents of change.

(5) Seize and keep control of the initiative in the democratization process. Only lead from strength and never introduce democratization measures in response to obvious pressure from more extreme radical opposition groups.

(6) Keep expectations low as to how far change can go; talk in terms of maintaining an ongoing process rather than achieving some fully elaborated democratic utopia.

(7) Encourage development of a responsible, moderate opposition party, which the key groups in society (including the military) will accept as a plausible nonthreatening alternative government.

(8) Create a sense of inevitability about the process of democratization so that it becomes widely accepted as a necessary and natural course of development even if to some people it remains an undesirable one.

REPLACEMENTS

Replacements involve a very different process from transformations. Reformers within the regime are weak or nonexistent. The dominant elements in government are standpatters staunchly opposed to regime change. Democratization consequently results from the opposition gaining strength and the government losing strength until the government collapses or is overthrown. The former opposition groups come to power and the conflict then often enters a new phase as groups in the new government struggle among themselves over the nature of the regime they should institute. Replacement, in short, involves three distinct phases: the struggle to produce the fall, the fall, and the struggle after the fall.

Most third wave democratizations required some cooperation from those in power. Only six replacements had occurred by 1990. Replacements were rare in transitions from one-party systems (one out of eleven) and military regimes (two out of sixteen) and more common in transitions from personal dictatorships (three out of seven). As we have pointed out, with some exceptions (Gandhi, Evren, Pinochet), leaders who created authoritarian regimes did not end those regimes. Changes of leadership within authoritarian systems were much more likely in military regimes through "second phase" coups or, in one-party systems, through regular succession or the action of constituted party bodies. Personal dictators, however, seldom retired voluntarily, and the nature of their power—personal rather than military or organizational—made it difficult for opponents within the regime to oust them and, indeed, made it unlikely that such opponents would exist in any significant numbers or strength. The personal dictator was thus likely to hang on until he died or until the regime itself came to an end. The life of the regime became the life of the dictator. Politically and at times literally (e.g., Franco, Ceausescu) the deaths of the dictator and the regime coincided.

Democratic reformers were notably weak in or missing from the authoritarian regimes that disappeared in replacements. In Argentina and Greece, the liberalizing leaders Viola and Papadopoulos were forced out of power and succeeded by military hard-liners. In Portugal Caetano initiated some liberalizing reforms and then backed away from them. In the Philippines, Romania, and East Germany, the entourages of Marcos, Ceausescu, and Honecker contained few if any democrats or even liberals. In all six cases standpatters monopolized power, and the possibility of initiating reform from within was almost totally absent.

An authoritarian system exists because the government is politically stronger than the opposition. It is replaced when the government becomes weaker than the opposition. Hence replacement requires the opposition to wear down the government and shift the balance of power in its favor. When they were initiated, the authoritarian regimes involved in the third wave were almost always popular and widely supported. They usually had the backing of a broad coalition of groups. Over time, however, as with any government, their strength deteriorated. The Greek and Argentine military regimes suffered the humiliation of military defeat. The Portuguese and Philippine regimes were unable to win counterinsurgency wars, and the Philippine regime created a martyr and stole an election. The Romanian regime followed policies that deeply antagonized its people and isolated itself from them; hence it was vulnerable to the cumulative snowballing of the antiauthoritarian movement throughout Eastern Europe. The case of East Germany was more ambiguous. Although the regime was relatively successful in some respects, the inevitable comparison with West Germany was an inherent weakness, and the opening of the transit corridor through Hungary dramatically undermined the regime's authority. The party leadership resigned in early December 1989, and a caretaker government took over. The regime's authority, however, evaporated, and with it the reasons for the East German state.

The erosion of support for the regime sometimes occurred openly, but, given the repressive character of authoritarian regimes, it was more likely to occur covertly. Authoritarian leaders were often unaware of how unpopular they were. Covert disaffection then manifested itself when some triggering event exposed the weakness of the regime. In Greece and Argentina it was military defeat. In Portugal and East Germany it was the explicit turning against the regime of its ultimate source of power—the army in Portugal, the Soviet Union in East Germany. The actions of the Turks, the British, the Portuguese military, and Gorbachev galvanized and brought into the open the disaffection from the regime of other groups in those societies. In all these cases, only a few weak groups rallied to the support of the regime. Many people had become disaffected from the regime but, because it was an authoritarian regime, a triggering event was required to crystalize the disaffection.

Students are the universal opposition; they oppose whatever regime exists in their society. By themselves, however, students do not bring down regimes. Lacking substantial support from other groups in the population, they were gunned down by the military and police in Greece in November 1973, Burma in September 1988, and China in June 1989. The military are the ultimate support of regimes. If they withdraw their support, if they carry out a coup against the regime, or if they refuse to use force against those who threaten to overthrow the regime, the regime falls. In between the perpetual opposition of the students and the necessary support of the military are other groups whose support for or opposition to the regime depends on circumstances. In noncommunist authoritarian systems, such as the Philippines, these groups tended to disaffect in sequence. The disaffection of the students was followed by that of intellectuals in general and then by the leaders of previously existing political parties, many of whom may have supported or acquiesced in the authoritarian takeover. Typically the broader reaches of the middle class—white-collar workers, professionals, small business proprietors—became alienated. In a Catholic country, Church leaders also were early and effective opponents of the regime. If labor unions existed and were not totally controlled by the government, at some point they joined the opposition. So also, and most important, did larger business groups and the bourgeoisie. In due course, the United States or other foreign sources of support became disaffected. Finally and conclusively, the military decided not to support the government or actively to side with the opposition against the government.

In five out of six replacements, consequently, the exception being Argentina, military disaffection was essential to bringing down the regime. In the personal dictatorships in Portugal, the Philippines, and Romania, this military disaffection was promoted by the dictator's policies weakening military professionalism, politicizing and corrupting the officer corps, and creating competing paramilitary and security forces. Opposition to the government normally (Portugal was the only exception) had to be widespread before the military deserted the government. If disaffection was not widespread, it was either because the most probable sources of opposition—the middle class, bourgeoisie, religious groups—were small and weak or because the regime had the support of these groups, usually as a result of successful policies for economic development. In Burma and China the armed forces brutally suppressed protests that were largely student-led. In societies that were more highly developed economically, opposition to authoritarianism commanded a wider range of support. When this opposition took to the streets in the Philippines, East Germany, and Romania, military units did not fire on broadly representative groups of their fellow citizens.

A popular image of democratic transitions is that repressive governments are brought down by "people power," the mass mobilization of outraged citizens demanding and eventually forcing a change of regime. Some form of mass action did take place in almost every third wave regime change. Mass demonstrations, protests, and strikes played central roles, however, in only about six transitions completed or underway at the end of the 1980s. These included the replacements in the Philippines, East Germany, and Romania, and the transplacements in Korea, Poland, and Czechoslovakia. In Chile frequent mass actions attempted, without success, to alter Pinochet's plan for transformation. In East Germany, uniquely, both "exit" and "voice," in Hirschman's terms, played major roles, with protest taking the form first of massive departure of citizens from the country and then of massive street demonstrations in Leipzig and Berlin.

In the Philippines, Portugal, Romania, and Greece, when the regime collapsed, it collapsed quickly. One day the authoritarian government was in power, the next day it was not. In Argentina and East Germany, the authoritarian regimes were quickly delegitimated but clung to power while attempting to negotiate terms for the change in regime. In Argentina, the successor military government of General Reynaldo Bignone, which took over in July 1982 immediately after the Falklands defeat, was "relatively successful" in maintaining some regime control over the transition for six months. In December 1982, however, mounting public opposition and the development of opposition organizations led to mass protests, a general strike, Bignone's scheduling of elections, and the rejection by the united opposition parties of the terms proposed by the military for the transfer of power. The authority of the lame-duck military regime continued to deteriorate until it was replaced by the Alfonsín government elected in October 1983. "The military government collapsed," one author observed; "it had no influence over the choice of candidates or the election itself, it excluded no one, and reserved neither powers nor veto prerogatives for itself in the future. In addition, it was unable to guarantee either its autonomy in relation to the future constitutional government or the promise of a future military policy, and, even less—given the winning candidate—the basis for an agreement on the ongoing struggle against the guerrillas."[28] In East Germany in early 1990 a somewhat similar situation existed, with a weak and discredited communist government clinging to power, and its prime minister, Hans Modrow, playing the role of Bignone.

The emphasis in transformations on procedural continuity and backward legitimacy was absent from replacements. The institutions, procedures, ideas, and individuals connected with the previous regime were instead considered tainted and the emphasis was on a sharp, clean break with the past. Those who succeeded the authoritarian rulers based their rule on "forward legitimacy," what they would bring about in the future and their lack of involvement in or connection with the previous regime.

In transformations and transplacements the leaders of the authoritarian regimes usually left politics and went back to the barracks or private life quietly and with some respect and dignity. Authoritarian leaders who lost power through replacements, in contrast, suffered unhappy fates. Marcos and Caetano were forced into exile. Ceausescu was summarily executed. The military officers who ran Greece and Argentina were tried and imprisoned. In East Germany punishments were threatened against Honecker and other former leaders in notable contrast to the absence of such action in Poland, Hungary, and Czechoslovakia. The dictators removed by foreign intervention in Grenada and Panama were similarly subjected to prosecution and punishment.

The peaceful collapse of an authoritarian regime usually produced a glorious if brief moment of public euphoria, of carnations and champagne, absent from transformations. The collapse also created a potential vacuum of authority absent from transformations. In Greece and the Philippines, the vacuum was quickly filled by the accession to power of Karamanlis and Aquino, popular political leaders who guided their countries to democracy. In Iran the authority vacuum was filled by the ayatollah, who guided Iran elsewhere. In Argentina and East Germany the Bignone and Modrow governments weakly filled the interim between the collapse of the authoritarian regimes and the election of democratic governments.

Before the fall, opposition groups are united by their desire to bring about the fall. After the fall, divisions appear among them and they struggle over the distribution of power and the nature of the new regime that must be established. The fate of democracy was determined by the relative power of democratic moderates and antidemocratic radicals. In Argentina and Greece, the authoritarian regimes had not been in power for long, political parties quickly reappeared, and an overwhelming consensus existed among political leaders and groups on the need quickly to reestablish democratic institutions. In the Philippines overt opposition to democracy, apart from the NPA insurgency, also was minimal.

In Nicaragua, Iran, Portugal and Romania the abrupt collapse of the dictatorships led to struggles among the former opposition groups and parties as to who would exercise power and what sort of regime would be created. In Nicaragua and Iran the democratic moderates lost out. In Portugal, as was noted on the opening pages of this book, a state of revolutionary ferment existed between April 1974 and November 1975. A consolidation of power by the antidemocratic Marxist-Leninist coalition of the Communist party and left-wing military officers was entirely possible. In the end, after intense struggles between military factions, mass mobilizations, demonstrations, and strikes, the military action by Eanes settled Portugal on a democratic course. "What started as a coup," as Robert Harvey observed, "became a revolution which was stopped by a reaction before it became an anarchy. Out of the tumult a democracy was born."[29]

The choices in Portugal were between bourgeois democracy and Marxist-Leninist dictatorship. The choices in Romania in 1990 were less clear, but democracy also was not inevitable. The lack of effectively organized opposition parties and groups, the absence of previous experience with democracy, the violence involved in the overthrow of Ceausescu, the deep desire for revenge against people associated with the dictatorship combined with the widespread involvement of much of the population with the dictatorship, the many leaders of the new government who had been part of the old regime—all did not augur well for the emergence of democracy. At the end of 1989 some Romanians enthusiastically compared what was happening in their country to what had happened two hundred years earlier in France. They might also have noted that the French Revolution ended in a military dictatorship.

Guidelines for Democratizers 2:
Overthrowing Authoritarian Regimes

The history of replacements suggests the following guidelines for opposition democratic moderates attempting to overthrow an authoritarian regime:*

*Myron Weiner has formulated a similar and more concise set of recommendations: "For those who seek democratization the lessons are these: mobilize large-scale non-violent opposition to the regime, seek support from the center and, if necessary, from the conservative right, restrain the left and keep them from dominating the agenda of the movement, woo sections of the military, seek sympathetic coverage from the western media, and press the United States for support." "Empirical Democratic Theory and the Transition from Authoritarianism to Democracy," *PS* 20 (Fall 1987), p. 866.

(1) Focus attention on the illegitimacy or dubious legitimacy of the authoritarian regime; that is its most vulnerable point. Attack the regime on general issues that are of widespread concern, such as corruption and brutality. If the regime is performing successfully (particularly economically) these attacks will not be effective. Once its performance falters (as it must), highlighting its illegitimacy becomes the single most important lever for dislodging it from power.

(2) Like democratic rulers, authoritarian rulers over time alienate erstwhile supporters. Encourage these disaffected groups to support democracy as the necessary alternative to the current system. Make particular efforts to enlist business leaders, middle-class professionals, religious figures, and political party leaders, most of whom probably supported creation of the authoritarian system. The more "respectable" and "responsible" the opposition appears, the easier it is to win more supporters.

(3) Cultivate generals. In the last analysis, whether the regime collapses or not depends on whether they support the regime, join you in opposition to it, or stand by on the sidelines. Support from the military could be helpful when the crisis comes, but all you really need is military unwillingness to defend the regime.

(4) Practice and preach nonviolence. (See pp. 196ff. below.) Among other things, this will make it easier for you to win over the security forces: soldiers do not tend to be sympathetic to people who have been hurling Molotov cocktails at them.

(5) Seize every opportunity to express opposition to the regime, including participation in elections it organizes. (See below, pp. 185ff.)

(6) Develop contacts with the global media, foreign human rights organizations, and transnational organizations such as churches. In particular, mobilize supporters in the United States. American congressmembers are always looking for moral causes to get publicity for themselves and to use against the American administration. Dramatize your cause to them and provide them with material for TV photo opportunities and headline-making speeches.

(7) Promote unity among opposition groups. Attempt to create comprehensive umbrella organizations that will facilitate cooperation among such groups. This will be difficult and, as the examples of the Philippines, Chile, Korea, and South Africa show, authoritarian rulers are often expert in promoting opposi-

tion disunity. One test of your qualifications to become a democratic leader of your country is your ability to overcome these obstacles and secure some measure of opposition unity. Remember Gabriel Almond's truth: "Great leaders are great coalition builders."[30]

(8) When the authoritarian regime falls, be prepared quickly to fill the vacuum of authority that results. This can be done by: pushing to the fore a popular, charismatic, democratically inclined leader; promptly organizing elections to provide popular legitimacy to a new government; and building international legitimacy by getting support of foreign and transnational actors (international organizations, the United States, the European Community, the Catholic Church). Recognize that some of your former coalition partners will want to establish a new dictatorship of their own and quietly organize the supporters of democracy to counter this effort if it materializes.

TRANSPLACEMENTS

In transplacements democratization is produced by the combined actions of government and opposition. Within the government the balance between standpatters and reformers is such that the government is willing to negotiate a change of regime—unlike the situation of standpatter dominance that leads to replacement—but it is unwilling to initiate a change of regime. It has to be pushed and/or pulled into formal or informal negotiations with the opposition. Within the opposition democratic moderates are strong enough to prevail over antidemocratic radicals, but they are not strong enough to overthrow the government. Hence they too see virtues in negotiation.

Approximately eleven of thirty-five liberalizations and democratizations that occurred or began in the 1970s and 1980s approximated the transplacement model. The most notable ones were in Poland, Czechoslovakia, Uruguay, and Korea; the regime changes in Bolivia, Honduras, El Salvador, and Nicaragua also involved significant elements of transplacement. In El Salvador and Honduras the negotiations were in part with the United States government, acting as a surrogate for democratic moderates. In 1989 and 1990, South Africa began a transplacement process, and Mongolia and Nepal appeared to be moving in that direction. Some features of transplacement were also present in Chile. The Pinochet regime was strong enough, however, to resist opposition pressure to negotiate democratization and stubbornly adhered to the schedule for regime change that it laid down in 1980.

In successful transplacements, the dominant groups in both government and opposition recognized that they were incapable of unilaterally determining the nature of the future political system in their society. Government and opposition leaders often developed these views after testing each other's strength and resolve in a political dialectic. Initially, the opposition usually believed that it would be able to bring about the downfall of the government at some point in the not too distant future. This belief was on occasion wildly unrealistic, but so long as opposition leaders held to it, serious negotiations with the government were impossible. In contrast, the government usually initially believed that it could effectively contain and suppress the opposition without incurring unacceptable costs. Transplacements occurred when the beliefs of both changed. The opposition realized that it was not strong enough to overthrow the government. The government realized that the opposition was strong enough to increase significantly the costs of nonnegotiation in terms of increased repression leading to further alienation of groups from the government, intensified divisions within the ruling coalition, increased possibility of a hard-line takeover of the government, and significant losses in international legitimacy.

The transplacement dialectic often involved a distinct sequence of steps. First, the government engaged in some liberalization and began to lose power and authority. Second, the opposition exploited this loosening by and weakening of the government to expand its support and intensify its activities with the hope and expectation it would shortly be able to bring down the government. Third, the government reacted forcefully to contain and suppress the mobilization of political power by the opposition. Fourth, government and opposition leaders perceived a standoff emerging and began to explore the possibilities of a negotiated transition. This fourth step was not, however, inevitable. Conceivably, the government, perhaps after a change of leadership, could brutally use its military and police forces to restore its power, at least temporarily. Or the opposition could continue to develop its strength, further eroding the power of the government and eventually bringing about its downfall. Transplacements thus required some rough equality of strength between government and opposition as well as uncertainty on each side as to who would prevail in a major test of strength. In these circumstances, the risks of negotiation and compromise appeared less than the risks of confrontation and catastrophe.

The political process leading to transplacement was thus often marked by a seesawing back and forth of strikes, protests, and demonstrations, on the one hand, and repression, jailings, police violence, states of siege, and martial law, on the other. Cycles of protest and repression in Poland, Czechoslovakia, Uruguay, Korea, and Chile eventually led to negotiated agreements between government and opposition in all cases except that of Chile.

In Uruguay, for instance, mounting protests and demonstrations in the fall of 1983 stimulated the negotiations leading to the military withdrawal from power. In Bolivia in 1978 "a series of conflicts and protest movements" preceded the military's agreeing to a timetable for elections.[31] In Korea as in Uruguay, the military regime had earlier forcefully suppressed protests. In the spring of 1987, however, the demonstrations became more massive and broad-based and increasingly involved the middle class. The government first reacted in its usual fashion but then shifted, agreed to negotiate, and accepted the central demands of the opposition. In Poland the 1988 strikes had a similar impact. As one commentator explained, "The strikes made the round table not only possible, but necessary—for both sides. Paradoxically, the strikes were strong enough to compel the communists to go to the round table, yet too weak to allow Solidarity's leaders to refuse negotiations. That's why the round table talks took place."[32]

In transplacements, the eyeball-to eyeball confrontation in the central square of the capital between massed protesters and serried ranks of police revealed each side's strengths and weaknesses. The opposition could mobilize massive support; the government could contain and withstand opposition pressure.

Politics in South Africa in the 1980s also evolved along the lines of the four-step model. In the late 1970s P. W. Botha began the process of liberalizing reform, arousing black expectations and then frustrating them when the 1983 constitution denied blacks a national political role. This led to uprisings in the black townships in 1984 and 1985, which stimulated black hopes that the collapse of the Afrikaner-dominated regime was imminent. The government's forceful and effective suppression of black and white dissent then compelled the opposition drastically to revise their hopes. At the same time, the uprisings attracted international attention, stimulated condemnation of both the apartheid system and the government's tactics, and led the United States and European governments to intensify economic sanctions against South Africa. As the hopes for revolution of the African National Congress (ANC) radicals declined, the worries of the National party government about international legitimacy and the economic future increased. In the mid-1970s, Joe Slovo, head of the South African Communist party and the ANC's military organization, argued that the ANC could overthrow the government and win power through sustained guerrilla warfare and revolution. In the late 1980s he remained committed to the use of violence, but saw negotiations as the more likely route for achieving ANC goals. After becoming president of South Africa in 1989, F. W. de Klerk also emphasized the importance of negotiations. The lesson of Rhodesia, he said, was that "When the opportunity was there for real, constructive negotiation, it was not grasped. . . . It went wrong because in the reality of their circumstances they waited too long before engaging in fundamental negotiation and dialogue. We must not make that mistake, and we are determined not to repeat that mistake."[33] The two political leaders were learning from their own experience and that of others.

In Chile, in contrast, the government was willing and able to avoid negotiation. Major strikes erupted in the spring of 1983, but a national general strike was suppressed by the government. Beginning in May 1983 the opposition organized massive monthly demonstrations on "Days of National Protest." These were broken up by the police, usually with several people being killed. Economic problems and the opposition protests forced the Pinochet government to initiate a dialogue with the opposition. The economy then began to recover, however, and the middle classes became alarmed at the breakdown of law and order. A national strike in October 1984 was put down with considerable bloodshed. Shortly thereafter the government reimposed the state of siege that had been cancelled in 1979. The opposition efforts thus failed to overthrow the government or to induce it to engage in meaningful negotiations. The opposition had "overestimated its strength and underestimated the government's."[34] It had also underestimated Pinochet's tenacity and political skill and the willingness of Chilean security forces to shoot unarmed civilian demonstrators.

Transplacements required leaders on both sides willing to risk negotiations. Divisions of opinion over negotiations usually existed within governing elites. At times, the top leaders had to be pressured by their colleagues and by circumstances to negotiate with the opposition. In 1989, for instance, Adam Michnik argued that Poland, like Hungary, was following "the Spanish way to democracy." At one level, he was right in that both the Spanish and Polish transitions were basically peaceful. At a more particular level, however, the Spanish analogy did not hold for Poland because Jaruzelski was not a Juan Carlos or Suarez (whereas Imre Pozsgay in Hungary in considerable measure was). Jaruzelski was a reluctant democrat who had to be pushed by the deterioration of his country and his regime into negotiations with Solidarity.[35] In Uruguay the president, General Gregorio Alvarez, wanted to prolong his power and postpone democratization and had to be forced by the other members of the military junta to move ahead with the regime change. In Chile, General Pinochet was somewhat similarly under pressure from other junta members, especially the air force commander, General Fernando Matthei, to be more forthcoming in dealing with the opposition, but Pinochet successfully resisted this pressure.

In other countries changes occurred in the top leadership before serious negotiations with the opposition began. In Korea the government of General Chun Doo Hwan followed a staunch standpatter policy of stonewalling opposition demands and suppressing opposition activity. In 1987, however, the governing party designated Roh Tae Woo as its candidate to succeed Chun. Roh dramatically reversed Chun's policies, announced a political opening, and entered into negotiations with the opposition leader.[36] In Czechoslovakia the long-in-power standpatter Communist party general secretary, Gustav Husak, was succeeded by the mildly reformist Milos Jakes in December 1987. Once the opposition became mobilized in the fall of 1989, however, Jakes was replaced by the reformer Karel Urbanek. Urbanek and the reformist prime minister, Ladislav Adamec, then negotiated arrangements for the transition to democracy with Vaclav Havel and the other leaders of the opposition Civic Forum. In South Africa, de Klerk moved beyond his predecessor's aborted transformation process from above to transplacement-type negotiations with black opposition leaders. Uncertainty, ambiguity, and division of opinion over democratization thus tended to characterize the ruling circles in transplacement situations. These regimes were not overwhelmingly committed either to holding on to power ruthlessly or to moving decisively toward democracy. Disagreement and uncertainty existed not only on the government side in transplacements. In fact, the one group more likely to be divided against itself than the leaders of a decaying authoritarian government are the opposition leaders who aspire to replace them. In replacement situations the government suppresses the opposition and the opposition has an overriding common interest in bringing down the government. As the Philippine and Nicaraguan examples indicate, even under these conditions securing unity among opposition leaders and parties may be extremely difficult, and the unity achieved is often tenuous and fragile. In transplacements, where it is a question not of overthrowing the government but of negotiating with it, opposition unity is even more difficult to achieve. It was not achieved in Korea, and hence the governmental candidate, Roh Tae Woo, was elected president with a minority of the vote, as the two opposition candidates split the antigovernment majority by opposing each other. In Uruguay, because its leader was still imprisoned, one opposition party—the National party—rejected the agreement reached between the two other parties and the military. In South Africa a major obstacle to democratic reform was the many divisions within the opposition between parliamentary and nonparliamentary groups, Afrikaner and English, black and white, and among black ideological and tribal groups. At no time before the 1990s did the South African government confront anything but a bewildering multiplicity of opposition groups whose differences among themselves were often as great as their differences with the government.

In Chile the opposition was seriously divided into a large number of parties, factions, and coalitions. In 1983, the moderate centrist opposition parties were able to join together in the Democratic Alliance. In August 1985 a broader group of a dozen parties joined in the National Accord calling for a transition to democracy. Yet conflicts over leadership and tactics continued. In 1986 the Chilean opposition mobilized massive protests, hoping to duplicate in Santiago what had just happened in Manila. The opposition, however, was divided and its militancy frightened conservatives. The problem, as one observer put it at the time, was that "the general is not being challenged by a moderate opposition movement that has got itself together under the leadership of a respected figure. There is no Chilean Cory."[37] In Poland, on the other hand, things were different. Lech Walesa was a Polish Cory, and Solidarity dominated the opposition for most of a decade. In Czechoslovakia the transplacement occurred so quickly that differences among opposition political groups did not have time to materialize.

In transplacements democratic moderates have to be sufficiently strong within the opposition to be credible negotiating partners with the government. Almost always some groups within the opposition reject negotiations with the government. They fear that negotiations will produce undesirable compromises and they hope that continued opposition pressure will bring about the collapse or the overthrow of the government. In Poland in 1988–89, right-wing opposition groups urged a boycott of the Round Table talks. In Chile left-wing opposition groups carried out terrorist attacks that undermined the efforts of the moderate opposition to negotiate with the government. Similarly, in Korea radicals rejected the agreement on elections reached by the government and the leading opposition groups. In Uruguay, the opposition was dominated by leaders of moderate political parties and extremists were less of a problem.

For negotiations to occur each party had to concede some degree of legitimacy to the other. The opposition had to recognize the government as a worthy partner in change and implicitly if not explicitly acquiesce in its current right to rule. The government, in turn, had to accept the opposition groups as legitimate representatives of significant segments of society. The government could do this more easily if the opposition groups had not engaged in violence. Negotiations were also easier if the opposition groups, such as political parties under a military regime, had previously been legitimate participants in the political process. It was easier for the opposition to negotiate if the government had used only limited violence against it and if there were some democratic reformers in the government whom it had reason to believe shared its goals.

In transplacements, unlike transformations and replacements, government leaders often negotiated the basic terms of the regime change with opposition leaders they had previously had under arrest: Lech Walesa, Vaclav Havel, Jorge Batlle Ibanez, Kim Dae Jung and Kim Young Sam, Walter Sisulu and Nelson Mandela. There were good reasons for this. Opposition leaders who have been in prison have not been fighting the government, violently or nonviolently; they have been living with it. They have also experienced the reality of government power. Governmental leaders who released their captives were usually interested in reform, and those released were usually moderate enough to be willing to negotiate with their former captors. Imprisonment also enhanced the moral authority of the former prisoners. This helped them to unite the opposition groups, at least temporarily, and to hold out the prospect to the government that they could secure the acquiescence of their followers to whatever agreement was reached.

At one point in the Brazilian transition, General Golbery reportedly told an opposition leader, "You get your radicals under control and we will control ours."[38] Getting radicals under control often requires the cooperation of the other side.

In transplacement negotiations, each party has an interest in strengthening the other party so that he can deal more effectively with the extremists on his side. In June 1990, for instance, Nelson Mandela commented on the problems F. W. de Klerk was having with white hard-liners and said that the ANC had appealed "to whites to assist de Klerk. We are also trying to address the problems of white opposition to him. Discussions have already been started with influential sectors in the right wing." At the same time, Mandela said that his own desire to meet with Chief Mengosuthu Buthelezi had been vetoed by militants within the ANC and that he had to accept that decision because he was "a loyal and disciplined member of the A.N.C."[39] De Klerk obviously had an interest in strengthening Mandela and helping him deal with his militant left-wing opposition.

Negotiations for regime change were at times preceded by "prenegotiations" about the conditions for entering into negotiations. In South Africa, the government precondition was that the ANC renounce violence. ANC preconditions were that the government urban opposition groups and release political prisoners. In some cases prenegotiations concerned which opposition individuals and groups would be involved in the negotiations.

Negotiations were sometimes lengthy and sometimes brief. They often were interrupted as one party or the other broke them off. As the negotiations continued, however, the political future of each of the parties became more engaged with their success. If the negotiations failed, standpatters within the governing coalition and radicals in the opposition stood ready to capitalize on that failure and to bring down the leaders who had engaged in negotiations. A common interest emerged and the sense of a common fate. "[I]n a way," Nelson Mandela observed in August 1990, "there is an alliance now" between the ANC and the National party. "We are on one boat, one ship," agreed National Party leader R. F. Botha, "and the sharks to the left and the sharks to the right are not

going to distinguish between us when we fall overboard."[40]
Consequently, as negotiations continued, the parties became
more willing to compromise in order to reach an agreement.
The agreements they reached often generated attacks from
others in government and opposition who thought the negotiators had conceded too much. The specific agreements reflected, of course, issues peculiar to their countries. Of central importance in almost all negotiations, however, was the
exchange of guarantees. In transformations former officials
of the authoritarian regime were almost never punished; in
replacements they almost always were. In transplacements
this was often an issue to be negotiated; the military leaders
in Uruguay and Korea, for instance, demanded guarantees
against prosecution and punishment for any human rights
violations. In other situations, negotiated guarantees involved arrangements for the sharing of power or for changes
in power through elections. In Poland each side was guaranteed an explicit share of the seats in the legislature. In
Czechoslovakia positions in the cabinet were divided between the two parties. In both these countries coalition governments reassured communists and the opposition that their
interests would be protected during the transition. In Korea
the governing party agreed to a direct, open election for the
presidency on the assumption, and possibly the understanding, that at least two major opposition candidates would run,
thereby making highly probable victory for the government
party's candidate.

The risks of confrontation and of losing thus impel government and opposition to negotiate with each other; and
guarantees that neither will lose everything become the basis
for agreement. Both get the opportunity to share in power
or to compete for power. Opposition leaders know they will
not be sent back to prison; government leaders know they
will not have to flee into exile. Mutual reduction in risk
prompts reformers and moderates to cooperate in establishing democracy.

Guidelines for Democratizers 3:
Negotiating Regime Changes

For democratic reformers in government:

(1) Following the guidelines for transforming authoritarian systems (see above, pp. 141–42), first isolate and weaken your standpatter opposition and consolidate your hold on the government and political machinery.

(2) Also following those guidelines, seize the initiative and surprise both opposition and standpatters with the concessions you are willing to make, but never make concessions under obvious opposition pressure.

(3) Secure endorsement of the concept of negotiations from leading generals or other top officials in the security establishment.

(4) Do what you can to enhance the stature, authority, and moderation of your principal opposition negotiating partner.

(5) Establish confidential and reliable back-channels for negotiating key central questions with opposition leaders.

(6) If the negotiation succeeds, you very probably will be in the opposition. Your prime concern, consequently, should be securing guarantees and safeguards for the rights of the opposition and of groups that have been associated with your government (e.g., the military). Everything else is negotiable.

For democratic moderates in the opposition:

(1) Be prepared to mobilize your supporters for demonstrations when these will weaken the standpatters in the government. Too many marches and protests, however, are likely to strengthen them, weaken your negotiating partner, and arouse middle-class concern about law and order.

(2) Be moderate; appear statesmanlike.

(3) Be prepared to negotiate and, if necessary, make concessions on all issues except the holding of free and fair elections.

(4) Recognize the high probability that you will win those elections and do not take actions that will seriously complicate your governing your country.

For both government and opposition democratizers:

(1) The political conditions favorable to a negotiated transition

will not last indefinitely. Seize the opportunity they present and move quickly to resolve the central issues.

(2) Recognize that your political future and that of your partner depend on your success in reaching agreement on the transition to democracy.

(3) Resist the demands of leaders and groups on your side that either delay the negotiating process or threaten the core interest of your negotiating partner.

(4) Recognize that that agreement you reach will be the only alternative; radicals and standpatters may denounce it, but they will not be able to produce an alternative that commands broad support.

(5) When in doubt, compromise.

CHAPTER 4

HOW? CHARACTERISTICS OF DEMOCRATIZATION

THE THIRD WAVE DEMOCRATIZATION SYNDROME

COUNTRIES TRANSITED TO DEMOCRACY in different ways. For all their differences, however, third wave transformations, replacements, and transplacements had important characteristics in common. Of the more than twenty-five democratizations that had occurred by or appeared to be underway in 1990, only two, Panama and Grenada, were the result of foreign invasion and imposition. Most of the other transitions were alike in what they lacked. With the partial and debatable exception of Nicaragua, no authoritarian regime was brought down by a prolonged guerrilla insurgency or civil war. What might be termed revolutionary upheavals occurred in two cases, Portugal and Romania, but the Portuguese revolution involved very little violence and the Romanian revolution was an urban uprising assisted by the armed forces and was very brief. Significant fighting between armed military units occurred only in Romania, the Philippines, Bolivia, and Nicaragua. Except in the Philippines, Romania, and East Germany, outraged mobs of citizens did not storm into presidential palaces.

How were democracies made? They were made by the methods of democracy; there was no other way. They were made through negotiations, compromises, and agreements.

They were made through demonstrations, campaigns, and elections, and through the nonviolent resolution of differences. They were made by political leaders in governments and oppositions who had the courage both to challenge the status quo and to subordinate the immediate interests of their followers to the longer-term needs of democracy. They were made by leaders in both government and opposition who withstood the provocations to violence of opposition radicals and government standpatters. They were made by leaders in government and opposition who had the wisdom to recognize that in politics no one has a monopoly on truth or virtue. Compromise, elections, and nonviolence were the third wave democratization syndrome. In varying degrees they characterized most of the transformations, replacements, and transplacements of that wave.

COMPROMISE AND THE PARTICIPATION/ MODERATION TRADE-OFF

Negotiations and compromise among political elites were at the heart of the democratization processes. The leaders of the key political forces and social groups in society bargained with each other, explicitly or implicitly, and worked out acceptable if not satisfying arrangements for the transition to democracy. Negotiation, compromise, and agreement between reformers and moderates were, of course, the central elements of transplacements. In transformations the process was often implicit, as the reformers in the government opened up the political process and opposition groups modified their demands and moderated their tactics to take part in that process. At times also explicit agreements were reached between reformers leading the transition and opposition moderates, whom they wished to coopt. In both replacements and transplacements democratic opposition groups negotiated agreements among themselves. Once in power through replacement, former opposition moderates normally steered middle courses making concessions as needed to reformers, standpatters, and radicals. Whether the initiative for democratization came from the government, from the opposition, or from both, at some point the key players reached agreements on the crucial aspects of the democratization process and the new system that was to be created.

The agreements on introducing democracy took many forms. The transitions in Brazil, Peru, Ecuador, and Bolivia were generally characterized by "tentative understandings between the opposition and an official caretaker coalition trying to manage the transition from the authoritarian regime." These understandings usually only involved "tacit agreement on some procedural—primarily electoral—ground rules for the transition." In other instances, regime changes resembled the second wave transitions in Colombia and Venezuela in 1957 and 1958 in which very explicit pacts were negotiated among the interested parties.[1] In Spain, the government under Juan Carlos and Suárez dominated the transition, but government and opposition engaged in "the politics of compromise" in reaching agreements in the constituent assembly on the constitutional framework for the new democracy and in the so-called Pact of Moncloa in October 1977. In this pact all the relevant political parties, including the Socialists and Communists, agreed on a comprehensive economic program including limitations on wages, currency devaluation, monetary policy, increased public investment, restrictions on social security, tax reform, trade union activities, control of nationalized industries, and other matters.[2] In Poland Solidarity and the Communist party negotiated the Round Table agreements in March and April 1989. In Hungary government and opposition leaders negotiated the "triangular" agreement during the summer of 1989. Later that fall government and opposition leaders arrived at arrangements for the transition in Czechoslovakia. In Uruguay the military and party leaders reached agreement in the Club Naval Pact of August 1984. In almost all cases the principal participants were the leaders of government and opposition political parties. In many instances, implicit or explicit agreements were also reached with the leaders of key social and institutional forces in the society, including, besides the military, the business community, labor unions, and, where appropriate, the church. Whether or not formal pacts were negotiated, agreement—implicit or explicit—was easier to reach when no vast discrepancy in power resources existed among the participants and when group leaders were able to exercise substantial control over their followers. Agreement also came more easily when the negotiations were carried out in secret among a relatively small number of leaders. In Spain, even in the constitutional assembly, key arrangements were negotiated, as the Spanish said, "behind the curtain."[3] In Poland the Round Table negotiations were relatively public, but the most important issues were discussed in "secret, parallel talks . . . conducted in isolation from the mass media" at a villa at Magdalenka outside Warsaw. "Many fewer people took part in the secret talks than in the open ones." The leaders of the negotiations, General Czeslaw Kiszczak and Lech Walesa, appeared occasionally at the open talks "only to depart soon thereafter for Magdalenka, where discussions continued in private." Concerning the private talks, only "Vague and highly diplomatic communiques were issued, as if by the ambassadors of two countries that had been at war until recently."[4] It was at these meetings that the basic agreements were reached between the Communist party and Solidarity.

The compromises reached in negotiations at times created problems for political leaders when, as in Spain, they "would have been unacceptable to their followers." In Spain, Suarez emphasized, it was necessary to break with the past pattern of "imposition by some Spaniards on the rest" and instead develop a broad-gauged consensus. Agreement among political parties, however, another government leader pointed out, led to "a process of disaffection of Spanish society from political parties, because political parties in Spain at that time were not adequately performing their function of representation of interests."[5] A Communist party journal commented on the "disenchantment within and outside our ranks" afflicting the party because "all parties are saying the same thing" and "there is no clear Communist identity in the PCE." In Bolivia in 1980 rank-and-file union members "widely criticized" the pact their leaders signed with the military and political leaders concerning transition elections; and in Nicaragua in 1990 anti-Sandinista labor union members similarly felt "betrayed" by President-Elect Violeta Chamorro's agreeing to appoint Humberto Ortega chief of the armed forces.[6] In Poland long-time supporters of both Solidarity and the Communist party were alienated by the compromises made by leaders of those two organizations. General Jaruzelski was attacked by Communist party conservatives "for having yielded too much power to the opposition" and for abandoning "fundamental Communist tenets." Lech Walesa, on the other hand, was attacked at union rallies for starting negotiations with the government and denounced by radicals who had "grown to abhor his striving for compromise with the Communist authorities." Solidarity supporters particularly objected to the union leadership's support for Jaruzelski as president of Poland. One leading Solidarity journalist commented that as a result of the 1989 negotiations over forming a government "both sides will be afraid of their respective electorates . . . and the logic of events will push the communist party and Solidarity into back-room arrangements hidden from the public."[7] In Hungary major elements of the agreement reached in September 1989 by the Communist party and the opposition Round Table were challenged by dissenting opposition groups and defeated in a referendum two months later.

The collapse of authoritarian regimes was almost always exhilarating; the creation of democratic regimes was often disillusioning. Few political leaders who put together the compromises creating those regimes escaped the charge of having "sold out" the interests of their constituents. The extent of this disaffection was, in a sense, a measure of their success.

"How is the state to be made democratic," asked the Polish scholar Wojtek Lamentowicz, "by two artificially united and oligarchically ruled constellations of political forces?" That, however, may be the most effective way. In the third wave, democracies were often made by leaders willing to betray the interests of their followers in order to achieve that goal.[8]

A central compromise in most cases of democratization was what might be termed "the democratic bargain," the trade-off between participation and moderation. Implicitly or explicitly in the negotiating processes leading to democratization, the scope of participation was broadened and more political figures and groups gained the opportunity to compete for power and to win power on the implicit or explicit understanding that they would be moderate in their tactics and policies. In this sense the third wave duplicated experiences of the first wave in Europe, when suffrage was extended to the working class and socialist parties abandoned their commitment to violent revolution and tempered their policies. In late nineteenth-century Italy Giovanni Giolitti pursued an explicit policy of "deradicalization by incorporation." In late twentieth-century Spain, Portugal, and Greece, moderation was "the price of power," and the socialist parties of those countries "won their victories and achieved the tolerance of their once intransigent foes by dint of deradicalization."[9]

Authoritarian regimes, by definition, drastically restrict political participation. The ruling groups in authoritarian systems often found particular opposition leaders and political parties especially anathema. Democratization required accepting these groups as legitimate participants in politics. For decades the military establishments of Peru and Argentina used force to prevent the Apristas and the Peronistas from achieving or exercising power. In the democratization processes in those countries in the 1980s, the military accepted not only the participation in politics of their old opponents but also eventually their acquisition of power. A few months after taking office in the Greek transition, Karamanlis legalized the

Greek Communist party. Facing a much more difficult situation and the severe threat of a right-wing coup, Suarez also legalized the Spanish Communist party in April 1977; Juan Carlos played a key role in securing the "grudging acceptance" of this by the armed forces. In Uruguay the Club Naval agreement legalized the leftist Broad Front.

In the Brazilian transition the ban on the old pre-1964 political leaders was lifted in 1979 and in 1985 the legislature legalized previously outlawed Marxist parties and gave illiterates the vote. In 1989 Chilean voters amended their constitution to legalize the Communist party.[10] In 1987 in Turkey first the parliament and then the electorate revoked the military-decreed bans that prevented one hundred politicians from engaging in politics. In South Africa in 1990 the African National Congress was unbanned, imprisoned political leaders were freed, and exiles were allowed to return to their country.

The other side of the democratic bargain was moderation in tactics and policies by the included leaders and groups. This often involved their agreeing to abandon violence and any commitment to revolution, to accept existing basic social, economic, and political institutions (e.g., private property and the market system, autonomy of the military, the privileges of the Catholic Church), and to work through elections and parliamentary procedures in order to achieve power and put through their policies.[11] In the Spanish transition, the army accepted the socialists and communists as participants in Spanish politics, the socialists accepted capitalism, and the communists abandoned their republicanism and accepted the monarchy as well as special arrangements for the Catholic Church. By persuading his socialist followers in 1979 to abandon their commitment to Marxism, Felipe González paved the way for their electoral victory three years later. In Portugal, Mário Soares similarly led the socialists to the center. Coming back into power in 1983 as the head of a coalition including conservative parties, he accepted the need "to abandon the Marxist, collectivist and—to a lesser extent—

etatist leanings, to which an important section of their party adhered," and imposed a rather severe austerity program. In Greece Papandreou distanced himself from the "more extreme and polemical positions" he had espoused in the past and acted with restraint in office.[12] In Peru APRA moved to the center; in Argentina the Peronists moved to the right; in Poland Solidarity moved first to the center and then to the right. In Brazil, the opposition party, the MDB, "cooperated with the government's political game. . . . the opposition was extraordinarily moderate. Even with successive *cassacoes*, the MDB effectively urged moderation on its more radical members." In the referendum campaign on Pinochet in 1988 in Chile the opposition coalition similarly pursued a consciously and explicitly moderate course.[13]

Transitions were thus helped by the deradicalization of new participants and former leftists. They were also helped if those who first came to power in the new regime were not far distant politically from the previous authoritarian rulers. Karamanlis was a reassuring moderate conservative to the anticommunist Greek military, and Soares was a reassuring moderate socialist to at least some elements of the radicalized Portuguese military. Juan Carlos and Suárez had indisputable conservative Francoist credentials. Aylwin, a Christian Democrat, was conservative enought to satisfy the Chilean military. By and large, the initial acquisition of power by conservative and centrist leaders eased the transition to democracy from noncommunist authoritarian regimes.[14] In somewhat similar fashion, the subsequent coming to power of socialist leaders often eased the introduction of economic reforms and austerity programs.

The willingness and ability of leaders to reach compromises were affected by the prevailing attitudes toward compromise in their society. Some cultures appear to be more favorable to compromise than are others, and the legitimacy of and value placed on compromise may vary over time in a society. Historically, Spaniards, Poles, and Koreans, for instance, were noted more for the value they placed on principle and honor than on compromise. It can at least be hypothesized that the tragic consequences of those emphases together with socio-economic development produced changes in their national values by the 1970s and 1980s. In all three countries political leaders manifested an appreciation of the need for compromise in order to move their countries toward democracy. When, for instance, the governing and opposition parties in Korea reached agreement on a new constitution, it was reported that the "committee of negotiators from the two parties did something today that Koreans themselves acknowledge is a rarity in their politics: They compromised." [15] Democratization occurs in a society when that rarity becomes a reality, and democracy is stabilized when that reality becomes commonplace.

Historically the first efforts to establish democracy in countries frequently fail; second efforts often succeed. One plausible reason for this pattern is that learning occurred, and that does appear to be the case in several instances. Venezuela was a dramatic example in the second wave. The first meaningful effort to establish democracy in Venezuelan history occurred during the so-called *trienio* of 1945–48. In 1945 a military coup overthrew the dictator and introduced democratic politics that for the next three years was dominated by the reformist Acción Democrática (AD). The AD government pursued radical policies that alienated many groups and led to extreme polarization. "Democracy in the *trienio* was flawed by the absence of a sense of trust and mutual guarantees among major social and political groups. . . . Secure in their majorities, AD's leaders discounted the need to compromise with intense minorities, no matter how small in size."

This first attempt at democracy ended in a coup in 1948. Ten years later, when the military dictatorship of Gen. Marcos Pérez Jiménez was dissolving, the leaders of AD and other democratic groups explicitly acted "to reduce inter-party tension and violence, to accentuate interests and procedures, and remove, insofar as possible, issues of survival and legitimacy from the political scene." The leaders of the successful democratization in 1958 were in large part those who had led the unsuccessful democratization of 1945. They had benefitted from their experience; their 1958 actions reflected their "recognition of the lessons learned from the breakdown of democracy during the *trienio* (1945–1948)."[16]

Similar learning experiences on the need for compromise and moderation occurred in third wave transitions. In Spain, for instance, Juan Carlos was reported by one political leader to be concerned with "why the monarchy collapsed in 1932. He wants to avoid making the same mistakes as his grandfather." The leaders of the Communist party were also convinced that the mistakes of the 1930s had to be avoided. "The memory of the past obliges us," one of them said, "to take these circumstances into account, that is, to follow a policy of moderation. . . . We cannot allow ourselves the luxury of expressing opinions that might be misunderstood, that could be, or appear to be, extremist."[17] The peaceful transition in Argentina in 1983 similarly "suggests that there may have been a tenuous learning process at work in Argentina in comparison to the transition of 1971–1973, when many sides of the political spectrum resorted to violence."[18] In Peru the military and APRA went through a similar learning process. In Poland in 1981 Solidarity moved in a radical direction, threatening the direct overthrow of the Marxist-Leninist system; the government reacted with a martial law crackdown, outlawing the union and imprisoning its leaders. Seven years later, both sides had learned their lessons: radicalism leads to repression, and repression does not work. They pursued policies of moderation and compromise in leading Poland toward democracy in 1988 and 1989.

Later democratizers not only received a snowballing impetus to regime change from those who had done it earlier, they also learned lessons from the previous experience of others. The Latin Americans and East Europeans took to heart the lessons in moderation of the Spanish model. In transplacements the groups dominant in both the government and the opposition have to be committed to compromise and moderation. Transplacements tended to occur more frequently in the later than in the earlier years of the third wave, which suggests that the groups involved may have learned the desirability of compromise from the earlier experiences of others. In Korea the opposition learned the lessons of peaceful people power from the Philippines, and the government learned the advantages of compromise from the fate of Marcos. The transplacement in Czechoslovakia was in some measure, as Timothy Garton Ash put it,

> the beneficiary, and what happened there the culmination, of a ten-year-long Central European learning process—with Poland being the first, but paying the heaviest price. A student occupation strike? Of course, as in Poland! Nonviolence? The First Commandment of all Central European oppositions. Puppet parties coming alive? As in East Germany. A "round table" to negotiate the transition? As in Poland and Hungary. And so on. Politically, Czechoslovakia had what economic historians call the "advantages of backwardness." They could learn from the others' examples; and from their mistakes.[19]

ELECTIONS: STUNNING AND OTHERWISE

Elections are the way democracy operates. In the third wave they were also a way of weakening and ending authoritarian regimes. They were a vehicle of democratization as well as the goal of democratization. Democratization was brought about by authoritarian rulers who, for one reason or another, ventured to hold elections, and by opposition groups who pushed for elections and participated in them. The lesson of the third wave is that elections are not only the life of democracy; they are also the death of dictatorship.

When their performance legitimacy declined, authoritarian rulers often came under increasing pressure and had increasing incentives to attempt to renew their legitimacy through elections. Rulers sponsored elections believing they would either prolong their regime or their rule or that of associates. The rulers were almost always disappointed. With very few exceptions, the parties or candidates associated with authoritarian regimes lost or did very poorly in the regime-sponsored elections. The results of these elections often surprised both the leaders of the opposition and the leaders of the government. In the first fifteen years of the third wave this "stunning election" pattern was a pervasive one. It occurred in all three types of transition processes. Consider the following:

(1) As part of his decompression policy General Geisel allowed fairly competitive congressional elections to be held in November 1974 in Brazil. The government party, the Aliança Nacional Renovadora (ARENA), expected an easy win against the opposition party, MDB, and as late as October "few informed political observers would have bet against them." The election results, however, "stunned everyone, including the most optimistic MDB strategists."[20] The MDB doubled its representation in the lower house of Congress, almost tripled its representation in the Senate, and increased its control of state legislatures from one to six.

(2) In January 1977 in India, Indira Gandhi, who had been exercising emergency powers, abruptly called parliamentary elections for March. Gandhi was the commanding figure in Indian politics, but the Janata opposition coalition won an overwhelming victory. For the first time in history the Congress party lost control of the national government, winning only 34 percent of the popular vote, the first time also that it had ever gotten less than 40 percent.

(3) In Peru's transition election in May 1980, the military government supported the APRA party and passed an electoral law designed to enhance its representation. The election, however, produced "surprising results." "APRA suffered an electoral collapse, obtaining 27 percent of the vote." Acción Popular, the opposition party most removed from the military, won "an astonishing victory," getting 45.5 percent of the vote and winning the presidency, a majority in the Assembly, and a plurality in the Senate.[21]

(4) In November 1980 the military government of Uruguay

held a referendum on a proposed new constitution that would have given the military an institutionalized permanent veto on government policies. "To the amazement of the army," the public rejected it by a vote of 57 percent to 43 percent. The result "stunned the military as much as the opposition."[22] Two years later the military government authorized election of delegates to conventions of the major parties. Opponents of the military swept the field, with one close associate of the military, former President Jorge Pacheco Areco, getting only 27.8 percent of the vote in his party.

(5) The transition military government in Argentina sponsored national elections in October 1983. The Radical party, led by Raúl Alfonsín, long a critic of the military, won a "stunning" victory with an unprecedented 52 percent of the popular vote. The candidate of the other major party, the Peronistas, had "the open or tacit support of various military sectors" and got 40 percent of the vote.[23] For the first time in Argentine history the Peronistas lost a free election.

(6) In November 1983 the military government in Turkey sponsored elections for a return to civilian rule, and the leaders of the government organized and explicitly backed the Nationalist Democratic party, headed by a retired general. "To the surprise of Turkey's military rulers," however, "the wrong man won."[24] The Nationalist Democrats ran a poor third, getting only 23 percent of the vote, while the opposition Motherland party swept into power with 45 percent of the vote.

(7) In the February 1985 elections for the National Assembly in Korea, the newly formed opposition party, the New Korea Democratic party, did "unexpectedly well," winning 102 of the 276 seats in the legislature.[25] This followed a campaign that "was tightly controlled by the government, and opposition parties charged that a fair vote was impossible."

(8) In 1985 the military ruler of Pakistan, General Zia-ul-Huq, organized parliamentary elections but initially prohibited political parties from nominating candidates. The parties formally boycotted the election. Despite these circumstances, a "large number of candidates who held high positions in the martial law regime or who were identified as supporters of Zia were defeated."[26]

(9) In Chile in October 1988 General Pinochet submitted himself to a yes or no vote on his continued rule. A year before the

referendum, informed opinion held that he would "win by a landslide."[27] Buoyed by an economic surge, the general himself was confident of victory. As the campaign progressed, however, the opposition mobilized public opinion against him. The electorate turned down General Pinochet's bid for eight more years in power by a vote of 55 percent to 43 percent.

(10) In March 1989, for the first time in over seventy years, Soviet voters had a chance to vote freely for members of their national legislature. The result was most surprising, "a mortifying rebuke to the high and mighty," including the defeat of the Leningrad party chief and Politburo members, the party chiefs in Moscow, Kiev, Lvov, and Minsk, several regional party bosses, at least two top military commanders, as well as other leading figures of the communist establishment.[28]

(11) In the June 1989 Polish elections Solidarity scored a totally unanticipated sweeping victory, winning 99 of 100 seats in the Senate and 160 of 161 seats for which it could compete in the lower house. Thirty-three of thirty-five high-level government candidates running unopposed did not get the necessary 50 percent of the votes required for election. The results were described as "stunning" and reportedly greeted with "disbelief" by both government and Solidarity supporters who were "unprepared" for them.[29]

(12) The February 1990 victory in Nicaragua of the National Opposition Union (UNO) under Violeta Chamorro was the most pervasively stunning election anywhere up to that date. It was variously described as a "stunning electoral defeat," a "stunning upset," a "stunning election defeat," and a "stunning expression of Nicaragua's popular will," which "stunned many political analysts" and produced "stunned Sandinistas."[30] Despite anticipations that the Sandinistas benefitting from their control of the government and access to its resources would win easily, Chamorro carried eight out of nine administrative regions and got 55.2 percent of the vote to 40.8 percent for Daniel Ortega.

(13) In May 1990 in Myanmar (formerly Burma) the military State Law and Order Restoration Council sponsored the first multiparty elections in thirty years. The result was "astounding" and "a surprise." The opposition National League for Democracy (NLD) won a "stunning landslide victory" and elected 392 of the 485 contested seats in the National Assembly; the military-backed National Unity Party won 10 seats. During the campaign

the NLD's leader and four hundred of its activists were under detention and the party was subjected to a variety of constraints and harassments.[31]

(14) In June 1990 in the first multi-party elections in Algeria's twenty-eight years of independence, the opposition Islamic Salvation Front "scored a stunning success," which was greeted by officials in North Africa and Europe with "stunned silence."[32] The Islamic Front won control of thirty-two provinces and 853 municipal councils. The previously dominant single party, the National Liberation Front, won fourteen provinces and 487 municipal councils.

In all these cases authoritarian rulers sponsored elections and lost or did much worse than they and others anticipated. Were there any exceptions to this pattern, where authoritarian rulers sponsored fair elections and they or their friends won fairly? One ambiguous case is the September 1980 referendum in Chile in which 68 percent of the voters approved a constitution proposed by General Pinochet. The opposition, however, was severely restricted, there was no electoral registration, and no meaningful way of monitoring fraud.[33] In Korea in 1987, the candidate backed by the military government, Roh Tae Woo, was elected president with a plurality of 36 percent against three other candidates. The two opposition candidates who had long campaigned against military rule got a combined total of 54 percent of the vote. If they had united their forces they probably would have won the election.

More significant deviations from the stunning election pattern occurred in the elections in Romania, Bulgaria, and Mongolia in May, June, and July 1990. In Romania, the National Salvation Front took over the government after the downfall of Ceausescu and five months later won a substantial victory in the May 1990 elections. In Bulgaria the Communist party, which had governed the country for decades, renamed itself the Socialist party and won control of the Grand National Assembly. In Mongolia the general secretary and other top leaders of the Communist party were replaced, opposition parties formed, and competitive elections held in which the communists won 60–70 percent of the seats in parliament. In all cases the leading figures on the winning side had been officials in the communist regimes.

How can these apparent departures from the stunning election pattern be explained? Three factors may have been relevant. First, the new leaders distanced themselves from the former authoritarian rulers. Clearly neither Ceausescu nor Todor Zhivkov could have won fair elections in their countries in 1990. Ion Iliescu, the leader of the National Salvation Front, had been an official in the Ceausescu regime, but was expelled from the Communist party's Central Committee. Petar Mladenov and his associates in Bulgaria had themselves thrown Zhivkov, the long-term dictator, out of office; they had been the reformers ousting the standpatters in the Bulgarian transformation process. A less dramatic change in leadership occurred in Mongolia.

Second, coercion and fraud in the conduct of the campaigns and the elections may have played a part. In Romania and Bulgaria international observers were divided as to the extent to which the governing groups unfairly attempted to influence the elections; such efforts were apparently more prevalent in Romania than in Bulgaria. In both cases, foreign observers identified certain elements of coercion and unfair practices, but their prevalent opinion was that these did not decisively affect the outcome of the elections.

The third, and most important, factor was the nature of the societies. As has been pointed out, urban middle-class groups were the principal forces pushing for democratization in third wave countries. In 1980 only 17 percent of the Romanian population lived in cities of over 500,000 people, compared, for instance, to 37 percent in Hungary. Both Bulgaria and Romania were still in considerable measure peasant societies and both were at lower levels of economic development than other Eastern and southern European third wave countries, as well as some East Asian and Latin American third wave countries. Mongolia was still in considerable mea-

population concentrations in cities vs. countryside

sure a pastoral society, with three-quarters of its population living outside its only major city and with less than 600 miles of surfaced roads. In all three countries, the opposition parties were strong in the cities; the successor parties to the communist regimes won in the countryside, which provided enough votes to return them to office. Whether a country produced a stunning result in an authoritarian-sponsored election was perhaps one test of whether it had reached a level of socioeconomic development that would be supportive of a democratic regime.

The frequency of the stunning election pattern in the transitions from authoritarianism to democracy raises three major questions.

First, why did authoritarian rulers or groups closely associated with them so consistently lose these elections? The most obvious and probably most valid answer is that they lost the elections for the same reasons that leaders and parties that have been in power for substantial periods of time lose elections in democratic states. All leaders eventually lose their initial support and legitimacy. Publics look for an alternative. In most stunning elections, the voters clearly were casting protest votes against the existing authoritarian rulers. They were probably voting against the existing authoritarian system. They may or may not have been casting affirmative votes in favor of democracy. They could not, however, vote against the incumbents without also voting against the system. The defeats of incumbents in a large number of industrialized democracies in the 1970s and early 1980s did not destroy democracy; they renewed it. The electoral defeat of authoritarian rulers, in contrast, usually meant the effective end of the authoritarian regime.

The protest character of the votes in the stunning elections is reflected in the tenuous nature of opposition unity. Individuals and groups representing very different political ideologies and with very different grievances against the regime came together to vote against the regime. The opposition was often a motley coalition of a large number of parties with little in common except their opposition to the incumbent rulers. In both Nicaragua and Chile, for instance, the opposition coalitions were composed of fourteen parties ranging in views from the extreme right to the extreme left. In Bulgaria, where the government party won, the opposition coalition included sixteen parties and movements. In many elections, the leading opposition party was a new and recently formed party that, whatever its predominant ideological view, could serve as a new and undiscredited vehicle for whatever resentments and frustrations voters had with the regime. It seems highly unlikely, for instance, that a majority of Algerians in 1990 were staunchly committed to Islamic fundamentalism. Voting for the Islamic Salvation Front, however, was the most effective way of expressing their opposition to the party that had governed Algeria for three decades. In addition, there was the widows and daughters phenomenon. Heterogeneous opposition groups coalesced around the surviving female relatives of martyred national heroes: Corazon Aquino, Benazir Bhutto, Violeta Chamorro, Aung San Suu Kyi. These leaders dramatized the issue of good versus the evil of the incumbent regime and provided a magnetic symbol and personality around which all manner of dissident groups could rally. Overall, publics rarely missed the opportunity to cast protest votes against long-term authoritarian incumbents.

Second, given this pattern of stunning defeats, why did authoritarian rulers sponsor elections they were so likely to lose? They appeared to be driven by a variety of factors, including perception of the need to revive their declining legitimacy at home, the prevalence of democratic norms globally and in their society, and the desire for international respect and legitimacy (symbolized by a formal welcome by the president on the White House lawn). In addition, in most cases, undoubtedly the risks of having an election seemed small. Authoritarian regimes normally provide few feedback mechanisms, and dictators naturally tended to believe that they had sufficient rapport with their publics to win their endorsement. The authoritarian leaders also, of course, controlled the government, whatever political organizations were allowed to exist, and substantial financial resources; hence it was reasonable to assume that they could overwhelm what usually appeared to be a weak, narrowly based, disorganized, and fragmented opposition. Authoritarian rulers naturally concluded, "How can I lose?" In considerable measure, third wave democratizations moved forward on the false confidence of dictators.

The confidence of authoritarian rulers that they could win the elections they sponsored was undoubtedly further bolstered by the extent to which they felt they could manipulate electoral procedures. Three devices were frequently employed. Some leaders attempted to affect the results of elections by affecting the timing of elections. Both they and their opponents usually thought that earlier elections would benefit the government because it was organized and commanded public attention, whereas later elections would benefit the opposition by giving it time to get organized, appeal to the public, and mobilize its supporters. Marcos called a "snap" election with the hope that the opposition would be disorganized and unprepared. In Brazil, the opposition supported the delay of the municipal elections scheduled for May 1980 because they feared they would not be ready for them.[34] In the Polish Round Table negotiations the government pushed for early elections, and Solidarity was viewed as making a major concession when it agreed to them. In Hungary the government wanted an early popular election for president because it assumed its probable candidate, Imre Pozsgay, had high visibility and a very good chance of winning. The opposition feared that would happen and pushed through a proposal for a referendum on the issue, in which the public approved parliament selecting the first president. In Czechoslovakia similar concerns were expressed about the advantage that early elections would give the communists; and in Romania in February 1990, opposition leaders said they wanted to delay the elections scheduled for May because they had inadequate resources and time to prepare for them.

The logic of these government and opposition positions on election timing seems obvious: opposition groups would benefit from more time to prepare for the election. Little empirical evidence exists, however, to support this logic. Back in Turkey's second wave democratization, for example, the government moved up elections to July 1946 in order "to catch the new [opposition] party before it could fully organize,"[35] but that party did extremely well in those elections. In the Korean elections in February 1985, the opposition New Korea Democratic Party, formed a few weeks before the election, won 29 percent of the vote and 67 of 184 elected seats in the National Assembly.[36] By all impartial accounts, Ferdinand Marcos lost his snap election, and Solidarity scored a sweeping victory in the early elections to which it had agreed very reluctantly. The evidence is not conclusive, but it clearly does not support the proposition that governments always benefitted from calling early elections and that oppositions suffered by participating in them.

Second, authoritarian rulers often rigged elections by establishing electoral systems highly favorable to the government, by harassing and intimidating the opposition, and by employing government resources in the campaign. If carried to an extreme, of course, these tactics ensured the government's victory but made a mockery of the election. In most of the stunning elections listed above, however, groups in power made efforts, at times extensive ones, to tilt the election in their favor, and yet did not succeed. Over the course of a decade, from 1974 to 1984, the Brazilian government regularly revised its laws on elections, parties, and campaigning in hopes of stopping the steady growth of opposition power. It did not succeed. Again the evidence is fragmentary, but what there is does suggest that, unless they were carried to an extreme, rigging tactics were unlikely to ensure government victory.

If manipulation of election timing and procedures did not suffice, the alternative remaining to authoritarian rulers was outright fraud and theft. Authoritarian rulers can steal elections if they want to. Often in the past they were able to steal elections quietly, in nonobvious ways, so that although everyone knew the elections were stolen, no one could prove it. In the July 1978 elections in Bolivia, for instance, General Banzer engaged in "massive fraud" in arranging for his candidate, Gen. Pereda Asbun, to receive exactly the required 50 percent of the vote.[37] As the third wave went on, however, democratization became a recognized phenomenon of global politics, the media paid more attention to it, and elections were increasingly subject to international monitoring.

By the late 1980s foreign observers had become a familiar and indispensable presence in almost all transition elections. In some instances such missions were sponsored by the United Nations, the Organization of American States, or other intergovernmental bodies. In other cases private organizations provided this service. By 1990 the National Democratic Institute for International Affairs had organized international observer missions for third wave elections in some thirteen countries. Delegations from the U.S. Congress and other legislatures were also present in some cases. Former President Jimmy Carter played an active role in and added his authority to several of these missions.

Foreign observers made it difficult if not impossible for governments quietly and secretly to steal an election. Blatant theft, as in the Philippines and Panama, however, defeated the purpose of having the election, which was to enhance the domestic and international legitimacy of the rulers. If, on the other hand, the government refused to allow "impartial" external observers to witness the vote, that in itself now became proof that it was rigging the election. The emergence and

prevalence of the foreign observer phenomenon was a major development of the 1980s and significantly enhanced the importance of elections in the democratization process. Authoritarian rulers who sponsored elections to bolster their declining legitimacy were in a no-win position. If they played the game fairly, they suffered a "stunning" defeat. If they manipulated timing and procedures in other than extreme fashion, they probably also were defeated. If they stole the election, they lost legitimacy rather than gaining it. The reasons that led them to hold elections—decreasing legitimacy and opposition pressure—were also the reasons they lost those elections. The insoluble dilemma they faced was neatly summed up by Gen. Fernando Matthei, commander of the Chilean air force, shortly before the 1988 election: "If the government's candidate wins everyone will say it was a fraud. If he loses everyone will say it was a fair election. So it is more in our interests than anyone else's to be able to show it was an absolutely fair election."[38] In 1990 the Sandinistas, similarly confident of victory, felt the need to have a fair election and invited masses of foreign observers who would be able to testify to both its fairness and their victory. The results of both elections underscored Matthei's point. Authoritarian rulers could only legitimate their regime through elections by ending their regime through elections.

Third, elections sponsored by authoritarian regimes also posed problems for opposition groups. Should they participate in the election or should they boycott it? Given the pattern of stunning defeats of authoritarian rulers, what, if any, was the rationale for the opposition not taking advantage of the opportunity offered by the authoritarian-sponsored election? These issues did not normally arise when a regime transition was clearly underway: if democratic reformers were in power and moving decisively forward in a transformation process, if the leaders of a military government explicitly said that they are returning to the barracks, if leaders of government and opposition were agreed on a transplacement pro-

end regimes through elections

cess. In these circumstances the principal opposition groups normally had no reason not to participate.

At the other extreme opposition democrats had little to gain by accepting appointed positions in authoritarian governments and thus lending legitimacy to those governments. If they did, they would divorce themselves from their constituencies and make themselves dependent on the authoritarian rulers. The Jaruzelski government in Poland and the Botha government in South Africa, for instance, both attempted to lure opposition leaders to positions on appointive consultative councils. From the viewpoint of promoting democracy, Polish and South African opposition leaders correctly refused to participate. Opposition democrats also generally did not participate in elections for legislatures that were powerless and simply government tools. In 1973, for instance, Papadopoulos attempted to bolster his foundering regime by promising parliamentary elections. The leaders of the Greek political parties refused to participate. George Mavors, head of the outlawed Center Union party, said it well: the promised "elections have a single purpose: to legitimize the dictatorship covering it by a castrated Parliament which will not have the power to debate, let alone decide, any of the nation's vital matters."[39]

In between those extremes, the boycott issue most often arose when elections were called either by a standpatter regime or by a liberalizing regime whose ultimate intentions with respect to democratization were unclear. Philippine opposition leaders, for instance, hotly debated and disagreed on the boycott issue with respect to the Marcos-sponsored 1978 and 1984 National Assembly elections and the 1986 presidential election. Most but not all black South African political leaders urged boycotts of the 1983 and 1988 municipal elections; coloured and Asian political leaders were divided about participation in the 1984 and 1989 parliamentary elections. Three out of four opposition parties urged boycott of the 1974 Dominican Republic presidential elections when it appeared that the Belaguer government had little or no intention of being willing to surrender power. At U.S. government urging, opposition groups boycotted the 1984 Nicaraguan elections. Pakistani party leaders urged a boycott of the 1985 National Assembly elections organized by the Zia regime as it began to liberalize. The two principal opposition parties (the Movement for Democracy in Algeria and the Socialist Forces Front) but not the Islamic Salvation Front urged abstention from the 1990 local and provincial elections in Algeria.

Standpatter or liberalizing governments sponsored elections to enhance their regime legitimacy and/or to extend their personal tenure in power. Participation in the elections by at least some opposition groups thus was essential to the governments. Marcos, for instance, welcomed Benigno Aquino's decision to run for the Assembly in 1978 while in prison under a death sentence "because it legitimized the exercise." Hence governments often tried to defeat boycott efforts. In the Pakistan assembly election of 1985, "propaganda against and instigation of the boycott of the polls was declared a cognizable offense" and "newspapers were ordered in February 1985 not to publish any statement in favor of the boycott campaign." In the 1988 municipal elections, the South African government similarly "clamped down on pro-boycott opposition groups and made it unlawful for individuals to urge a boycott."[40]

Boycott campaigns changed the election issue from whom to vote for to whether to vote. The success of these efforts varied, depending on the unity of the opposition groups in support of the boycott, public perception of the intentions of the government, and the public's previous experience with voting. Most South African blacks had never voted previously, so it is not surprising that only 20 percent of potential black voters voted in the municipal elections in 1983 and about 30 percent in 1988. Thirty percent of coloured voters and 20 percent of Indian voters participated in the 1984 parliamentary election in South Africa and voting in 1989 was comparably low. In the Dominican Republic in 1974 the abstention rate was again about 70 percent.

Some boycott efforts were less successful. The principal opposition groups urged Spanish voters to boycott the referendum on political reform in December 1976, but 77 percent of the voters went to the polls. This election, however, was sponsored by a government clearly committed to democratic reform. In the May 1984 national assembly elections in the Philippines, 80 percent of the electorate voted despite the appeals of leftist opposition groups that they not do so. In the 1985 Pakistani National Assembly elections boycotted by the political parties, many opposition candidates were elected, and the parties subsequently admitted they had made a mistake in urging abstention. About 40 percent of the potential voters abstained from the 1990 Algerian local and provincial elections.[41]

What then were the efficacy and wisdom of boycotts as a strategy for the democratic opposition? A successful boycott did not end the authoritarian regime or remove the government from power. It did reduce its legitimacy, which was one reason why governments responded so vigorously against boycott efforts. Unsuccessful boycotts, on the other hand, were evidence of opposition weakness. More important, boycotts often meant opportunities foregone, choosing nonproductive exit instead of meaningful voice. Participation in an election campaign itself often furnished an opportunity, depending on government restrictions, to criticize the government, mobilize and organize opposition supporters, and appeal to the public. It was an incentive to political activity, and authoritarian regimes are only changed or brought down by political activity. If the election was conducted with minimal fairness, the opposition often did extraordinarily well. In the best of circumstances it won a "stunning" victory and toppled the government. Short of this, opposition candidates made effective campaigns in authoritarian-sponsored elections in Brazil, Taiwan, Mexico, the Philippines, Pakistan, and the Soviet Union.

Even modest opposition electoral successes could be capitalized upon to weaken the government. Peping Cojuangco argued that the Philippine opposition should contest the 1984 National Assembly elections, although they clearly would not win a majority, because "If you get thirty [National Assembly seats] this time, then people will believe it can be done, and in the next election that thirty will multiply." In Brazil in the 1970s the government restricted opposition electoral campaigning and changed electoral rules to hamper the opposition. The opposition party, the MDB, however, contested every election as best it could, gradually expanded its strength in and control of legislative bodies, used these positions to pressure the government to move forward in democratization, and, as a result, increasingly came to be viewed as a responsible alternative government.[42] At the same time its activity strengthened the hand of the democratic reformers in the government in dealing with the strong standpatter resistance within the military.

In South Africa boycott proponents greatly reduced participation in the elections to the coloured and Indian houses of Parliament in 1984. At least some of those who were elected, however, made effective use of their positions in the campaign against apartheid. The 1985 session of Parliament repealed the laws prohibiting interracial marriage and sex and preventing formation of multiracial political parties. It also loosened restrictions on black residence and employment in urban areas. Coloured and Indian members of Parliament gave "impetus" to these changes. Allan Hendrickse, leader of the coloured Labour party, "forced Mr. Botha's hand against the law which prevents the formation of multiracial parties, by putting up Coloured candidates for the Indian chambers. The Labour party may also have helped to relax the 'pass laws,' which control the movement of non-whites, and encouraged one black community to resist the government's plans to displace it from its ancestral home."[43] Subsequently, Hendrickse used his control of the coloured house of Parliament to demand that President Botha repeal the Group Areas Act in return for Hendrickse agreeing to amend the constitution so as to postpone parliamentary elections from 1989 to 1992. Botha refused to agree to the deal, and the elections were held in 1989. In South Africa and elsewhere, elected representatives found ways to lobby the government and to bargain with it in the interests of democratic reforms.

Those most prone to boycott elections were radical opposition groups opposed to democracy. Marxist-Leninist insurgents in the Philippines and El Salvador spurned elections. Opposition groups, such as the Palestine Liberation Organization (PLO) and the ANC in the 1980s, which refused to participate in elections, however limited or unfair, were likely to be dominated by leaders not adverse to replacing one undemocratic regime with another. In the 1984 Philippine elections the communist-dominated National Democratic Front led the boycott campaign against Corazon Aquino and the other democratic candidates who participated in the election against the Marcos regime. They also intensified their use of violence during the campaign. "The opposition running in these elections," one Communist party leader said, "are only opportunists. The real opposition are the boycotters."[44] He was right. His "real opposition" opposed both the Marcos regime and democracy. His political opportunists were using ballots rather than bullets to revive Philippine democracy.

The lesson of the third wave seems clear: authoritarian leaders who wanted to stay in power should not have called elections; opposition groups who wanted democracy should not have boycotted the elections authoritarian leaders did call.

In the course of the transitions to democracy, elections also tended to promote political moderation. They provided incentives to move toward the center for both opposition parties that wished to gain power and government parties that wished to retain power. In their first election in April 1975 Portuguese voters decisively rejected radical Marxist alternatives and gave their support to moderate centrist parties. Two years later Spanish voters acted similarly in their first election, which was appropriately described as "a triumph for moderation *and* for the desire for change."[45] Voters in Greece, El Salvador, Peru, the Philippines, and elsewhere similarly gave only minuscule electoral support to leftist revolutionaries, and, of course, Nicaraguan voters ousted the leftists from power. With only a few exceptions, publics consistently rejected the old authoritarian regimes and those who had been associated with them and also rejected extremist alternatives to those regimes. "No dictators, no revolutionaries," was, in effect, the maxim of voters in third wave transition elections.

Elections were one road away from authoritarianism. Revolution was the other. Revolutionaries rejected elections. "We shall not allow puppet organizations to put up candidates," the head of the ANC military wing said in connection with the 1988 municipal elections in South Africa. "We shall use revolutionary violence to prevent blacks from collaborating." The contrast between the two paths was well summed up by Alvaro Cunhal, head of the Portuguese Communist party, in 1976:

> In the Portuguese Revolution two processes have intervened, two dynamics, with completely different characteristics. On one side, the revolutionary dynamic, created by the intervention of material force—popular and military—directly transforming situations, conquering and exercising liberties, defeating and throwing out the fascists, opposing the counterrevolutionary attempts, bringing about profound social and economic transformations, attempting to create a state in service of the Revolution, and the creation of organs of power (including military organs) which will guarantee the democratic process and correspond to the revolutionary transformation.

On the other side, the electoral process, understood as the
choice by universal suffrage of the organs of power, tending to
subordinate any social transformation to a previous constitutional legality, and not recognizing the intervention of the military in political life, or the creative, predominant intervention
of the masses in the revolutionary process.[46]

In the third wave the "electoral dynamic" led from authoritarianism to democracy; the "revolutionary dynamic" led
from one form of authoritarianism to another.

LOW LEVELS OF VIOLENCE

Major political changes almost always involve violence. The
third wave was no exception. Almost every democratization
between 1974 and 1990 involved some violence, yet the overall level of violence was not high. Taking place as they did
through compromise and elections, most third wave democratizations were relatively peaceful compared to other regime
transitions.

Political violence involves people doing physical injury to
persons or property in order to affect the composition or behavior of government. An imperfect but widely used measure
of political violence is the number of deaths that occur for
political reasons during a particular time or in connection
with a particular event. Estimating with even very rough accuracy the number of political deaths in the third wave is extraordinarily difficult. Conceptually, violence that is part of
democratization has to be distinguished from violence that
may occur during democratization, such as the routine murder by government of presumed opponents (which is an
inherent characteristic of many authoritarian regimes), and
from ethnic conflict, which may be a product of liberalization
and democratization.

In a minority of countries democratization efforts were accompanied by major violence. The most extensive violence
occurred where there was sustained armed conflict between
governments and opposition guerrilla movements over an

extended period of time. In Guatemala, El Salvador, the Philippines, and Peru, Marxist-Leninists waged insurgent wars against authoritarian governments; these regimes were replaced by democratically elected governments; the insurgencies, however, continued. In at least Guatemala and El Salvador the political deaths resulting from the insurgencies against the authoritarian regimes were considerable. Estimates of those killed in Guatemala between 1978 and the election of Vinicio Cerezo in 1985 range from 40,000 to 100,000. Political killings in El Salvador between the 1978 reform coup and the coming into office of Duarte in 1984 have been estimated at 30,000 to 45,000. These killings were the result of the often brutal and indiscriminate application of violence by the security forces defending authoritarian governments in wars against insurgent movements attempting to overthrow those governments and establish Marxist-Leninist regimes. The killings were a product not of democratization efforts by either government or opposition but of a war between two nondemocratic groups. In Nicaragua 23,000 people are estimated to have been killed in the civil war between 1981 and 1990. Whether or not a *contra* military victory would have produced a democratic government in Nicaragua is uncertain. The *contra* insurgency, however, was one of the many factors that induced the Sandinista regime to call elections. After a democratic regime came into office, the *contras*, unlike the Marxist-Leninists in Guatemala and El Salvador, ended their insurgency and disbanded. The casualties in the Nicaraguan civil war, unlike those in El Salvador, Guatemala, the Philippines, and Peru, thus may be appropriately viewed as part of the costs of democratization.

Nicaragua stands alone among third wave countries in the number of people killed in the struggle to democratize. For the period 1974–90, South Africa probably ranked second. In South Africa 575 people were killed in the Soweto massacre in 1976; some 207 were killed by government forces, the ANC, and others between 1977 and 1984; about 3,500 are estimated to have been killed in the uprisings in the black townships from 1984 to 1988, and from 3,500 to 5,000 more in the fighting between black groups from 1985 to 1990. Overall perhaps 9,500 to 10,000 South Africans died in political violence between 1976 and 1990.

Individual incidents or actions also produced significant numbers of deaths in some countries. U.S. invasions resulted in the killing of some 120 to 150 people in Grenada, and at least 550 and possibly as many as 800 in Panama. The Korean army killed at least 200 and possibly up to 1,000 people in the Kwangju incident of May 1980. Probably 1,000 and perhaps as many as 3,000 people were killed by the Burmese military when they suppressed the democracy movement in August and September 1980. Somewhere between 400 and 1,000 people were killed in Beijing in the Chinese government's crackdown in June 1989. At least 746 people were killed in political violence in Bucharest in December 1989 and probably several hundred others were killed in Timisoara and elsewhere. Apparently more than 200 people were killed in the coups d'etat in Bolivia in 1979 and 1980.[47]

In the great majority of third wave countries, however, the overall levels of violence were quite low. Such was clearly the case in the first transitions in southern Europe. In the coup that began the third wave in Portugal, for instance, 5 people were killed and 15 wounded. In the year that followed less than a dozen people died in political violence. Several more people were apparently killed in peasant anticommunist upheavals in northern Portugal in the summer of 1975. One soldier was killed in the abortive right-wing coup of March 11, 1975, and 3 more in the November 25, 1975, coup and countercoup.[48] In a year and a half of revolutionary upheaval in Portugal, however, total political deaths probably numbered less than 100. The Spanish transition also was relatively nonviolent. During the four years from 1975 through 1978, 205 political deaths were reported: 13 by extreme right-wing groups, 23 by Marxist-Leninist groups, 62 by the police and Civil Guard, and 107 by the ETA Basque leftist separatists.[49] Apart from the army killing 34 people in the Polytechnic incident, the Greek transition was relatively free of violence. The transitions from military regimes in the South American countries, with the partial exception of Chile, were also generally peaceful. Virtually no blood was shed during the regime changes in Poland, East Germany, Hungary, and Czechoslovakia. These transitions were, as Timothy Garton Ash put it, "remarkable for their almost complete lack of violence. . . . No bastilles were stormed, no guillotines erected. Lamp posts were used only for street lighting."[50] In Taiwan the most dramatic event in the struggle over democratization was the so-called "Kaohsiung incident," in which no one was killed but 183 unarmed policemen were injured. In the Philippines, a country with what is generally considered a violence-prone culture, both the Marcos regime and the Marxist insurgents killed people, but the numbers were limited and the principal opposition groups did not employ violence. In Korea, after the Kwangju incident, violence was restrained and very few political deaths occurred. The return to democracy in India and Turkey, after their brief experience with authoritarian rule, also involved minimal violence, as did the transition in Nigeria.

Violence obviously occurred in the third wave, but overall it was quite limited. The total political deaths in more than thirty democratization efforts apart from Nicaragua between 1974 and 1990 probably numbered about 20,000 and were heavily concentrated in South Africa and mainland Asia. It was, obviously, tragic that these people were killed. Compared, however, to the hundreds of thousands of people killed in individual communal conflicts, civil wars, and international wars, and considering the positive results achieved in terms of political change, the cost in human lives of the third wave was extraordinarily low. Democratization accounted for an infinitesimal portion of the political deaths in the world beteen 1974 and 1990. From the "revolution of the carnations" in Lisbon to the "velvet revolution" in Prague, the third wave was overwhelmingly a peaceful wave. What explains the low levels of violence in these regime changes?

First, the experience of some countries with substantial civil violence before democratization began or early in the process of democratization encouraged both government and opposition to abjure violence. Spain and Greece suffered bloody and divisive civil wars before and after World War II. Military governments in Brazil, Uruguay, and Argentina fought ruthless "dirty wars" against terrorist groups in the 1960s and 1970s. One effect of these wars was to reduce drastically or to eliminate extremist radical opposition of the Marighella type, committed exclusively to violence.[51] A second effect was to produce in all sectors of society the reaction of "nunca más." In December 1982, for instance, Argentina's transition was marred when some participants in an authorized protest charged police barriers in front of the presidential palace; the police responded with tear gas, and one person was shot by a government security agent. President Bignone and opposition party leaders reacted promptly to prevent further violence and the Church declared a "Day of National Reconciliation." After this, the Argentine transition continued to be "relatively peaceful compared to those in many other countries."[52] Somewhat similarly, in the Korean protests of 1986 and 1987, the police were careful to avoid using firearms so as not to replicate the Kwangju massacre. In Taiwan both opposition and government tactics were similarly heavily affected by memories of the Kaohsiung incident. In December 1986, for instance, the principal leaders of the Taiwan opposition condemned those members of a crowd who had stoned police cars at the airport, announced that "security should be first and freedom second," and cancelled plans for twenty rallies. In Leipzig in East Germany in October 1989, both communist authorities and opposition leaders recognized the need to avoid "another Beijing."[53]

Second, different levels of violence were, in some measure, associated with different processes of transition. About half the transitions between 1974 and 1990 were transformations in which democratic reformers in the government were strong enough to initiate and in considerable measure to control the process of regime change. The government thus had little incentive to resort to violence, and the opposition had little opportunity to do so. One notable exception was Chile, where the government adhered to a rigid schedule for regime transformation and the opposition used massive demonstrations to attempt to accelerate change and to force the government to negotiate. In transplacements democratic reformers dominant in the government and democratic moderates dominant in the opposition had a common interest in minimizing violence as they struggled to agree on the terms for transition. Among replacements, the record was more varied, and the two military interventions caused significant bloodshed in two small countries. The prevalence of transformations and, to a lesser degree, transplacements, however, minimized violence in the third wave.

Third, the willingness of standpatter governments to order the use of violence against opposition groups varied considerably, as did the willingness of the security forces to carry out such orders. In China, Burma, South Africa, and Chile, tough-minded leaders endorsed the use of force, and police and military units ruthlessly employed violence to suppress peaceful and not-so-peaceful opposition demonstrations. In other cases, however, government leaders did not act decisively and seemed reluctant to direct the use of force against their own citizens. Like the shah of Iran, Marcos waffled back and forth in his instructions to his military as opposition protests mounted after the February 1986 election. In Poland, East Germany, and Czechoslovakia, the communist governments for many years did not hesitate to use force to suppress opposition. At the crucial moments of regime transition in 1988 and 1989, however, they refrained from doing so. In Leipzig on October 9, 1989, the situation was apparently one of touch and go: a massive opposition demonstration was planned and "riot police, state security forces, and members of the paramilitary factory 'combat groups' stood ready to clear East Germany's Tienanmen Square with truncheons and, it was subsequently reported, live ammunition."[54] The order to use force against the 70,000 demonstrators, however, never came. This was apparently the result of action by the local civic and party leaders with the belated endorsement of the national Communist leader, Egon Krenz. Overall, in East Europe, apart from Romania, there was, as Garton Ash noted, an amazing absence of "major *counter*revolutionary violence."[55] In both the Philippines and East Europe, probably the principal reason behind the reluctance of government leaders to use force at the crisis moments in the democratization process was the expressed opposition to such use by the governments of the relevant superpowers. In contrast, the influence of restraining superpowers was totally absent in China, Burma, Romania, and South Africa, and was very weak in Chile.

When governments do authorize the use of violence, the violence only becomes real when those orders are obeyed. *Ultima ratio regum* is not guns but the willingness of those who have guns to use them on behalf of the regime. That willingness also varied considerably. Armies generally do not like to train their weapons on the citizens whom they have a duty to defend. Police and internal security troops were normally more willing than regular military units to use violence to quell disorder and protest. Authoritarian rulers often created special security forces—the Securitate in Romania, "dignity battalions" in Panama, interior ministry troops in many countries—especially recruited and trained to support the regime.

Soldiers and police were less likely to obey orders to use violence if they could identify with the people they were ordered to shoot. Authoritarian regimes, consequently, attempted to ensure that there were social, ethnic, or racial differences between the users and targets of regime violence. The South African government regularly assigned black policemen to tribal areas different from their own. The Soviet government attempted to pursue a similar policy with respect to that country's nationalities. The Chinese government used peasant armies from distant provinces against the students in Tiananmen Square. The more homogeneous a society was, the more difficult it was for the regime to use violence to suppress opposition. The same principle also probably explains in part the relatively high casualties produced by U.S. forces in their invasions of Grenada and Panama.

In a similar vein, the more broad-gauged and representative of mainstream citizenry a mass demonstration was, the more reluctant military and police units were to use violence against it. In September 1984 the Manila police used "guns, clubs, and tear gas" to break up an antigovernment demonstration of 3,000 people, composed largely of students and leftists, with 34 people (12 with shotgun wounds) being hospitalized.[56] The following month the police did not interfere with a demonstration of 30,000 people organized by business groups and Cardinal Sin. In the confrontation outside Camp Craeme in February 1986, Filipino army units clearly did not wish to fire on the massed religious workers, professionals, and housewives. Similarly, Korean security forces were much more willing to use force against radical student demonstrators than against middle-class clerical workers, technicians, and businesspeople. In Czechoslovakia the defense minister assured leaders of the Civic Forum that the Czech army would not shoot Czech citizens. In Romania, army units refused to fire on demonstrators in Timisoara; and the army then turned against the regime and played a crucial role in suppressing the Securitate, which remained loyal to the

Ceausescus. Even in China, some army units apparently refused to fire on civilians, and their officers were subsequently
investigated and court-martialed.[57]

The use of force against the opposition was thus likely to
be more effective if (1) the society was socially or communally
heterogeneous, or (2) it was at a relatively low level of socio-
economic development. Authoritarian regimes in societies in
which economic development had produced a substantial
middle class sympathetic to democratization were more reluctant to order the use of force to suppress dissent, and the
security troops of those regimes were less likely to carry out
such orders.

Fourth, opposition groups also varied widely in the extent
to which they used, tolerated, or rejected the use of violence.
This issue posed in a much more critical and dramatic way
some of the same questions that came up in the debates over
whether or not to boycott regime-sponsored elections. In
many cases, the police and security forces of the regime imprisoned hundreds or thousands of people and tortured or
murdered them. The activities of the official forces were often supplemented by those of the semiofficial, paramilitary
"death squads." Under these circumstances the temptation
was strong to dramatize and further the opposition cause
by blowing up government installations, throwing Molotov
cocktails at government vehicles, shooting at soldiers and police, kidnapping and executing notoriously brutal officials. To
what extent should a democratic opposition resort to these
tactics against a repressive regime that uses violence? The answers of opposition groups varied across the spectrum from
never to sometimes to always. The answers correlated highly
with the overall commitment of the groups to democracy.
Democratic moderates rejected violence; radical groups advocated violence.

In most third wave countries the principal mainstream
opposition groups pursued democracy through nonviolent

means. The Catholic Church, as we have seen, was a major force pushing for democratization in many countries, and the Pope, local bishops, and most clergy also vigorously espoused nonviolence.[58] Middle-class urban businesspeople, professionals, and clerical workers, who often dominated the democratic opposition, usually rejected violence and attempted to minimize violence. Political party leaders had a stake in employing the methods in which they were presumably skilled—negotiations, compromise, elections—and in avoiding the tactics of terrorism and insurgency in which others would excel. The social sources of the moderate opposition movements thus shaped not only their support for democracy but also their support for nonviolent means of realizing democracy.

The extent to which the opposition was committed to nonviolence varied among countries. "In a revolution," Benigno Aquino said in the speech he drafted for delivery at Manila Airport, "there can really be no victors, only victims. We do not have to destroy in order to build."[59] In the years following his murder, Corazon Aquino firmly maintained this commitment to nonviolence which, of course, culminated in the massive demonstration of people power by businesspeople, students, and nuns that brought down the Marcos regime in February 1986. In Eastern Europe, Solidarity from the start opposed revolutionary tactics and supported nonviolence. As one Solidarity leader put it during the organization's underground phase, when the temptation to use violence was presumably strongest, Solidarity was "against any acts of violence, street battles, hit squads, acts of terror, armed organization—and we do not accept any responsibility for violent acts." "We know lots of revolutions, great revolutions, and magnificent people," said Walesa, "who after taking over power, produced systems that were much worse than the ones they destroyed." Those who start by storming bastilles, Adam Michnik similarly warned, end up building their own.[60]

Solidarity provided the model for nonviolent opposition movements that brought about the transitions in East Germany and Czechoslovakia.

In South Africa, the African National Congress adhered to a policy of nonviolence for almost a half century until the Sharpeville massacre in 1960, after which the ANC changed its policy, espoused the use of violence, and created its own military organization, Umkhonto we Sizwe. Other black leaders, such as Archbishop Desmond Tutu and Chief Mengosuthu Buthelezi, continued to adhere to nonviolence. "Bloody revolutions fought against terrible oppression," Buthelezi warned, "do not automatically bring about great improvements."[61] In Korea, also, the principal opposition groups rejected the use of violence, although their demonstrations in the mid-1980s were often accompanied by violence produced by radical students.

In many countries some opposition groups were, of course, firmly committed to the use of violence against the nondemocratic regimes they confronted. These included Marxist-Leninist and Maoist opposition groups in El Salvador, the Philippines, Peru, and Guatemala that fought against authoritarian regimes and their democratic successors. The Communist party and associated leftist revolutionary organizations in Chile engaged in sustained violence against the Pinochet regime, and from 1960 to 1990 the African National Congress employed violence against the South African regime. Opposition groups used violence against three types of targets: (1) government officials (political leaders, police officers, soldiers) and installations (police stations, electrical pylons, depots, communications facilities); (2) "collaborators," that is, individuals who ostensibly supported the opposition or belonged to social or radical groups supporting the opposition but who also allegedly acted as informers, agents, or officials for the nondemocratic regime; (3) random civilian facilities, such as stores, shopping centers, and theaters, which were attacked presumably with a view to demonstrating the strength of the opposition and the inability of the government to provide security. Much debate went on within opposition groups as to the relative merits of these different types of targets and particularly over the morality and effectiveness of random terrorist attacks against civilians. In addition, opposition groups committed to violence debated the relative merits of rural and urban guerrilla warfare and the desirability and timing of major offensives and popular uprisings.

In the 1970s and 1980s, leaders of the African National Congress repeatedly affirmed the role of violence as a tactic in their struggle against apartheid. "Violence," as ANC leader Thabo Mbeki said in 1987, "is a very important element to achieve change."[62] Initially the ANC focused on government installations: police stations, electrical pylons, power plants, and other facilities. Between October 1976 and December 1984, the ANC reportedly carried out 262 armed attacks largely against such targets. In the three years following the start in September 1984 of sustained unrest in black townships, the number of attacks reportedly quadrupled, and blacks associated with the regime increasingly became targets. After police fired on demonstrators in Sharpeville in September 1984, mobs killed six black councilors, including the deputy mayor of Sharpeville. In the following years blacks killed hundreds of other blacks suspected to be collaborators. During the nine months after September 1984, black radicals attacked 120 black councilors, killed five, and burned down the homes of seventy-five. In July 1985 only two of thirty-eight councils were reported to be still operating. Finally in late 1985 and 1986 a major increase occurred in the third type of attack, with more assaults against "soft" civilian targets occurring in the first six months of 1986 than in the previous three years combined. Statements by ANC leaders suggested that serious differences existed among them as to the wisdom of these bombings.[63]

In Chile the radical opposition groups concentrated primarily on government installations and officials. During the first three months of 1984, for instance, reportedly there were eighty bombings of rail lines, utilities, and radio stations, with the central area of the country being blacked out three times as a result. On October 29, 1984, twelve bombings in five cities damaged government offices, banks, and telephone centers. All in all, apparently over 400 terrorist attacks occurred in Chile during 1984, and some 1,000 during a twelve-month period in 1985–86.[64] Chilean opposition violence culminated in the September 1986 effort by the Manuel Rodriguez Patriotic Front (MRPF) to assassinate Pinochet, in which the general escaped serious harm though five of his bodyguards were killed.

In virtually all countries a central tactic of the opposition was the mass rally, march, or demonstration against the regime. Such demonstrations mobilize and focus discontent, enable the opposition to test the breadth of its support and the effectiveness of its organization, generate publicity that is often international in scope, enhance divisions within the regime on the appropriate response, and, if the regime responds violently, can create martyrs and new causes for outrage. Opposition mass protests were typically called on four types of occasions:

(1) In some instances, opposition groups organized demonstrations on a recurring basis. In Chile in 1983–84, for instance, the opposition held monthly protest demonstrations that involved significant violence by both police and protesters. In Leipzig in 1989 there were weekly Monday evening peaceful demonstrations against the regime.

(2) Opposition groups organized demonstrations on the anniversaries of notable events, such as the Sharpeville and Soweto massacres in South Africa, the Kwangju massacre in Korea, the coup against Salvador Allende in Chile, and the murder of Benigno Aquino in the Philippines.

(3) Demonstrations were organized as part of a campaign to induce or compel the government to acquiesce in opposition demands. In both Brazil and Korea, for instance, a series of massive

demonstrations supported the opposition's demands for direct popular election of the president.

(4) Finally, opposition groups organized demonstrations in response to government outrages, such as the killing of peaceful demonstrators or political prisoners or other particularly infamous acts of police brutality. In some instances, most notably in South Africa, an act of brutality would lead to a demonstration, often in the form of the funeral for the victim of the brutality, which would then provoke new acts of brutality, giving rise for the need for further funeral demonstrations. This sequence of events led the South African government to ban funeral processions in August 1985.

Whatever occasioned them, mass demonstrations almost invariably provided a setting for violence. Even when moderate mainstream organizers of demonstrations were firmly committed to nonviolence, at least some participants in the demonstrations were susceptible to violence. Radicals would take advantage of the cover and protective support provided by the demonstrations to throw stones or gasoline bombs at police and government vehicles. Often violence-prone groups would split off from the main demonstration to launch attacks on government targets. On the other side, even a peaceful demonstration could and frequently did furnish an excuse for the police to resort to violence. Mass protests, in short, at times (1) inadvertently generated violence, (2) provided an opportunity for radicals to use violence, (3) provided an opportunity for regime standpatters to use violence, and (4) provided an opportunity for standpatter agents to attack the police and thus create a justification for massive government violence against the opposition.

The use of violence was a major issue between radical and moderate opposition groups. Those committed to violence usually were younger and more likely to be students than were those supporting nonviolent tactics. They typically criticized the adherents to nonviolence as "opportunistic" and as de facto collaborators with the regime. In Korea, for instance, a major gulf existed between Kim Dae Jung, Kim Young Sam, and other leaders of the mainstream opposition parties, on the one side, and, on the other, the young radical students and associated toughs who filled the ranks of the protest marches and used those occasions for attacks on the police. At times student demonstrators denounced moderate opposition leaders as much as they denounced the leaders of the government. These denunciations, according to Kim Dae Jung, "astonished" the moderate leaders.[65] They placed those leaders in the difficult position of wanting to dissociate themselves from the tactics the students were using while at the same time wishing to mobilize the students for the massive peaceful demonstrations by which they hoped to bring down the regime. When the government agreed to a popular free election in 1987, the students remained unsatisfied, alienated, and committed to using protests and violence to promote socialist reforms and the end of American influence in Korea.

In Chile, the mainstream opposition political leaders similarly attempted to distance themselves from the communist party, the MRPF, and other groups using violence against the regime. In the Philippines the Aquino forces rejected both the use of violence and cooperation with those who were using violence. In South Africa, in contrast, opposition groups and leaders pursuing nonviolence, such as Tutu and other religious leaders, Buthelezi, and the liberal coalition—the United Democratic Front, had little choice but to cooperate with the ANC.

Inevitably, opposition radicals and angry crowds were tempted to resort to violence, and mainstream leaders were often hard put to restrain them. Adam Michnik and Desmond Tutu shared the experience of having been imprisoned by the nondemocratic regimes in their countries. They also shared the experience of risking their own lives to prevent the lynching of government agents by outraged opposition mobs.

A variety of factors thus reduced the levels of violence in

third wave democratizations. In considerable measure these factors also contributed to the success of the democratization efforts. Violent external intervention produced democracy in several cases in the second wave and in Grenada and Panama in the third wave. Violence by groups within a society did not have the same result. The leaders of authoritarian regimes can successfully use violence to sustain their rule; their radical opponents may successfully use violence to overthrow those regimes. The former action prevents democracy from coming into being; the latter kills it at birth. Throughout history armed revolts have almost never produced democratic regimes. In nine out of eleven unsuccessful efforts at democratization between 1860 and 1960, substantial civil violence had occurred during the twenty years preceding the democratization attempt. Only two of eight successful efforts at democratization during the same period had been preceded by substantial civil violence.[66] Similarly, between 1974 and 1990 violent upheavals ended authoritarian regimes in Nicaragua, Yemen, Ethiopia, Iran, Haiti, Romania, and elsewhere. In no case, with the possible but highly problematic exception of Romania, did democracy result. The resort to violence increased the power of the specialists in violence in both government and the opposition. Governments created by moderation and compromise ruled by moderation and compromise. Governments produced by violence ruled by violence.

CHAPTER 5

HOW LONG?

CONSOLIDATION AND ITS PROBLEMS

THE DEMOCRATIC REFORMERS in Country A have achieved power and begun the transformation of their country's political system. The standpatter dictator in Country B has flown into exile on a U.S. Air Force jet, generating wild euphoria among his people, and the moderate democrats of the former opposition now face the challenges of governing. Government and opposition democratizers in Country C have sacrificed the immediate interests of their constituents and agreed on the essentials of a new democratic system. In all three countries for the first time in years free and fair elections have produced a popularly chosen government.

What then? What problems do the new democratic systems confront? Does democracy endure? Do the new systems consolidate or collapse?[1] In both the first and second reverse waves twenty countries with democratic political systems shifted to authoritarian forms of government. How many of the thirty countries that transited to democracy in the 1970s and 1980s are likely to shift back to some form of authoritarianism? Two reversals occurred in Africa in the 1980s: Nigeria in 1984 and the Sudan in 1989. Were these idiosyncratic or the first manifestations of what would be a much more extensive collapse of new democratic governments?

Speculations about the future are rarely illuminating; predictions about the future are often embarrassing. Previous chapters have examined the what, why, and how of third wave transitions to democracy. This chapter attempts to continue this empirical approach by analyzing: (1) two major transition problems confronting the new democracies; (2) the steps involved in the development of democratic political institutions and a democratic political culture; and (3) the factors that may plausibly affect the probability of democratic consolidation.

Countries confronted three types of problems in developing and consolidating their new democratic political systems. *Transition problems* stemmed directly from the phenomenon of regime change from authoritarianism to democracy. They included the problems of establishing new constitutional and electoral systems, weeding out proauthoritarian officials and replacing them with democratic ones, repealing or modifying laws that were unsuitable for democracy, abolishing or drastically changing authoritarian agencies such as the secret police, and, in former one-party systems, separating party and government property, functions, and personnel. Two key transition problems in many countries concerned (1) how to treat authoritarian officials who had blatantly violated human rights, "the torturer problem" and (2) how to reduce military involvement in politics and establish a professional pattern of civil-military relations, "the praetorian problem."

A second category of problems might be termed *contextual problems*. These stemmed from the nature of the society, its economy, culture, and history, and were in some degree endemic to the country, whatever its form of government. The authoritarian rulers did not resolve these problems and, in all probability, neither would the democratic rulers. As these problems were specific to individual countries and not to the common phenomenon of transition, they obviously differed from country to country. Among those that were prevalent among third wave democracies, however, were insurgencies, communal conflict, regional antagonisms, poverty, socioeconomic inequality, inflation, external debt, low rates of economic growth. Commentators often stressed the threats these problems posed to the consolidation of new democracies. In fact, however, apart from a low level of economic development, the number and severity of a country's contextual problems appeared to be only modestly related to its success or failure in consolidating democracy.

Finally, as the new democracies became consolidated and achieved a certain stability, they would confront *systemic problems* stemming from the workings of a democratic system. Authoritarian political systems suffer from problems that derive from their particular nature, such as overly concentrated decision making, deficient feedback, dependence on performance legitimacy. Other problems tend to be peculiarly characteristic of democratic systems: stalemate, the inability to reach decisions, susceptibility to demagoguery, domination by vested economic interests. These problems have afflicted long-standing democracies, and new third wave democracies presumably would not be immune to them. The timing of these three types of problems is presented schematically in Figure 5.1.

The following sections of this chapter deal with the problems posed by torturers and soldiers and then discuss the role of contextual problems in the consolidation process. No effort will be made to analyze the systemic problems arising from the workings of a democracy as they are, in a sense, largely a postconsolidation phenomenon.

Type of problem:	Political Evolution		
	Authoritarian System	Transition Phase	Democratic System
Contextual	██		
Transitional		████████████████████████	
Systemic	██████████████████ c		██████████

Figure 5.1. Problems Confronting Third Wave Countries

THE TORTURER PROBLEM:
PROSECUTE AND PUNISH VS. FORGIVE AND FORGET

Among other things, new democratic regimes had to decide what to do with the symbols, doctrines, organizations, laws, civil servants, and leaders of the authoritarian system. Beneath these issues often lay fundamental questions of national identity and political legitimacy. One common issue concerned crimes committed by officials of the predecessor regime.[2] Democratic governments succeeding each other seize opportunities to expose and prosecute incompetence, corruption, and fraud by officials of the predecessor government. Democratic governments succeeding authoritarian governments faced a much more serious, emotion-charged, and politically sensitive issue. How should the democratic government respond to charges of gross violations of human rights—murder, kidnapping, torture, rape, imprisonment without trial—committed by the officials of the authoritarian regimes? Was the appropriate course to prosecute and punish or to forgive and forget?

The authoritarian regimes of the 1970s and 1980s provided ample reason for this issue to emerge. During the years of military rule, almost 9,000 Argentines disappeared, presumably murdered by the security forces, and many others were kidnapped and tortured. During its years of military rule Uruguay had, according to one estimate, the highest proportion of political prisoners of any country in the world. One out of every 50 Uruguayans was detained at one point or another, and many were tortured. About 200 people disappeared or were killed in detention. In Greece those tortured or otherwise abused apparently numbered in the hundreds. In Chile, about 800 civilians were killed during or immediately after the coup in 1973 and another 1,200 were killed in later years. When an amnesty was declared in 1979, some 7,000 political prisoners were freed from jail. The Ceausescu regime violated basic human rights of thousands of Romanians. Central American dictatorships of both the Right and the Left treated their populations, particularly racial minorities, in similarly brutal fashion. Even in Brazil, some 81 civilians were killed and 45 disappeared in the war against the urban guerrillas between 1966 and 1975.[3] Acts against particular individuals were at times supplemented by mass violence against demonstrators, as in the Kwangju and Polytechnic killings in Korea and Greece.

These actions by the authoritarian governments of the late twentieth century did not differ greatly from those of earlier authoritarian regimes. Their behavior became a central issue in their societies largely because of the development of global concern about human rights in the 1970s. This manifested itself in the human rights legislation of the U.S. Congress, the emergence of human rights organizations such as Amnesty International, Freedom House, Americas Watch, and CSCE-related organizations, the more active role of intergovernmental human rights organizations, and the Carter administration's effectively putting human rights on the world's agenda. As a result, once democratic governments came to power they could not avoid confronting violations of human rights by their predecessor regimes, even if, as was usually the case, efforts at punishment would be unprecedented in their societies.

The central importance of human rights is reflected in the nature of the charges that were brought against authoritarian officials. The leaders of the Greek military regime were charged with carrying out a coup d'etat and were convicted of high treason. In virtually every other country, however, the charges and indictments concerned the murder, kidnapping, and torture of individuals. In many countries there had been broad popular support for the creation of the authoritarian system and hence it would have been politically embarrassing and difficult to prosecute people for creating that system. The global concern with human rights focused outrage not on the illegality of the regime but on the illegal actions of its agents. Authoritarian officials were prosecuted not because they killed constitutional democracy but because they killed individual people.

In those countries where there had been egregious violations of human rights, major debates took place over the action the democratic regime should take. It was argued that the perpetrators of such crimes should be prosecuted and punished because:

(1) Truth and justice require it; the successor regime has the moral duty to punish vicious crimes against humanity.

(2) Prosecution is a moral obligation owed to the victims and their families.

(3) Democracy is based on law, and the point must be made that neither high officials nor military or police officers are above the law. As one Uruguayan judge put it, criticizing the democratic government's amnesty proposal, "Democracy isn't just freedom of opinion, the right to hold elections, and so forth. It's the rule of law. Without equal application of the law, democracy is dead. The government is acting like a husband whose wife is cheating on him. He knows it, everybody knows it, but he goes on insisting that everything is fine and praying every day that he isn't going to be forced to confront the truth, because then he'd have to do something about it."[4]

(4) Prosecution is necessary to deter future violations of human rights by security officials.

(5) Prosecution is essential to establish the viability of the democratic system. If the military and police establishments can prevent prosecution through political influence or the threat of a coup, democracy does not really exist in the country, and the struggle to establish democracy must go on.

(6) Prosecution is necessary to assert the supremacy of democratic values and norms and to encourage the public to believe in them. "Unless major crimes are investigated and punished, there can be no real growth of trust, no 'implanting' of democratic norms in the society at large; and therefore no genuine 'consolidation' of democracy."[5]

(7) Even if most authoritarian crimes are not prosecuted, at a

very minimum it is necessary to bring into the open the extent of the crimes and the identity of those responsible and thus establish a full and unchallengeable public record. The principle of accountability is essential to democracy, and accountability requires "exposing the truth" and insisting "that people not be sacrificed for the greater good; that their suffering should be disclosed and the responsibility of the state and its agents for causing that suffering be made clear."[6]

Those opposed to prosecution made countering arguments:

(1) Democracy has to be based on reconciliation, on the major groups in society setting aside the divisions of the past.

(2) The process of democratization involves the explicit or implicit understanding among groups that there will be no retribution for past outrages.

(3) In many cases, both opposition groups and government forces grossly violated human rights. A general amnesty for all provides a far stronger base for democracy than efforts to prosecute one side or the other or both.

(4) The crimes of the authoritarian officials were justified at the time by the overriding need to suppress terrorism, defeat Marxist-Leninist guerrillas, and restore law and order to the society, and their actions were widely supported by the public at that time.

(5) Many people and groups in the society shared in the guilt for the crimes committed by the authoritarian regime. "We have all become used to the totalitarian system," argued Vaclav Havel, "and accepted it as an immutable fact, thus helping to perpetuate it. In other words, we are all—though naturally to various degrees—responsible for the creation of the totalitarian machinery. None of us is just its victim; we are all responsible for it."[7]

(6) Amnesty is necessary to establish the new democracy on a solid basis. Even if a legal and moral argument could be made for prosecution, that would fall before the moral imperative of creating a stable democracy. The consolidation of democracy should take precedence over the punishment of individuals. Or as President Sanguinetti of Uruguay put it: "What is more just—to consolidate the peace of a country where human rights are guaranteed today or to seek retroactive justice that could compromise that peace?"[8]

Such, in summary, were the arguments for and against prosecution of authoritarian crimes in third wave countries. In actual practice what happened was little affected by moral and legal considerations. It was shaped almost exclusively by politics, by the nature of the democratization process, and by the distribution of political power during and after the transition. In the end, the working of politics in the third wave countries undermined the efforts to prosecute and punish authoritarian criminals. In a few countries, summary justice was meted out to a few individuals; in almost all countries, no effective prosecution and punishment occurred. In the countries that democratized before 1990, only in Greece were there a substantial number of authoritarian officials subjected to meaningful trial and punishment.

Given the heated political debate and the emotional intensity of this issue, how can this result be explained?

First, about half of the pre-1990 democratizations were transformations initiated and guided by the leaders of the existing authoritarian regimes. These leaders were usually democratic reformers who had, in most cases, displaced previous standpatter leaders. The latter obviously did not wish to be prosecuted for crimes they may have committed. The reformers wanted to induce the standpatters to acquiesce in the democratization process, and assuring them that they would not be punished by the successor democratic regime was essential to achieving that. In addition, authoritarian regimes in which reformers were able to displace standpatters in power were likely to have been responsible for fewer and less heinous human rights violations than those regimes where standpatters stayed in power to the bitter end. Hence virtually every authoritarian regime that initiated its transformation to democracy also decreed an amnesty as a part of that process. These amnesties typically applied to any crimes committed during a specified period of time by either the agents of the regime or members of the opposition. The Brazilian and Chilean regimes enacted such amnesties in 1979.

Guatemala did so in 1986. The Turkish generals guaranteed their immunity against prosecution before allowing a democratic government to be elected in 1983.

In these and other cases of transformation, the authoritarian regimes not only acted in their own interests in legislating amnesty, they also had the power to make the amnesties stick. The argument can be and has been made that as a result the successor democratic regimes were not real democracies because they lacked the power to bring to justice those in the authoritarian regimes who committed crimes. In Guatemala, for instance, the military declared an amnesty for themselves four days before turning over the government to the democratically elected civilian president, Vinicio Cerezo, in January 1986. Cerezo accepted the amnesty, extended it further, and readily admitted that he would not long continue as president if he attempted to prosecute any Guatemalan soldiers for the apparently numerous human rights violations that occurred during the military regime. Hence, it was argued, the Cerezo government was not "a democratic government or even a government that is making a transition to democracy."[9]

The same charge could be and was made against the post-Pinochet regime in Chile. The multi-party coalition backing Patricio Aylwin for president in the 1989 election adopted a program urging legislation to overturn the 1979 amnesty law and to set aside for one year the ten-year statute of limitations for prosecutions for murder and other violent crimes. Chilean military leaders warned of the consequences if efforts were made to act along these lines. In October 1989, while still president, General Pinochet declared: "The day they touch any of my men will be the end of the state law." The commander of the Chilean air force, Gen. Fernando Matthei, for ten years had struggled with Pinochet and urged the desirability of speedier democratization. Efforts to repeal the amnesty law, however, he warned in 1989, would threaten that process. The armed forces will "not accept" prosecutions: "If they are going to try to put us in the pillory, as in Argentina, that is going to have the most grave consequences." Leftist opposition leaders continued to insist on the possibility of prosecutions; moderate democratic leaders, however, emphasized only the desirability of investigations. A few days before becoming president, Aylwin went out of his way to reassure the military. "The idea of a trial is not in my mind," he said. "It is not my intention to promote trials. . . . [I am not in the mood] to persecute or to antagonize General Pinochet or anyone else."[10] In keeping with his theme of national reconciliation, immediately after taking office Aylwin freed political prisoners imprisoned by the Pinochet regime who had not committed acts of violence.

The creation of a democratic system always involves compromises among the politically powerful groups as to what that government can and cannot do. The establishment of Venezuelan democracy in the late 1950s required commitments to honor the privileges of the Church, to respect private property, and to undertake land reform. Was the resulting political system undemocratic because of these constraints? Is a system undemocratic because the government lacks either the power or the will to prosecute criminals in the predecessor authoritarian regime? If it is, then no democratic system established through transformation is democratic because clearly no authoritarian leaders will make their system democratic if they expect themselves or their associates to be prosecuted and punished as a result. Governments that are strong enough to bring about transformations are strong enough to exact that price. If they had not been, possibly half of the pre-1990 third wave transitions would not have occurred. To reject amnesty in these cases is to exclude the most prevalent form of democratization.

The situation was quite different with authoritarian regimes that did not exit with strength but were replaced from weakness. Normally such regimes did not anticipate their end and hence did not attempt to protect their members by enacting amnesties. The most notable exception was Argentina, where General Bignone led an interim military regime for sixteen months from the downfall of the junta to the election of a democratic government. His government made successive efforts, all of which failed, to protect the military and police from prosecution. It first attempted to negotiate an agreement on nonprosecution with civilian leaders; this effort "was widely ridiculed." It then issued a televised report on its war against leftist terrorists in the hopes of justifying its actions; this "backfired badly." It next attempted to negotiate a secret agreement with conservative union leaders in the Peronist movement, but this was exposed by other opposition leaders and had to be abandoned.[11] Finally, a few weeks before the elections, Bignone's government decreed a "Law of National Pacification" which granted immunity from prosecution and investigation to all military and police officers for virtually any actions, including "common crimes and related military crimes," taken during the war against terrorism. The amnesty also applied to a small number of terrorists, perhaps a dozen, who had not been arrested and convicted and who were not in exile. This law was immediately denounced by all opposition political leaders. The democratic government repealed the amnesty law two weeks after taking office in December 1983.

Officials of authoritarian governments that collapsed or were overthrown were targets for punishment. After their removal from power by U.S. military forces, Bernard Coard and thirteen other leaders of the Grenadan communist regime were convicted of murder and other crimes and received long jail sentences. If Noriega had not been taken to the United States for prosecution on drug charges, he would have faced a variety of charges in his own country. The Ceausescus got rather summary justice. Before her election, Corazon Aquino threatened Marcos with prosecution, which he escaped by flying into exile. Honecker and his associates initially avoided serious punishment by being old and sick, but at the end of

1990 Honecker was charged with ordering the killing of East Germans who had attempted to escape over the Berlin Wall. The most extensive and serious efforts to prosecute and punish authoritarian criminals were made in Greece and Argentina. The situation in these two countries seems on the surface to have been rather similar. Both military governments were clearly guilty of substantial violations of human rights. Both governments collapsed after suffering military humiliation in external conflicts. In both cases, the successor democratic governments were fully controlled by one party and headed by a highly respected and popular leader. In both cases also, when the democratic government was elected, public opinion overwhelmingly supported prosecution and punishment of those guilty of human rights violations. In Greece, as one analyst put it, this was "the most sensitive and explosive of popular demands."[12] The same could be said of Argentina. Both new governments attempted to respond to popular demand and moral imperative by developing a program to deal with human rights violations.

Both governments also confronted similar problems in developing their policies. They had to determine who should be prosecuted for what crimes, in what manner, when, and before which tribunals. When personal dictatorships were overthrown in Colombia, Venezuela, the Philippines, and Romania, prosecution and punishment were largely limited to the dictator, his family, and close associates. The replacement of a military regime provided a more difficult challenge. In both Argentina and Greece it was clearly necessary to prosecute the top leaders of the military government. But how far down the military and police hierarchies should the prosecution go? The Alfonsín government attempted to deal with this issue by dividing those potentially guilty into three categories:

(1) those who gave orders to violate human rights;
(2) those who carried out the orders;
(3) those who engaged in human rights violations beyond the actions they were ordered to take.

Under the government's policies military and police officers who fell into categories (1) and (3) would be indicted and tried; those in category (2) would be tried only if they knew that the orders they were given were clearly illegitimate.

The conditions that confronted the Alfonsín and Karamanlis governments were thus quite similar. The results the two governments achieved were very different. By August 1975, nine months after Karamanlis had been elected prime minister, the eighteen top officials of the military government had been indicted, tried, and convicted of high treason. In the first torture trial that immediately followed, thirty-two military police (fourteen officers and eighteen enlisted men) were indicted and sixteen were convicted. Three other military, naval, and police trials in 1975, two more in late 1976, and a trial of the top military government leaders for the Polytechnic massacre produced additional convictions and prison sentences. All in all, between 100 and 400 trials for torture were apparently held throughout Greece, and a large number of people were convicted of human rights violations in those trials.[13] By the end of 1976, two years after the democratic government came to power, substantial justice had been done and the prosecution and punishment issue laid to rest in Greek politics.

Human rights violations in Argentina were significantly greater absolutely and proportionally than they were in Greece. The investigation commission appointed by Alfonsín concluded that the security forces had "forcibly disappeared" at least 8,960 people, that they had maintained a network of 340 secret detention and torture centers, that about 200 officers, whom it named, had been identified as directly involved in these operations, and that many more had also participated in the repression.[14] For seven years after Alfonsin came to power, the issue of how to handle human rights violations agitated and at times convulsed Argentine politics, stimulating at least three military coup attempts. When all was said and done, a total of sixteen officers (including members of the

ruling military juntas) were brought to trial and ten were convicted of human rights violations. In contrast to Greece, the efforts to prosecute and punish in Argentina served neither justice nor democracy and instead produced a moral and political shambles. In 1990 the issue was still a highly divisive factor in Argentine politics. Argentina was left with memories of the civic trauma caused by the efforts to prosecute authoritarian criminals that counterbalanced memories of the civic and personal trauma caused by the horrendous crimes they committed.

How can the difference in the Argentine and Greek outcomes be explained? In part it was due to the fact that a serious internal security threat had existed in Argentina, that the Peronist government preceding the military junta had directed the military to "eliminate" the terrorists, and that major sectors of the Argentine public had quietly accepted and in some measure approved the ruthless tactics the military employed in successfully accomplishing that mission. The less substantial human rights violations of the Greek military also had less justification. In addition, the Greek military regime had been a colonels' regime, opposed by some more senior officers. Hence elements of the Greek military were supportive of the government's prosecution efforts, while the Argentine military, whatever their other differences, unanimously opposed such efforts. These factors, however, explain only part of the difference between Greek success and Argentine failure in dealing with this issue. Far more important were the policies and strategies of the two governments.

Karamanlis did two things. First, he moved quickly when popular support was greatest. His was a "policy of swift, decisive, credible, but also contained and circumscribed retribution."[15] Confirmed in office by elections in 1974, Karamanlis prepared plans for prosecution of human rights violators. Support for such action was greatly increased by a serious military coup attempt against him in February 1975. Capitalizing on the popular reaction against this, he moved quickly to launch indictments and trials through the normal civilian courts, with the result that the process was substantially concluded within eighteen months. Second, Karamanlis acted to reassure the officer corps that he was not challenging it institutionally. His "policy of shielding the officer corps from criticism and his sensitivity to its professional demands and requirements forestalled a possible backlash by officers on active duty. The policy of a limited purge of junta principals conducted under regular legal procedures and after public passion had subsided also relieved much of the anxiety of the officer corps." The torturer issue then virtually disappeared from Greek politics for fourteen years only to be revived briefly in December 1990 when the conservative government announced that it would pardon seven of the eight junta members in prison. The government reversed itself quickly, however, following public outcry and the reported refusal of President Karamanlis to sign the decree.[16]

The failure of the efforts at prosecution in Argentina and the serious crises they generated for Argentine democracy largely resulted from the policies of the Alfonsín government. These produced an extended delay in the trial and punishment of the human rights violators and encouraged the military to resist this process. As time went on, public outrage and support for prosecution gave way to indifference, and the military regained influence and status from their humiliation of 1982–1983.

Immediately on taking office, Alfonsín repealed the Bignone government amnesty, appointed a civilian commission led by Ernesto Sabato, a novelist, to investigate military crimes, initiated the prosecution of nine top military officers, and secured passage of legislation providing the legal basis for prosecuting human rights violators throughout the military and police hierarchies. These actions provoked fear, concern, and opposition within the military establishment. At the same time, however, Alfonsín also secured legislation that military officers charged with human rights violations would be initially tried in military courts. He thus provided the military first with the incentive and then with the means to obstruct prosecutions.

The case of the nine generals and admirals went before the Armed Forces Supreme Council in early 1984. Eight months later, in September, the Council reported that it had found "nothing objectionable" about the actions of the junta members. The case was then transferred to the civilian Federal Appeals Court. The trial there lasted another year with a judgment in December 1985 convicting five and acquitting four of the junta members. During 1986 seven more high-ranking officers were indicted and five were eventually convicted of human rights violations. Meanwhile, investigations were proceeding and indictments being drawn up against many other officers.

Public opinion polls in 1984 and 1985 showed widespread support for prosecutions, particularly of the top military commanders. Yet concern with this issue also began to fade. A year after Alfonsín took office, it was reported that "Already, many Argentines may be losing interest in *desaparecidos*." The demonstrations supporting prosecution were smaller. One activist complained, "we are always the same bunch."[17] Public opinion was changing, military resistance was growing, and in December 1986 Alfonsín proposed a *punto final* or "full stop" bill that would prohibit initiation of additional cases. Human rights groups denounced this proposal, but most Argentines were indifferent, and an effort to mobilize a 24-hour protest against the bill failed. Congress passed the bill and deadline charges were filed against some 200 officers, including many on active duty. The military made clear that they strongly opposed trying the latter. At the same time, the most prominent prosecution group, the Mothers of the Plaza de Mayo, split, and its weekly marches came to resemble "a reunion of aging cousins or old friends, many accompanied by husbands, children and grandchildren."[18]

In April 1987 an effort to compel the appearance of an officer in court produced the so-called Easter Rebellion, in which army units on two bases mutinied and made several demands on the government. Alfonsín successfully induced the insurgents to surrender but acquiesced to their principal demands. He fired the army chief of staff and, over the vigorous objections of human rights groups, secured passage of a "due obedience" law, which effectively barred prosecution of everyone except a handful of retired officers. In January and December 1988 additional military uprisings were suppressed, but these put more pressure on the government to forego prosecutions. In 1989 the Peronist candidate, Carlos Menem, was elected president. The Peronist party by then had developed close ties to the military, and Menem appointed a supporter of amnesty as minister of defense and a favorite of the military mutineers as army chief of staff. In October 1989 Menem pardoned sixty guerrillas and all the military and police officers charged or potentially chargeable with human rights violations, except for the five junta members still in prison. On December 29, 1990, Menem pardoned the five junta members, another general extradited from the United States in 1988 and awaiting trial on thirty-eight charges of murder, and a Montenero guerrilla leader. His action stimulated intense bitterness, antagonism, and outrage. Almost 50,000 people protested in Buenos Aires. "This is," said former President Alfonsín, "the saddest day in Argentine history." [19]

In Greece the confrontation between the democratic government and the military came to a climax in an attempted coup three months after the government was elected. In Argentina the climax came in an attempted coup three and a half years after the government was elected. The coup attempt in Greece provided legitimation and generated support for prosecution. The coup attempt in Argentina induced the government to give up prosecution. Alfonsín's failure to move quickly and decisively in 1984, when public opinion supported action, made human rights prosecutions the victim of changes in power relationships and public attitudes. The result, as Ernesto Sabato put it, was that "A man who steals a pocketbook is thrown into jail, and the man who has tortured goes free." [20]

In contrast to what happened in transformations and replacements, in transplacements the terms of amnesty were negotiated explicitly or implicitly between government and opposition. In Nicaragua, for instance, the Sandinistas advanced one amnesty proposal but then modified it to meet the objections of the democratic opposition. In Korea President Chun Doo Hwan undoubtedly backed his colleague Roh Tae Woo for president on the assumption and with an implicit understanding that he and his associates would not be prosecuted for any actions they took during their seven years of authoritarian rule. Once Roh was elected, however, demands arose for an accounting for crimes committed by Chun government officials. These included, most notably, the Kwangju massacre, but in addition there were "many well-documented allegations of torture, victimization and unexplained deaths while in custody." [21] Opposition assemblymen demanded punishment for Chun and five others they held responsible for the massacre. During 1988 and 1989 the issue was intensely debated in Korea. In November 1988 Chun made a public apology and then retired to an isolated Buddhist monastery. Meanwhile, equally intense negotiations went on between the Roh government and the opposition, focused on hearings, prosecutions, and possible reparations to the Kwangju victims. In the end, a "backroom deal" was reached under which Chun testified in a televised hearing before the Assembly. This somewhat raucous affair did not satisfy the opposition but it did help Roh to distinguish his government from that of his predecessor.

In Nicaragua and Korea negotiations occurred between government and opposition after a government had been elected democratically. In other instances, an understanding was reached between authoritarian and opposition leaders before a new government was elected. In Uruguay, for instance, the military and some political leaders negotiated arrangements for the transition to democracy at the Club Naval in the summer of 1984. Controversy exists as to what extent the military received guarantees against prosecution. Subsequently both General Medina and President Sanguinetti said that the issue was never discussed. Some civilians said that the military were assured that the government would not prosecute them, although it would not prevent private citizens from bringing suits. Others said the military were assured that these actions too would be blocked, and Wilson Ferreira, leader of the opposition Blanco party, subsequently justified abandoning his opposition to amnesty on the grounds that the military had received guarantees against prosecution in the Club Naval negotiations (in which he had not taken part because he was in prison).[22]

The Uruguayan generals were under considerable domestic and international pressure (from the United States and the Argentine and Brazilian democratizations) to end their rule. They were not, however, driven from office. They negotiated their way out, and, as one Uruguayan political columnist remarked, "The generals believe they are leaving office with heads high and flags flying."[23] It was certainly widely assumed at the time that some understanding concerning prosecution had been reached at the Club Naval. Given the scope and seriousness of the human rights violations, it seems likely that the generals surrendered power either because they received some assurance or because both sides assumed serious prosecutions were out of the question.

In the year and a half after the elected government took office in March 1985, Uruguayan citizens initiated thirty-eight cases against 150 officials alleging murder, torture, kidnapping, rape, and other crimes. The military declared they would not allow their members to appear in court. Wishing to avoid a major confrontation, which could have meant the end of his regime, Sanguinetti proposed a blanket amnesty for the military, justified in part by the fact that he had already pardoned the terrorists and other political prisoners the military had imprisoned. The opposition parties in the legislature defeated his proposal and submitted a plan for a partial amnesty, which also was defeated. The first trial at which military officers were supposed to appear in court was scheduled for December 23. At the last moment, the opposition political leadership shifted its position, the legislature worked into the night of December 22, a general amnesty bill was approved, the first trial was cancelled, and no further trials were held.

The political battle in Uruguay, however, was only just beginning. When the amnesty bill was being debated, public opinion polls showed 72 percent of the public supporting punishment of those convicted of human rights violations.[24] Two months after the bill was passed a broad coalition of opposition politicians, human rights activists, victims and their families, clergymen, journalists, lawyers and others started a campaign to submit the amnesty law to a referendum. This required the signatures on petitions of one quarter of the voters in the last election, or 555,701 signatures from a total population of slightly over 3,000,000. The campaign to get those signatures dominated Uruguayan politics for two years. The government, Electoral Court, the military, and some opposition political leaders made strenuous efforts, by fair means and foul, to obstruct the gathering and the verification of the signatures. In the end, in December 1988, the Electoral Court held that referendum supporters had produced 187 more valid signatures than were required, and the Congress scheduled the referendum for April 16, 1989. After a bitter campaign that included not-so-veiled threats from the military that it would not acquiesce in repeal of the law, the Uruguayan public voted 53 percent to 40 percent in favor of amnesty. This outcome resolved the issue but satisfied no one. Those opposed to amnesty lost; but on the other side, there was, as President Sanguinetti said, "no sense of triumph."[25] It was nine years after the beginning of the democratization process and almost five years after a democratically elected government had assumed power.

In Eastern Europe, apart from Romania and East Germany, the initial overall tendency was to forgive and forget. The issue of punishment never really arose in Hungary; and Havel in Czechoslovakia, Mazowiecki in Poland, and Yakolev in the Soviet Union all argued against criminal charges. In several countries, however, demands arose for investigation and prosecution of those responsible for the most notorious crimes. The former communist leader in Prague was tried and sentenced to four years in prison for using violence against demonstrators. Two generals in the Polish secret police were arrested and charged with "instigating and directing" the murder of Father Jerzy Popieluszko in 1984. Todor Zhivkov was taken into custody in Bulgaria for six months and then released in July 1990, with charges against him still being investigated.

The record of democratic governments in bringing to justice authoritarian officials who had committed crimes yields some indisputable conclusions. Justice was a function of political power. Officials of strong authoritarian regimes that voluntarily ended themselves were not prosecuted; officials of weak authoritarian regimes that collapsed were punished, if they were promptly prosecuted by the new democratic government. "Justice," Ernesto Sabato once remarked, "works in this way. It is slow. The only quick justice belongs to totalitarian and despotic countries." [26] He was wrong. Democratic justice cannot be summary justice of the sort meted out to the Ceausescus, but it also cannot be slow justice. The popular support and indignation necessary to make justice a political reality fade; the discredited groups associated with the authoritarian regime reestablish their legitimacy and influence. In new democratic regimes, justice comes quickly or it does not come at all.

With the end of authoritarian regimes, there were demands for truth as well as for justice. In Argentina this demand was met by the report in September 1984 of the Sabato commission, appointed by President Alfonsín the previous December. The commission heard extensive testimony from victims, their families, officials, and others, exhaustively mined official records, and visited detention and torture centers. Its 400 page summary report was backed by 50,000 pages of documentation. The revelations and evidence in the report increased the probability that the promise of its title would be realized: "Nunca Más" (Never Again). In the Philippines, President Aquino appointed a Presidential Committee on Human Rights to investigate primarily abuses by the police rather than the military, who had, after all, helped her come to power. The chairman of the committee died shortly after his appointment, and the committee disbanded in less than a year without having had much impact. In Brazil, the transformation process and the much lower level of criminal violence precluded the successor democratic government from undertaking an investigation like that in Argentina. The Archdiocese of São Paulo, however, did produce a report based on official records that was somewhat similar to the Sabato report and had the same title: "Nunca Mais." In Chile, Aylwin opposed prosecution but determined that the truth should out. The government appointed a Commission for Truth and Reconciliation which was to be the "moral conscience of the nation" and investigate and report fully on political killings and disappearances during the military rule. The assumption was that those responsible for these crimes would not be prosecuted but that victims and their families would be compensated.[27]

In Uruguay the desirability of "truth" as well as of "justice" was the subject of debate. The supporters of amnesty also argued against investigation and exposure of authoritarian crimes. Forgetting was essential, as well as forgiving. "Amnesty does not mean that the crimes did not take place; it means forgetting them," argued Sen. Jorge Batlle. "The bottom line," Sanguinetti said, "is that either we're going to look to the future or to the past. . . . If the French were still thinking about the Night of St. Bartholomew, they'd be slaughtering each other to this day." [28] Others in Uruguay and elsewhere argued that truth was, if anything, more important than justice; that it was essential to lay bare all the facts of what happened in order to provide some consolation to the victims and their families, to expose and humiliate the torturers, and to develop a public conscience and determination that would ensure that such actions would indeed never happen again. Aryeh Neier concisely laid out this case: "By knowing what happened, a nation is able to debate honestly why and how dreadful crimes came to be committed. To identify those responsible, and to show what they did, is to mark them with a public stigma that is a punishment in itself, and to identify the victims, and recall how they were tortured and killed, is a way of acknowledging their worth and dignity." [29]

The main constraint on both prosecution and disclosure in the former communist countries was the pervasiveness of the communist regime, the extent to which so many people accepted it and collaborated with it, and the fear of what prosecutions or investgations might reveal. Zhivkov's scheduled testimony before the Bulgarian parliament was repeatedly postponed because of the people he might name. The most acute problem was posed by the immense files of the secret police. Should these be generally opened up, made available only to prosecutors, locked up, or destroyed? The East German files reportedly included the names of six million people, and in 1990 several parliamentarians and ministers in the successor regime were exposed as collaborators with the police. Many feared that an unselective opening of the files could poison public life in the new democracies, and a general opening of those in East Germany could also have effects on West Germany. In Romania the huge files of the Securitate were kept at a secret location under military guard. "If we publish the files as some people have suggested," a government official observed, "there could literally be something worse than a civil war with friend turning against friend once they find out what is contained in them."[30] In some respects, truth as well as justice was a threat to democracy.

Guidelines for Democratizers 4: Dealing with Authoritarian Crimes

(1) If transformation or transplacement occurred, do not attempt to prosecute authoritarian officials for human rights violations. The political costs of such an effort will outweigh any moral gains.

(2) If replacement occurred and you feel it is morally and politically desirable, prosecute the leaders of the authoritarian regime promptly (within one year of your coming into power) while making clear that you will not prosecute middle- and lower-ranking officials.

(3) Devise a means to achieve a full and dispassionate public accounting of how and why the crimes were committed.

(4) Recognize that on the issue of "prosecute and punish vs. forgive and forget", each alternative presents grave problems, and that the least unsatisfactory course may well be: do not prosecute, do not punish, do not forgive, and, above all, do not forget.

THE PRAETORIAN PROBLEM: REBELLIOUS AND POWERFUL MILITARIES

The problem of dealing with the criminal actions of authoritarian officials overlapped with a broader, more lasting, and politically more serious problem confronting many new democracies: the need to curb the political power of the military establishment and to make the armed forces into a professional body committed to providing for the external security of the country. The civil-military problems of the new democracies took one of three forms, depending on the type of authoritarian regime, the power of the military establishment, and the nature of the transition process.

The military forces of one-party dictatorships, with the glaring exception of Nicaragua and the partial exception of Poland, had generally been under the firm control of the party. They did not attempt coups and did not play a major role in the politics of the regime. In communist states, and to a lesser degree in the Republic of China, most military officers belonged to the ruling party, party cells and organizations permeated the military hierarchy, and the top party bodies shaped military as well as other policies. The problem in the successor democratic states to these regimes was to separate party from army and to replace military subordination to one party with military subordination to a democratic multiparty system. In Eastern European countries the separation of party and army went relatively smoothly. In the Soviet Union intense debates occurred over "departization" of the military; legislation passed in 1990 changed the functions of the Main Political Administration but left intact the structure of party cells despite arguments that "There are no organs in the armies of democratic countries that implant the ideology of a single party."[31] In general, however, the democratic successors to one-party dictatorships faced fewer difficulties in establishing civilian control than the democracies that followed military regimes and personal dictatorships.

Different and more serious problems arose from military establishments that had been replaced (that is, overthrown) in the transition process or had become highly politicized in personal dictatorships. The middle- and lower-ranking officers in these establishments often had well-developed political views or ideologies, greatly resented their loss of power and status, and felt threatened by the forces active in and dominant in the new democratic politics. Hence they often engaged in a variety of political activities designed to bring down the new democratic regime or to force changes in its leadership or policies. The most dramatic political actions were, of course, military uprisings and attempted coups d'etat. Coups were attempted or seriously planned in at least ten countries that democratized between the mid-1970s and the late-1980s. In Nigeria and the Sudan, the coups were successful, and military regimes were reestablished where they had ended a few years earlier. A distinction, however, should be made between coups that are reactions to the perceived failures of a democratic system and coups that are reactions to the prospective success of democratization. Both the Nigerian and Sudanese coups partake of more of the former than of the latter. The Nigerian coup came after a disputed election that returned to power a president widely regarded as corrupt and ineffective; the Sudanese coup followed three years of inept civilian government during which the economic and insurgency problems of the country had greatly worsened. Coup attempts also occurred in Guatemala and Ecuador, where the military had voluntarily exited from power. These efforts appear to have been related to intramilitary struggles. In Guatemala the elected civilian government clearly held power at the sufferance of the armed forces, and the attempted coups of May 1988 and May 1989 were quickly suppressed by the government and the military leadership, with many people wondering about the motives of the coup makers. As one leading Guatemalan politician commented, "The only explanation is that this is a very isolated group. The army is the power that designed this process [of democratization]. They are not crazy—they are in control."[32]

Coup attempts were most frequent in countries at the opposite extreme from Guatemala, countries where the armed forces had been humiliated by defeat or politicized by personal dictators. Seven coup attempts or conspiracies are reported to have occurred in Greece; seven coups or military uprisings were attempted in the Philippines; five in Argentina; three in Spain. Between 1974 and 1990, however, except for the ambiguous cases of Nigeria and the Sudan, no democratizing government was overthrown by a military coup d'etat.

Given the apparent fragility of new democracies, why was this the case? Overthrowing a government by coup d'etat normally requires support from either the military high command, or important civilian groups, or an influential foreign actor, or some combination of these. The antidemocratization coup makers were mostly middle-ranking officers. The same officers often led successive coup efforts: Lt. Col. Aldo Rico and Lt. Col. Mohammed Ali Seineldin in Argentina, Col. Gregorio Honasan in the Philippines, Lt. Col. Antonio Tejero Molina and Lt. Gen. Jaime Milans del Bosch in Spain. In virtually all cases, the top military leadership supported the government or at least did not back the coup attempt. The coup makers also were generally unable to mobilize the support of significant civilian groups or of influential foreign governments. In these respects, the transition coup attempts of the third democratization wave differed significantly from the successful coups of the second reverse wave. One of the most serious antidemocratization coup efforts, for instance, occurred in the Philippines in December 1989 and involved extensive fighting and casualties. Some political leaders tacitly supported the coup but they were not active in their support; key civilian groups opposed it. So also did Minister of Defense Gen. Fidel V. Ramos and the military high command. And at a critical moment, the United States decisively intervened, with American fighter planes taking to the air to deter the procoup forces.

In general, the vulnerability of elected governments to overthrow by coups varied with the level of socio-economic development of the society. In rural societies and in poor societies, coup-prone military officers could often find active support and cooperation among civilian elites. As the power of landowners and primary resource extractors declined and that of the bourgeoisie and middle class grew, the social basis for military coups withered. In Peru the agrarian reforms of the Velasco military regime wiped out the landowning elite and hence greatly reduced the coup threat to the subsequent democratic regime. In Spain, business leaders and other civilian elites opposed military coups and supported democracy. Alfonsín argued that coups in Argentina "have always been civilian-military in character" and that the key to preventing them was to break the link between the military and civilian groups.[33] The true key, however, was the changing balance of forces among civilian groups in Argentine society and the emerging numerical dominance of the middle classes, who no longer would have to rely on the military to protect themselves against the organized power of Peronist labor unions. Thus, when coups threatened in May 1985 and in the Easter Week crisis of April 1987 Alfonsín was able to mobilize hundreds of thousands of supporters to demonstrate on his behalf in the streets of Buenos Aires. Massed people power countered military firepower. In August 1974 in the first phase of the Greek transition, military leaders initially defied Karamanlis' demand that certain tank units be removed from Athens. Karamanlis replied, "Either you take the tanks out of Athens, or the people will decide the issue at Constitution Square."[34] The tanks left. If the politically dominant civilian group in Greece had still been landlords and the numerically dominant group had still been peasants, the outcome very likely would have been different.

The efforts to overthrow new democratic governments failed because coup makers were unable to win to their side middle-class and other groups in the political coalition that had made democratization possible. The coup attempts were, in effect, desperate rearguard actions by minority standpatter elements in the military. Like the December 1944 Ardennes offensive, they were efforts to reverse the course of events after the war had been lost. A coup attempt against a new democratic regime is a sign that democratization is working. The failure of that attempt is a sign that democratization is working successfully. While no government was overthrown by a transition coup between 1974 and 1990, coup efforts and military uprisings did on occasion affect government action. The coup attempts in Guatemala in May 1988 and in Argentina in April 1987 and December 1988 were aimed at, among other things, forcing changes in the top military leadership. In the latter two cases, they achieved their objectives. The April 1987 Easter Rebellion in Argentina also led the government to enact its "due obedience" law, effectively precluding prosecution of active duty officers for human rights violations. Coup attempts were thus one way by which dissident officers could pressure governments to change officials or policies. Governments also were generally lenient in their treatment of coup makers. In Spain, Tejero and Milans del Bosch were sentenced to thirty years in prison, but this was exceptional. When prosecuted and convicted, leaders of coup efforts normally received fairly minimal punishments, and rank-and-file participants in such efforts were normally not punished at all.

Coup efforts were the most extreme form of political action by disgruntled officers. At times, such officers also engaged in other, more normal forms of political activity. Midway between the February 1981 and October 1982 coup attempts in Spain, for instance, discontent manifested itself among middle- and lower-ranking officers, with 100 junior and noncommissioned officers signing a public manifesto protesting press treatment of the military and arguing that the military "in order to better fulfill their mission, do not need to be professionalized, democratized, or purged." Reportedly only vigorous action by the top military officers prevented several hundred other officers from signing this declaration.[35] In Guatemala, for several weeks before the May 1988 coup effort, an anonymous military group issued communiqués from "the Officers of the Mountains."

The Portuguese and Philippine armed forces became heavily

politicized during the period of authoritarian rule. In both cases middle-ranking officers formed associations to promote reform and democracy, the Movimento das Forcas Armadas (MFA) in Portugal and the Reform of the Armed Forces Movement (RAM) in the Philippines. The MFA was the key group in ending the Caetano regime; the RAM would have been the key group in overthrowing the Marcos regime, if it had not been preempted by Aquino's electoral victory. Once regime changes occurred in both countries, many of the officers that had been in the forefront opposing the dictatorships also came to oppose the successor democratic governments. This continuity of military opposition was epitomized in the Philippines by Col. Gregorio Honasan, a leading RAM member, who led two coups against the Aquino government, and in Portugal by Col. Otelo Saraiva de Carvalho, the intellectual leader of the MFA, who after 1980 was associated with the April 25 Popular Forces (PF-25), an underground group that waged a terrorist campaign against Portuguese democracy. In 1983 other officers formed a nonviolent parallel organization, the Association of the 25th of April, to keep alive the original radical and revolutionary goals of the MFA. This organization reportedly had substantial support among both active and retired military officers.

Over time the coup attempts against new democratic regimes became less frequent. One important measure of democratic consolidation (see below, pp. 256ff.) is the turnover of governmental control from one party to another as the result of elections. In Greece and Spain, the prospective victories of leftist parties, the Panellinio Sosialistiko Kinima (PASOK) and the Socialists, stimulated coup rumors and, apparently, coup conspiracies. The acquisition of power in Portugal by the conservative Social Democratic party promoted similar speculation, as the result of the dominance of Marxist and leftist ideologies among the Portuguese military. By the mid-1980s, however, all three countries had moved beyond the point where transition coup attempts were feasible. This did not necessarily mean that coups were forever impossible in those countries. If the democratic system failed to produce minimally effective government, or if important groups deserted the prodemocracy coalition, coups might again be attempted. They would not, however, be transition coups. Their target would be democracy, not democratization.

Democratic regimes that followed military regimes that left office voluntarily usually faced a different set of problems. They were confronted not by possible coups by alienated and discontented officers who opposed democratization, but rather by the continuing power and influence of the military leaders who had made democratization possible. As has been noted, such military leaders in effect defined their terms for giving up office. The problem for the elected leaders of the new democracy was to reduce the power and privileges of the military establishment to a level compatible with the functioning of a constitutional democracy. In countries at lower levels of economic and social development, such as Guatemala and El Salvador, this was difficult if not impossible to accomplish. Whatever curbing of military influence occurred in El Salvador was, in considerable measure, a product of U.S. government power rather than the power of civilian Presidents Duarte and Alfredo Cristiani. In other countries where the military had been the sponsors of democratization, over time new governments reduced military privileges, just as in countries where the military had been the victims of democratization, over time new governments reduced military coup attempts.

In Turkey, Brazil, Chile, Portugal, Nicaragua, and other countries, powerful military establishments attempted to continue into the posttransition period powers and prerogatives that might be considered "abnormal" for a constitutional democracy. First, they insisted that special provisions be included in constitutions assigning to the military responsibility to provide for law and order and national security, "to guarantee the institutional order of the republic" (Chile), or to "preserve the conquests of the revolution" (Portugal). Implicit in these provisions was the possibility that on their own initiative military leaders could intervene in politics and take action (including, conceivably, superseding an elected government) to ensure that these responsibilities were met.

Second, actions of the military regime were in some cases made irreversible. In Turkey, for instance, the military decreed that 631 laws they had enacted during their rule between 1980 and 1983 could not be changed or criticized. The power to revoke martial law was given to the head of the armed forces. In Chile the military government passed laws assigning to the military establishment power to buy and sell equipment and property without securing the approval of the government.

Third, new governmental bodies dominated by the military were sometimes created. The Portuguese constitution, for example, provided for a Council of the Revolution, the members of which came from the armed forces, to advise the government and to judge the constitutionality of laws. In Turkey, the National Security Council that had been the center of power in the military regime was reconstituted with a membership of retired military officers as an advisory council to the president.[36]

Fourth, top military officers themselves at times assumed key positions in new democratic governments. In countries with American-style presidential systems, military officers might occupy cabinet positions under a civilian president; in Brazil, six out of twenty-two to twenty-six cabinet members were military officers. In parliamentary or semiparliamentary regimes, military officers like Eanes in Portugal and Evren in Turkey, both of whom had directed the transition to democracy, became president and engaged in struggles with civilian prime ministers over the powers of their respective offices. In

Chile, the president in the authoritarian government, General Pinochet, stayed on as commander in chief of the army in the democratic government. In Nicaragua, the defense minister of the authoritarian government, Gen. Humberto Ortega, stayed on as army chief in the democratic government, and the Sandinistas maintained their dominance in and control of the officer corps.

Fifth, the military often attempted to guarantee the future autonomy of the armed forces, particularly the independence of their personnel and finances, from control by the elected civilian government. In Brazil the military ensured that they would have full control over promotions. The Chilean military decreed that the chiefs of the armed forces and the police could not be removed for seven years, that the newly elected government could not reduce the size of the military, and that the armed forces could set their own budget. The Chilean example impressed the Nicaraguan military. "In discussing the models that might be followed in creating a post-election balance between their military forces and the newly elected government, Sandinista leaders and officials speak openly about such countries as Chile—casting themselves in the role of that country's military dictator, Augusto Pinochet." The Sandinistas, however, outdid Pinochet and promulgated a law (dated before they surrendered power but possibly written afterward) that perpetuated and enhanced the power of the Sandinista army. This law gave the commander in chief of the armed forces rather than the president the power to appoint the new commander; the commander in chief was also given, among other things, the power to appoint all military officers, to procure arms, equipment, and other assets, to organize and deploy the military, to acquire and construct facilities, to establish businesses to meet the needs of the armed forces, and to prepare the military budget.[37]

Arrangements such as these were significant infringements on the normal authority of elected governments. Overall, it was probably easier for new democratic regimes to establish their control over rebellious militaries that were weak than over cooperative militaries that were strong. Yet while militaries that cooperated in democratization might attempt to prolong their power, the record suggests that in countries at middle levels of economic development military power tended to diminish over time. In Portugal, for instance, the military overthrew the dictatorship on their own initiative, dominated the government for two years thereafter, and had great prestige with the Portuguese public. Yet the institutional manifestation of military power, the Council of the Revolution, was abolished in 1982, a Law of National Defense was passed subordinating the military to a cabinet responsible to parliament, the powers of the president were curbed, and Mário Soares, the great opponent of Colonel Eanes, succeeded him as president. Ten years after the revolution civil-military relations in Portugal were "approximating the desired model of objective civilian control."[38]

In Brazil the military gave up control of government with flags flying, their power and prestige intact. Yet Brazil's first postmilitary popularly elected president, Fernando Collor, arrested one leading general for making political statements, reprimanded another, the brother of a former military president, for defending that general, and reduced military representation in the cabinet from six to four. In addition, he reduced the size of the principal intelligence agency, the Serviçio Nacional de Informaçês (SNI), which had always been headed by a general, and put a civilian in charge. Civilians replaced military officers on the presidential staff and were placed in key positions dealing with nuclear power and the Amazon, two issues of great concern to the military. President Collor also drastically cut the military budget and refused to grant cost-of-living increases to the military, generating considerable grumbling and protests within the ranks. The disgruntled officers threatened the government, however, not with a coup but with a lawsuit.[39] In Peru the military were also historically a major political force; yet on assuming power in July 1990, President Alberto Fujimori abruptly fired the heads of the navy and air force. In Chile, less than a year after surrendering the presidency, the redoubtable General Pinochet suffered from allegations of corruption by members of his family and reportedly considered retiring as army commander. "Pinochet is a cat, not a tiger," observed one leading Chilean politician."[39]

In Turkey the military have been consistently viewed as a revered national institution and identified with the values of the Kemalist secular republic. Yet in 1987, four years after the military gave up political office, a referendum restored political rights to those civilian political leaders, including two former prime ministers, whom the military had banned from politics. The chief of staff under the civilian government ended martial law in July 1987. Simultaneously, Prime Minister Turgut Ozal sacked the incoming new chief of staff of the armed forces and replaced him with another officer more to his liking. "Three years ago, when the civilians had just returned, questioning of the military was unthinkable," one Turkish observer commented. "Now, people are showing a little more courage, more self-confidence." In 1989 Turkey duplicated the shift in position that occurred in Portugal: the civilian prime minister, Ozal, replaced the general, Evren, as president of the republic. Historically in Turkey in conflicts over policy between the military chiefs and civilian leaders, the latter would give way. In 1990, however, in an unprecedented action, the Chief of the General Staff resigned in protest against President Ozal's policies concerning the Persian Gulf crisis and Islamic fundamentalism. Six years after they gave up power clearly "the soldiers' traditional prerogatives" were "being eroded by a steady flow of criticism and actions."[40]

In countries with weak and politicized militaries, the workings of democracy over time reduced the number of coup attempts. In countries with strong and cooperative military establishments, the workings of democracy over time reduced the powers and privileges the military inherited from authoritarian rule. In both situations, the development of a "normal" pattern of civil-military relations was significantly affected by the policies and actions of the new democratic governments toward their armed forces. In several countries the first or second democratic governments initiated fairly comprehensive programs to establish civilian control of the armed forces, to professionalize those forces, to reorient them from internal to external security missions, to eliminate overstaffing and nonmilitary responsibilities, and to ensure that they would have the status and respect that their professionalism deserved. Karamanlis and Papandreou, González and his defense minister Narcís Serra, Alfonsín, García, and Aquino all pushed for comprehensive programs of military modernization and professionalization. These programs usually were a combination of carrots and sticks affecting at least five aspects of the military establishment. [41]

(1) *Professionalism.* Like other institutions armies develop distinctive sets of values, beliefs, and attitudes. In professionalized military establishments, these normally approximate a conservative military outlook that recognizes the limited functions of the military and is compatible with civilian control. In many authoritarian systems, however, the military had much more politicized outlooks. Under Franco, the Spanish military developed an intense right-wing ideology, different from the "normal conservatism" of most armies and stressing *patria*, centralism, antiliberalism, anticommunism, Roman Catholicism, and traditional social values. Spanish officers provided little support for democracy: in the 1979 election more than 50 percent of the military vote went to right-wing parties that received 7 percent of the total vote. In 1981, it is estimated, perhaps 10 percent of Spanish officers were

committed democrats.[42] In Portugal, the dominant groups in
the officer corps adhered to leftist, revolutionary, and Marxist-Leninist ideologies. Philippine military officers in RAM
wanted drastic reform of their society, government, and
armed forces, and had mixed views on whether this could
be accomplished by democratic means. In Argentina and
elsewhere in Latin America, military establishments were
pervaded with intense anticommunism, which usually also
meant antisocialism and antiliberalism. In South Africa, for
four decades the military had been the willing defenders of
the institutions and ideology of an apartheid state. The Turkish military were the staunchest supporters in Turkish society
of the Kemalist secular, national, and statist ideology, and the
Nicaraguan military, obviously, were totally committed to
Sandinista revolutionary dogma. The East European militaries were filled with officers who at least professed to be committed communists.

The replacement of these highly political outlooks by a
nonpolitical professional ethic was a top priority for the new
democratic governments. Achieving it required immense effort, much time, and some risk. The new governments attempted to promote professional values and the importance
of military abstention from politics by exhortation and indoc-
trination, training, curriculum changes in military schools,
and the revision of promotion systems. In Greece both Karamanlis and Papandreou articulated the need for strict professionalism, and Evangelos Averoff, defense minister under
Karamanlis, once commented that "I brainwashed them [the
military] extensively on the merit of democracy. I think there
is not a single officer in front of whom I did not speak personally at least three times." The importance of a depoliticized
military was also a constant theme with Papandreou. "The
Government," as he said at one point, "is determined not to
allow any undermining of the work of the armed forces
through political activity within its ranks, and this is a warn-

ing in all directions, without exception." In his first months in office, President Aylwin of Chile rather abruptly told General Pinochet "to keep the army out of politics." The agreement reached between the Sandinistas and the incoming UNO government specified that "The armed forces will have a professional character and will not belong to any political party."[43] Juan Carlos, Alfonsín, and Aquino also repeatedly stressed the need for total military abstention from politics.

To reinforce this point, new democratic leaders attempted to alter military training and educational systems. Papandreou moved to reorganize the curricula in the military schools so as to emphasize professionalism and to warn of the dangers of totalitarianism. Alfonsín promoted changes in the doctrines taught at Argentine military schools and introduced in the war colleges courses taught by civilians on the role of the armed forces in a democracy. The Aquino government created a new national training center to strengthen professionalism and combat skills in the Philippine military. González promoted the education of Spanish officers in an effort to bring them up to the professional levels of their allies in the North Atlantic Treaty Organization (NATO). In Spain, Greece, and elsewhere, democratic leaders encouraged the retirement of older officers, accelerated the promotion of younger, more professionally oriented officers, and emphasized merit rather than seniority as a criterion for promotion.

(2) *Mission*. To depoliticize the military, it was necessary to orient them to the performance of purely military missions. In many countries the armed forces had a variety of miscellaneous functions not related to military security. Almost without exception new democratic governments attempted to remove nonmilitary and internal security functions from their armed forces and to direct their attention to the mission of defending the external security of the country. In Argentina, Alfonsín acted to give civilians rather than the armed forces control of Fabricaciones Militares, a huge industrial com-

plex—the country's largest employer—that operated domestic airlines and manufactured many civilian goods as well as military equipment. His successor, Carlos Menem, in 1990 prepared plans to sell off military shares of eight companies including an iron- and steelworks, a shipyard, and several petrochemical companies. In Greece, the government moved to end military control of a radio station and a bank. Comparable moves in Brazil on the other hand, were precluded by the continued influence of the military after democratization.

The reorientation of the military was obviously easier to carry out if plausible external security threats existed. The rapidity with which the Turkish military relinquished power after its interventions in 1960, 1971, and 1980 was, in some measure, related to its preoccupation with the perceived Soviet military threat. After giving up power in 1974, the Greek military could be fully occupied not only with their NATO responsibilities but, much more important, with the threat posed by their NATO ally Turkey. Both Karamanlis and Papandreou adopted highly nationalistic stances designed to find favor with the military. They stressed Greece's independent role in NATO and attempted to reduce their military's identification with and dependence on the United States. Papandreou put great emphasis on the Turkish threat and the resulting need for the Greek military to cultivate its professional expertise. His policies were designed "to create a climate that would force the military to be preoccupied with matters related to military preparedness for the possibility of war with the perennial 'enemy' to the east."[44]

NATO was the functional equivalent for the Spanish military of Turkey for the Greek military. It was the source of an external security mission and of an extensive round of new demands on and new activities for the Spanish forces, stimulating military morale and prestige. As one defense analyst in Madrid put it, NATO "served as occupational therapy for the armed forces. For decades under Franco, they had been ostracized by civilized countries. Then suddenly they were allowed to sit alongside the top brass from other NATO countries, they were invited to join in war games, they were given new weapons to play with. They were respectable."[45] The Philippine, Peruvian, and Salvadoran military clearly had major internal insurgencies to deal with, although experience suggests that the frustrations and overwhelmingly political character of counterinsurgency warfare often generate within officer corps political ideologies and incentives to play political roles.

In keeping with the reorientation of their military toward security threats, new democratic governments attempted to redeploy military forces so that they were better located to defend the nation than to overthrow its government. Alfonsín disbanded the Argentine First Army based in Buenos Aires and transferred its units to other bases about the country. Felipe González's defense minister, Narcís Serra, moved to reduce the number of military regions in Spain from nine to six, established a number of mobile brigades, and shifted military units away from major cities. Intense resistance from the officer corps forced postponement of the implementation of these plans. By late 1987 the Aquino government had moved many divisional and brigade headquarters away from cities and out to the countryside to deal more effectively with the communist insurgency. In Portugal, however, ten years after the revolution the army lacked any significant security mission and was still primarily deployed on "bases just outside Lisbon and the main cities."[46]

Democratic governments, we have noted, are not necessarily more peaceful than authoritarian governments. Democracies, however, almost never fight other democracies, and new democratic governments often attempted to resolve longstanding international disputes. Under the Alfonsín and Menem governments, Argentine relations improved with both Great Britain and Chile. With the advent of democracy in Spain, Gibraltar became less of an issue in Anglo-Spanish relations. To the extent that democratic governments resolve international disputes, however, they may also deprive their armed forces of external missions that would reduce the probability of those forces intervening in internal politics. From the standpoint of civilian control, happy is the country with a traditional enemy.

(3) *Leadership and organization.* Initial and succeeding democratic governments usually replaced the top leadership of the armed forces. This was most important with respect to weak and politicized militaries because it was essential that the new democratic leaders be able to rely on the loyalty of the top military leaders. It was less necessary where the top military leadership had voluntarily given up office, as they presumably had a stake in the success of the democratic regime that followed. Democratic leaders in both situations, however, usually acted promptly to remove the existing military leaders and replace them with ones whose loyalty they could trust. This happened in Greece, Spain, Portugal, Argentina, the Philippines, Pakistan, Turkey, and Poland. In Argentina, however, Alfonsín was also compelled by military pressure, including attempted coups, to replace some of his appointees with officers more acceptable to the military establishment.

Democratic leaders also strengthened their control by altering the structure of their defense establishments. In Spain, the first democratic government created a joint chiefs of staff in February 1977 to promote this objective. To further this goal its successor created the posts of minster of defense and chief of the defense staff and clarified the power of the prime minister to "administer, direct, and coordinate" the military services. In Peru the García government created a minister of defense, and President Collor promised to do so in Brazil. In Portugal the anomalous military-membered Council of the Revolution was abolished. In Nicaragua, the outgoing Sandinistas and the incoming Chamorro government agreed that the military would "come under the orders of the President of the Republic, as set out in the Constitution and the law," and President Chamorro herself took the position of minister of defense.[47] In Greece, Papandreou similarly became defense minister as well as prime minister. In Chile, however, General Pinochet insisted that as commander in chief of the army he would report to the president, not to the civilian minister of defense.

In creating the post of minister of defense, the new democratic governments established a position to which they could more easily appoint a civilian than they could to the individual service ministries, whose occupants, at least in Latin America, had always been military officers. By establishing a central chief of the defense staff, the new governments created a position that they would have greater flexibility in filling than the posts of service chief, and to which they could appoint an officer clearly supportive of democracy. In Greece and in Spain, the democratic governments appointed admirals to these posts as a counter to the dominant influence of the army and as a product of a service less inclined toward coups d'etat.

(4) *Size and equipment.* The armed forces of authoritarian states tended to be oversized and underequipped. With the notable exception of Greece, new democratic leaders generally moved to reduce military money and manpower. The overall size of the military establishment was significantly cut back in Spain, Argentina, Nicaragua, Peru, Uruguay, and Portugal. In Spain, Argentina, and Greece, large numbers of senior officers were retired, significantly cutting the numbers of their rather bloated officer corps. Military budgets were slashed in many countries; that of the Argentine military, for instance, dropped from over 6 percent of the GNP to about 2 percent of the GNP. In Greece, however, the first two democratic governments maintained the military budgets and manpower on the grounds of the continuing confrontation over Cyprus. In Chile, the terms of democratization did not permit a cutback in the armed forces. In Nicaragua, however, leaders of the Chamorro government, including the Sandinista holdover as army chief, Gen. Humberto Ortega, committed them-

selves to reducing their military manpower from 70,000 to 35,000–40,000.

In Peru the García government cut several major weapons procurement programs, including an order for twenty-six Mirage 2000 jet fighters. For most new democratic governments, however, modernization of their armed forces was a high priority and they carried through and even expanded purchases of new equipment. This was designed both to reinforce the external orientation of their military and to promote military satisfaction with and support for the new regime. In Spain, for instance, the equipment of the army under Franco had been inferior and obsolete, and the democratic governments inaugurated major programs of investment and modernization. In Greece, Papandreou "attempted to diversify and improve the quality of arms, equipment, organization, and system of communications" of the armed forces. In Argentina, Alfonsín carried through major purchases of new equipment that had been ordered by the military junta.[48]

(5) *Status.* In all countries military officers are deeply concerned with their material status—pay, housing, medical care, and other benefits—and with their perceived status and reputation among the public in their country. New democratic governments were generally sensitive to these concerns. They did not, however, follow any uniform policies with respect to material benefits. The García government reduced officers' salaries, and low salaries along with other grievances among the military stimulated coup rumors in early 1989. In Argentina military pay decreased 50 percent in real terms during the first four years of democratic government, which presumably added to the unhappiness and coup-proneness of Argentine officers. González in Spain and Aquino in the Philippines increased the pay of their military. Karamanlis and Papandreou increased the pay and the housing, medical, and retirement benefits of the Greek military.[49]

Democratic leaders also made efforts to enhance the pres-

tige and morale of the military and to assure the officers that the government and the nation appreciated their services. In Greece, Karamanlis and his defense minister repeatedly "praised the armed forces' patriotism and devotion to legality and the constitutional process," and Papandreou not only appointed himself defense minister but "paid almost daily visits to the armed forces' headquarters, where he also has an office." He also asked Karamanlis, as president, "to take a more visible role in military affairs."[50] After their first months in office, leaders of the Alfonsín government recognized the need to correct the military's perception that the new democratic government and civilian society viewed them with contempt and hostility. Juan Carlos, Aquino, Alfonsín, Collor, and other leaders of new democracies seized opportunities to identify themselves symbolically with the military, emphasizing the military dimensions of their offices, visiting military installations, participating in military events, and, in the case of Juan Carlos, wearing the military uniform. During his first nine months in office, Collor attended approximately fifty military ceremonies.[51]

Overall, between 1975 and 1990 third wave governments were generally successful in defeating coups d'etat, reducing coup attempts, gradually cutting back military political influence and nonmilitary roles, developing military professionalism, and inaugurating patterns of civil-military relations similar to those existing in Western industrialized democracies.

Guidelines for Democratizers 5:
Curbing Military Power, Promoting
Military Professionalism*

(1) Promptly purge or retire all potentially disloyal officers, including both leading supporters of the authoritarian regime *and*

**The *Economist* has offered somewhat similar advice to leaders of new democracies in dealing with their military:

Forgive past sins—or at least do not seek to punish them . . .
Be strong and tactful too . . .

military reformers who may have helped you to bring about the democratic regime. The latter are more likely to lose their taste for democracy than their taste for intervening in politics.

(2) Ruthlessly punish the leaders of attempted coups against your new government, *pour décourager les autres.*

(3) Clarify and consolidate the chain of command over the armed forces. Remove ambiguities or anomalies, making clear that the civilian head of the government is the commander of the military.

(4) Make major reductions in the size of your military forces. An army that has been running a government will be too large and, in all probability, have far too many officers.

(5) Your military officers think that they are badly paid, badly housed, and badly provided for—and they are probably right. Use the money saved by reducing the size of the military to increase salaries, pensions, and benefits, and to improve living conditions. It will pay off.

(6) Reorient your military forces to military missions. For good reasons you may wish to resolve conflicts with other countries. The absence of a foreign threat, however, may leave your military devoid of a legitimate military mission and enhance their inclination to think about politics. Balance gains from the removal of foreign threats against the potential costs in instability at home.

(7) In line with refocusing the military on military purposes, drastically reduce the number of troops stationed in or around your capital. Move them to the frontiers or other relatively distant unpopulated places.

(8) Give them toys. That is, provide them with new and fancy tanks, planes, armored cars, artillery, and sophisticated electronic equipment (ships are less important; navies do not make coups). New equipment will make them happy and keep them busy trying to learn how to operate it. By playing your cards

---

Treat them generously . . .
Keep them busy . . .
Teach them respect for democracy . . .
Get the people on your side—but beware of promising more than you can deliver . . .
If all else fails, abolish the army.

Economist, August 29, 1987, p. 36.

right and making a good impression in Washington, you will also be able to shift much of the cost to the American taxpayer. You then gain the added benefit that you can warn the military that they will only continue to get these toys if they behave themselves because nasty U.S. legislators take a dim view of military intervention in politics.

(9) Because soldiers, like everyone else, love to be loved, seize every opportunity to identify yourself with the armed forces. Attend military ceremonies; award medals; praise the soldiers as embodying the highest values of the nation; and, if it is constitutionally appropriate, appear yourself in uniform.

(10) Develop and maintain a political organization that is capable of mobilizing your supporters in the streets of the capital if a military coup is attempted.

If you follow these ten rules, you may not prevent coup attempts, but you are likely to defeat them. At least up until the end of 1990, Suárez and González, Karamanlis and Papandreou, García and Fujimori, Alfonsín, and Menem, Collor, Ozal, and Aquino had generally followed these rules and had remained in office. In their societies, that was no mean achievement.

CONTEXTUAL PROBLEMS, DISILLUSIONMENT, AND AUTHORITARIAN NOSTALGIA

If new democratic regimes are to be consolidated, they have to deal in some way with transitional problems such as coping with the legacy of authoritarianism and establishing effective control of the military. More persistent challenges come from the contextual problems endemic to individual countries. In some countries these were neither numerous nor severe; in others they were both. A very rough listing of the major contextual problems confronting third wave democracies in the 1970s and 1980s and the countries in which those were most severe might go as follows:

(1) major insurgencies: El Salvador, Guatemala, Peru, Philippines;

(2) ethnic/communal conflicts (apart from insurgencies): India, Nigeria, Pakistan, Romania, Sudan, Turkey;

(3) extreme poverty (low per capita GNP): Bolivia, El Salvador, Guatemala, Honduras, India, Mongolia, Nigeria, Pakistan, Philippines, Sudan;

(4) severe socio-economic inequality: Brazil, El Salvador, Guatemala, Honduras, India, Pakistan, Peru, Philippines;

(5) chronic inflation: Argentina, Bolivia, Brazil, Nicaragua, Peru;

(6) substantial external debt: Argentina, Brazil, Hungary, Nigeria, Peru, Philippines, Poland, Uruguay;

(7) terrorism (apart from insurgency): Spain, Turkey;

(8) extensive state involvement in economy: Argentina, Brazil, Bulgaria, Czechoslovakia, East Germany, Hungary, India, Mongolia, Nicaragua, Peru, Philippines, Poland, Romania, Spain, Turkey.

The eight problems listed above are a reasonable list of the major contextual problems that confronted new democracies of the third wave. The judgments as to the countries where these problems are severe are casual and ad hoc. If, however, the judgments have any validity at all, they suggest that these twenty-nine third wave countries could be grouped into three categories in terms of the number of severe contextual problems they face:

(1) four or more major contextual problems: Brazil, India, Philippines, Peru;

(2) two or three major contextual problems: Argentina, Bolivia, El Salvador, Guatemala, Honduras, Hungary, Mongolia, Nicaragua, Nigeria, Pakistan, Poland, Romania, Spain, Sudan, Turkey;

(3) less than two major contextual problems: Bulgaria, Chile, Czechoslovakia, East Germany, Ecuador, Greece, Grenada, Korea, Portugal, Uruguay.

Many have argued that the new democracies facing severe contextual problems have to cope successfully with those problems in order to develop the legitimacy essential to the consolidation of democracy. This general proposition has been reinforced by arguments that failure to solve the country's most serious problem—be it debt, poverty, inflation, or insurgency—would mean the end of democracy in that country. If this is the case, the key question then becomes: Will the new third wave democracies confronted with severe contextual problems (which also bedeviled their authoritarian predecessors) successfully resolve those problems? In some cases new democratic regimes may deal successfully with individual problems. In the overwhelming majority of cases, however, it seems highly likely that third wave democratic regimes will not handle these problems effectively and that they will, in all probability, be no more or less successful in doing this than their authoritarian predecessors. Insurgencies, inflation, poverty, debt, inequality, and/or bloated bureaucracies will continue more or less as they have in previous decades. Does this then mean an inevitably bleak future for third wave democracies?

For some it may well mean that. Clearly democracy was under great stress in countries such as the Philippines, Peru, and Guatemala. The problems are numerous and severe; they will not go away, and they will not be solved. Other countries confront only slightly less challenging sets of contextual problems.

Unresolved and seemingly unresolvable contextual problems reinforced tendencies toward disillusionment in the new democracies. In most countries the struggle to create democracy was seen as moral, dangerous, and important. The collapse of authoritarianism generated enthusiasm and euphoria. The political struggles in democracy, in contrast, rapidly came to be seen as amoral, routine, and petty. The workings of democracy and the failure of new democratic governments to resolve the problems endemic to society generated indifference, frustration, and disillusionment.

A short time after the inauguration of democratic government disappointment over its operation became widespread in Spain, Portugal, Argentina, Uruguay, Brazil, Peru, Turkey,

Pakistan, the Philippines, and most East European countries. This phenomenon first appeared in 1979 and 1980 in Spain, where it was labeled *el desencanto* (disillusionment), a term that then spread throughout Latin America. In 1984, ten years after the overthrow of the Portuguese dictatorship, the "excitement and creative enthusiasm that accompanied the transition to democracy" had disappeared and the "predominant political mood" was "one of apathy and disenchantment." By 1987, euphoria over democratization in Latin America had "given way across the restless continent to frustration and disappointment with the results so far." In 1989, it was reported that "a groundswell of public disillusionment with Brazil's political leadership and an explosive mood of social discontent have replaced the high hopes of 1985 when millions of Brazilians celebrated the restoration of democratic government after two decades of military rule." In Pakistan, less than a year after the transition, "a sense of impatience and sadness" had "replaced the euphoria that greeted the country's return to democracy." Within a year of the collapse of dictatorships in Eastern Europe, observers were speaking of the phenomenon of "post-totalitarian depression" and the mood of "disappointment and disillusion" that was sweeping the region.[52]

Politically, the years after the first democratic government came to power were usually characterized by the fragmentation of the democratic coalition that had produced the transition, the decline in the effectiveness of the initial leaders of the democratic governments, and the growing realization that the advent of democracy would not, in itself, produce solutions to the major economic and social problems confronting the country. The intractability of problems, the constraints of the democratic process, the shortcomings of political leaders—these became the order of the day. The leaders of the new democracies often came to be viewed as arrogant, incompetent, or corrupt, or some combination of all three.

A related response to democracy was "authoritarian nostalgia." This was not significant in countries where the authoritarian regimes had been extremely harsh, incompetent, or corrupt, or where they had been unwilling to give up power. It was more prevalent where the dictatorship had been mild, where there had been some economic success, and where the regimes were more or less voluntarily transformed by their leaders into democracies. In these countries, memories of repression faded and were in some measure replaced by images of order, prosperity, and economic growth during the authoritarian period. In Spain, for instance, the ratings of the Franco government in terms of general satisfaction, living standards, law and order, and social equity all increased between 1978 and 1984: "memories of Franco have become rosier, the farther the dictator fades into the past." This "absence-makes-the-heart-grow-fonder" effect also appeared in Brazil. In 1989, reassessment of the rule of General Geisel was reported to be "in full swing. Today his rule is remembered fondly as a time when annual inflation was running well below 100 percent, instead of quadruple digits, and it was safe to walk the streets of Rio de Janeiro at night." In 1978, when asked which government or regime governed Portugal best, three times as many Portuguese citizens chose the Caetano dictatorship as chose the democratic regimes of Mário Soares. In 1987, seven years after the inauguration of democracy in Peru, residents of Lima picked Gen. Juan Velasco, military dictator of Peru from 1968 to 1975, as the best president of the country since 1950. By 1990 the reputations of both General Zia and General Ayub Khan were on the rise in Pakistan.[53]

The intractability of problems and the disillusionment of publics were pervasive characteristics of the new democracies. They dramatically posed the issue of the survivability of the new regimes: Would they consolidate or collapse? The essence of democracy is the choosing of rulers in regular, fair, open, competitive elections in which the bulk of the population can vote. One criterion of the strength of democracy

[handwritten note: When authoritarian regimes aren't that bad, why go to democracy?]

would be the extent to which political elites and publics firmly believe that rulers should be chosen this way, that is, an attitudinal test of the development of a democratic political culture in the country. A second criterion would be the extent to which political elites and publics do indeed choose leaders through elections, that is, a behavioral test of the institutionalization of democratic practices in the politics of the country.

DEVELOPING A DEMOCRATIC POLITICAL CULTURE

The democratic culture issue focuses attention on the relation between the performance or effectiveness of new democratic governments and their legitimacy—in other words, the extent to which elites and publics believe in the value of the democratic system. In an essentially pessimistic argument about this relationship, Diamond, Linz, and Lipset held that a primary reason for the instability of democratic and other regimes in the Third World, was "the combination and interaction of low legitimacy and low effectiveness." Regimes begin with low legitimacy and hence find it difficult to be effective, and regimes "which lack effectiveness, especially, in economic growth, tend to continue to be low in legitimacy."[54] New democracies are, in effect, in a catch-22 situation: lacking legitimacy they cannot become effective; lacking effectiveness, they cannot develop legitimacy.

To what extent is this pessimistic hypothesis justified?

The inability of new democratic regimes to solve longstanding, severe contextual problems does not necessarily mean the collapse of those regimes. The legitimacy of authoritarian regimes (including, in the end, communist regimes) came to rest almost entirely on performance. The legitimacy of democratic regimes clearly rests in part on performance. It also rests, however, on processes and procedures. The legitimacy of particular rulers or governments may depend on what they can deliver; the legitimacy of the regime derives from the electoral processes by which the governments are constituted. Performance legitimacy plays a role in demo-

cratic regimes, but it is nowhere near as important as the role
it plays in authoritarian regimes and it is secondary to procedural legitimacy. What determines whether or not new democracies survive is not primarily the severity of the problems they face or their ability to solve those problems. It is
the way in which political leaders respond to their inability to
solve the problems confronting their country.

Democratic regimes faced by extraordinarily severe contextual problems survived in the past. As Linz and Stepan have
emphasized, the argument that economic crisis necessarily
undermines democratic regimes is belied by the experience of
the 1930s in Europe. Democratic systems survived the Great
Depression in all countries except Germany and Austria, including countries that suffered much more economic hardship than those two did. They survived because, in the words
of Ekkart Zimmerman, of "the ability of group leaders to
come together, form new coalitions, sometimes on the basis
of reaffirming older ones (such as Belgium), and then settle
on how to steer the economy." Similarly, new democratic regimes in Colombia and Venezuela faced challenges in the
1960s fully as severe as those later confronted by third wave
democracies. The lesson of their cases, as Robert Dix neatly
summarized it, is that "political engineering can in substantial measure substitute for the dearth of more deterministic
economic and sociological conditions of democracy in Third
World nations."[55]

The stability of democratic regimes depends, first, on the
ability of the principal political elites—party leaders, military
leaders, business leaders—to work together to deal with the
problems confronting their society and to refrain from ex-
ploiting those problems for their own immediate material or
political advantage. New democratic regimes could not and
did not rid their countries of long-standing terrorism and insurgencies. The crucial question for stability was how political elites and publics responded to this situation. In the 1960s,
the elites in Colombia and Venezuela collaborated in attempt-

ing to cope with these problems. Similar developments occurred in the third wave democracies. Spain, for instance,
confronted the continuing problem of extremist Basque terrorism. No national political party, however, attempted to
exploit the issue in order "to delegitimize the democratic
regime. . . . no party persisted in blaming the various governments for creating the problem. No party claimed that the
problem could be handled better outside of a democratic regime." In Peru, somewhat similarly, experience showed that
"a guerilla movement can unite key political actors behind
democracy as the only alternative to civil war."[56]

Second, the stability of democracy depends on the ability
of publics to distinguish between the regime and the government or rulers. In 1983, for instance, twenty-five years after
the inauguration of the second wave democratic regime in
Venezuela, public opinion had become quite disillusioned
with the performance of the elected rulers of Venezuela but
not with the system of electing them. Despite, as one study
reported, the "discontent with government there is nothing
to indicate similar discontent with the method of selecting the
government." While a substantial proportion (34.2 percent)
of Venezuelans in 1983 believed the situation in their country
justified a coup, only about 15 percent supported a specific
alternative to a democratic regime. Fewer people than in 1973
believed that the government would be better without politicians and that politicians were indifferent to the country's
problems. In 1983, "Venezuelans remained very supportive
of the manner in which their governments come to office, increasingly dissatisfied with what they do once they get there,
and convinced that the suffrage is the only way to improve
things."[57] Overall, despite the continued inability of elected
governments to deal effectively with the problems confronting their country, Venezuelans were more strongly committed to democracy in 1983 than they had been in 1973.

During the six years after 1983, Venezuela confronted intensifying economic problems stemming largely from declining oil prices. By 1989 the economic crisis had created a situation "where expectations have remained constant while the capability of the government to meet them has declined." Yet this did not pose a threat to democracy:

> The high level of frustration is not channeled into illegal, violent political activism, but rather in legal, peaceful system-maintaining mechanisms and processes. We find that the middle and lower class Venezuelans have turned to mainly four ways to cope psychologically with the crisis they are facing: legal protest, adaptation, resignation or emigration.[58]

The distinction between support for democracy and support for the governments that democratic elections produce was also manifest in Spain. Between 1978 and 1984, there was a "gradual dissociation of support for the democratic regime from satisfaction with what seems to be the mere effectiveness of democracy."[59] In the last years of the Franco regime, unemployment was among the lowest in Europe (averaging 3 percent) and the economic growth rate was one of the highest in the world (averaging about 7 percent). In the first years of democracy in the late 1970s and early 1980s, unemployment rose to 20 percent and economic growth dropped to less than 2 percent. Confidence in the ability of democracy to resolve these problems varied widely. In 1978, 68 percent of the public thought democracy would allow resolution of the problems confronting the country. In 1980 and 1981, pluralities of the public thought democracy could not solve the country's problems. In late 1982 and in 1983, however, substantial majorities (55 percent and 60 percent) of the public once again had confidence in the ability of democracy to deal with Spain's problems. Yet despite these fluctuations in the public's confidence that democracy could solve their problems, support for democracy remained consistently high and even increased. In 1978, 77 percent of the Spanish public believed that democracy was the best political system for Spain. That figure dipped to 69 percent in 1980, but rose to 81 percent in 1981 and to 85 percent in 1983.[60]

How can this consistent widespread support for democracy as a political system be reconciled with the variations in confidence in the ability of democratic governments to deal with problems? The answer, of course, is the electoral cycle. In 1978, voters still had confidence in the new Suárez government. By 1980 and 1981, with increasing economic hardship, they had lost confidence in that government, and in 1982 they swept Felipe González and the Socialists into office. Having done that, their confidence in the ability of democracy to solve Spain's problems soared upward. Like Venezuelan voters, Spanish voters thus separated their support for democracy as a political system from their evaluation of the performance of the party in power. That distinction is crucial to the functioning of democracy.

Under some circumstances, authoritarian nostalgia could conceivably pave the way for the "slow death" of a democratic regime, with the military or other authoritarian forces resuming power.[61] Nostalgia, however, is a sentiment, not a movement. More generally, authoritarian nostalgia was further evidence of the tendency of publics to distinguish between rulers and regimes. The citizens of Spain, Portugal, Brazil, and Peru simultaneously saw Franco, Caetano, Geisel, and Velasco as effective rulers and yet also overwhelmingly supported democracy as a better system of government.

Disillusionment with democratic rulers and nostalgia for authoritarian ones were an essential first step in the process of democratic consolidation. They also were a sign that elites and publics were coming down from the euphoric and ephemeral "high" of democratization and were adapting to the grubby and plodding "low" of democracy. They were learning that democracy rests on the premise that governments will fail and that hence institutionalized ways have to exist for changing them. Democracy does not mean that problems will be solved; it does mean that rulers can be removed; and the essence of democratic behavior is doing the latter because it is impossible to do the former. Disillusionment and the lowered expectations it produces are the foundation of democratic stability. Democracies become consolidated when people learn that democracy is a solution to the problem of tyranny, but not necessarily to anything else.

A striking feature of the first fifteen years of the third wave was the virtual absence of major antidemocratic movements in the new democracies. Authoritarian holdover groups (both standpatter and extremist) existed in many countries. Authoritarian nostalgia materialized in several. Enthusiasm for democracy, participation in electoral politics, and the popularity of democratic leaders all declined significantly. Yet in the first fifteen years of the third wave, in no country did a large-scale mass political movement develop challenging the legitimacy of the new democratic regime and posing an explicit authoritarian alternative to that regime. In at least those countries that had transited to democracy early in the third wave, the consensus on the desirability of democracy seemed to be overwhelming. In Spain, as was indicated above, in five polls between 1977 and 1983 substantial majorities of the public agreed that democracy was the best political system for a country like theirs. As one study concluded, "the bases of support for the democratic regime are much more variegated— broader and more ambiguous—than is the case for the exclusionary regime that preceded it. The democratic regime is less strictly tied to particular interests; in this respect it enjoys relative autonomy." Broad support for democracy was not limited to Spain. In Peru, for instance, in four polls between 1982 and 1988 the citizens of Lima endorsed democracy by majorities of between 66 percent to 88 percent, and 75 percent of a 1988 nationwide sample chose democracy as the most desirable system for their country.[62] More fragmentary evidence suggests similar levels of support for democracy in other third wave countries.

This broad consensus on democracy in the third wave countries immediately after regime change contrasts rather markedly with the relatively slow development in Germany and Japan after World War II of support for both democracy and the values and attitudes associated with democracy. In the early 1950s, over a third of Germans indicated that they would support or be indifferent to an attempt by a new Nazi party to seize power and just under a third supported restoration of the monarchy. When asked to identify the period when Germany had been best off, 45 percent chose the pre-1914 empire, 42 percent the Third Reich, 7 percent the Weimar Republic, and 2 percent the new Federal Republic. Support for the Federal Republic rose to 42 percent in 1959 and to 81 percent in 1970. In 1953, 50 percent of the German public thought democracy was the best form of government for Germany; by 1972, 90 percent did. The development of support for democracy and of the attitudes of trust and civic competence that go with democracy thus occurred slowly over the course of two decades.[63] In still slower and less complete fashion a somewhat similar shift in opinion toward a more prodemocratic position occurred in Japan during the 1950s and 1960s.

Why was there almost instant consensus on democracy after the end of dictatorships in Spain and Peru while it took two decades for comparable consensuses to develop after the collapse of authoritarianism in Germany and Japan? In Germany and Japan, in some degree people changed their opinions, but to a much larger degree the people changed. Younger and better educated people were more prodemocratic. Support for democracy in Germany approached unanimity when the German public had come to be composed of people who had been educated and spent their adult lives in the Federal Republic.[64] In Spain and Peru, in contrast, widespread support for democracy shortly after the inauguration of democratic regimes either meant that such broad support existed under the authoritarian regime, or meant that people who had supported or at least acquiesced in authoritarianism before the transition changed their minds very quickly after the transition. Neither alternative is exactly a happy one for democracy. If the first alternative holds, authoritarian regimes existed in those societies even when there was overwhelming support for democracy. If the second holds, people who changed their opinions very quickly in a prodemocratic direction after the transition quite conceivably could shift equally quickly in an antidemocratic direction if circumstances warranted. In Germany and Japan broad support for democracy was the product of *generational change*, and hence was likely to be irreversible in the short run. In Spain and Peru, broad support for democracy was, apparently, the result of *opinion change*, and hence could be more reversible in the short run.

INSTITUTIONALIZING DEMOCRATIC POLITICAL BEHAVIOR

The disillusionment that developed in the new democratic systems manifested itself behaviorally in four ways. First, it often led to resignation, cynicism, and withdrawal from politics. In most new democracies, voting levels were high during the transition but declined, sometimes quite drastically, in subsequent elections. Decreased political participation may have been undesirable in terms of democratic theory, but it did not, in itself, threaten the stability of the new democracies.

Second, disillusionment manifested itself in an anti-incumbent reaction. As in Spain, voters could oust the ruling party and replace it in office by an alternative group of rulers. This is, of course, the familiar democratic response, and it occurred frequently in the new third wave democracies. Incumbent leaders and parties were more often than not defeated when they attempted to win reelection. The parties that thus came to power in the first and second turnovers after the establishment of democracy usually pursued moderate policies well within the mainstream of opinion in their country. In particular, parties identified with the Left—the socialists in Portugal and Spain, PASOK in Greece, the Peronists in Argentina—generally adopted highly conservative and orthodox economic and financial policies when in office (the major exception was García's APRA government in Peru).

Third, disillusionment with democracy at times produced an antiestablishment response. In this case, voters not only rejected the incumbent party; they also rejected the principal alternative party or group within the political establishment and threw their support to a political outsider. This response was more frequent in presidential systems, where candidates for the top office run more on an individual than a party basis; hence it tended to be more prevalent in Latin America, where it was identified as populism. Notable examples of the populist antiestablishment response were the successful candidacies of Fernando Collor in Brazil and Alberto Fujimori in Peru. The candidacy of Carlos Menem in Argentina had some populist characteristics, although he was also the candidate of what was arguably the strongest established political party in the country. Successful populist candidates won office on the basis of "outsider" antiestablishment political appeals, with little or no backing from established political parties and with broad, multiclass support from the public. Once in office, however, successful populist candidates generally did not follow populist economic policies but instead launched rigorous austerity programs designed to cut government spending, promote competition, and hold down wages.

Anti-incumbent and antiestablishment responses are the classic democratic reactions to policy failure and disillusionment. Through elections one set of rulers is removed from office and another is installed in office, leading to changes if not improvements in government policy. Democracy is consolidated to the extent these in-system responses become institutionalized.

One criterion for measuring this consolidation is the two-turnover test. By this test, a democracy may be viewed as consolidated if the party or group that takes power in the initial election at the time of transition loses a subsequent election and turns over power to those election winners, and if those election winners then peacefully turn over power to the winners of a later election. Selecting rulers through elections is the heart of democracy, and democracy is real only if rulers are willing to give up power as a result of elections. The first electoral turnover often has symbolic significance. The 1989 transition in Argentina was the first turnover since 1916 from an elected president of one party to an elected president from another party. The 1985 and 1990 Peruvian elections marked the second and third times in the twentieth century in Peru that one elected president has transferred power to another.

A second turnover shows two things. First, two major groups of political leaders in the society are sufficiently committed to democracy to surrender office and power after losing an election. Second, both elites and publics are operating within the democratic system; when things go wrong, you change the rulers, not the regime. Two turnovers is a tough test of democracy. The United States did not clearly meet it until the Jacksonian Democrats surrendered office to the Whigs in 1840. Japan was universally and properly viewed as a democratic nation after World War II, but it did not meet this test and, indeed, effectively never has had even one electoral turnover. Between 1950 and 1990, Turkey had three military interventions and several first turnovers but never a second one.

In three countries (Sudan, Nigeria, Pakistan) of twenty-nine that had transition elections between 1974 and 1990, the governments installed by those elections were removed by military or executive coups. In ten other countries with transition elections in 1986 or later, no other national election was held before the end of 1990. In fifteen of the sixteen remaining countries that held one or more elections after the transition election, a first turnover had occurred, the exception being Turkey. In six of eight countries that had two or more national elections after the transition election, a second turnover occurred, the exceptions being Spain and Honduras. In twenty-two of the total of twenty-eight elections in the sixteen countries incumbent candidates or parties were defeated and the opposition came to power. The democratic process, in short, was operating: voters regularly ousted the ins and the ins always yielded office to the new choices of the voters. Apart from the three cases of democratic governments overturned by coups, in terms of institutionalizing the electoral process democracy in 1990 was alive and well in third wave countries.

A fourth and most extreme political manifestation of discontent would be a response, directed not at the groups in office or at the establishment generally, but at the democratic system itself. Concrete political forces opposed to democracy included both surviving standpatter groups from the authoritarian regime and continuing extremist groups from the anti-authoritarian regime opposition. Standpatter groups included in some cases elements among the military, but, as was pointed out above, these were normally discontented middle-ranking officers opposed by the military leadership and unable to mobilize significant support from civilian groups. In formerly communist countries, elements of the party and state bureaucracies, including the secret police, also fought rearguard actions against democratization. In Nicaragua, the standpatter Sandinista-controlled labor unions overtly challenged the elected democratic government, threatening to "govern from below."

Extremist opposition groups also attempted to challenge the new democratic regimes. By their very nature, however, radical groups employing violence, such as the Shining Path in Peru, the NPA in the Philippines, or the FMLN (Farabundo Martí National Liberation Front) in El Salvador, were not able to mobilize extensive support among the publics of the new democracies. Extremist groups that employed more peaceful tactics also had little success. In May 1990 in Korea, for instance, radical students organized demonstrations and riots to commemorate the tenth anniversary of the Kwangju massacre. One demonstration involved almost 100,000 people, others numbered between 2,000 and 10,000. These were the largest demonstrations since those in 1987 that impelled the ruling party to agree to elections. The 1990 demonstrations against an elected government, however, did not draw the broad support that the 1987 ones did against the authoritarian regime. Only a "tiny fraction" of Korea's large student population joined the 1990 demonstrations and the middle class abstained because of its "broad lack of confidence in the opposition's ability to form an alternative government." "The middle class," it was reported, "prefers to grumble at home in front of television sets."[65] In general, holdover standpatter and extremist groups tended to be isolated on the margins of politics in the new democracies in the 1970s and 1980s.

The prevalence of democratic political practices in third wave democracies reflected the absence of authoritarian alternatives. Military juntas, personal dictators, and Marxist-Leninist parties had been tried and had failed. As a result, democracy was the only alternative. The crucial question, of course, was whether or not this would remain the case, or whether new movements would appear promoting new forms of authoritarianism. The extent to which such movements did materialize and develop significant support would presumably depend on the extent to which democratic behavior, including electoral turnovers, had become institutionalized.

In addition, however, there was the possibility that over time within-system democratic alternatives would become exhausted. How many times would a public be willing to replace one party or coalition with another in the hopes that one of them would resolve the problems confronting the country? How often would voters be willing to elect charismatic, populist outsiders believing they would work economic and social miracles? At some point, publics could become disillusioned not only with the failures of democratic governments but also with the failures of democratic processes. They might be willing to shift from anti-incumbent and antiestablishment responses to antisystem responses. If democratic options appeared to be exhausted, ambitious political leaders would have powerful incentives to produce new authoritarian alternatives.

CONDITIONS FAVORING
CONSOLIDATION OF NEW DEMOCRACIES

What conditions promote the consolidation of democratic political institutions and of a democratic political culture in third wave countries? As of 1990, the third wave was only fifteen years old, the returns on this issue were not in, and no definitive answer was possible. Two bodies of potentially relevant evidence, however, were available. First, the experience of the consolidation of first and second wave democracies could yield lessons for the third wave. Second, as has been pointed out, the factors promoting the inauguration of democratic regimes did not necessarily promote their consolidation. Yet some may do so. In addition, it may be possible reasonably to conclude that some developments will be more supportive of democratic consolidation than others. It would be folly to attempt to predict in which countries democracy will consolidate and in which countries it will not, and no attempt will be made here to make that prediction. It may, however, be useful, if speculative, to attempt to identify variables that could affect democratic consolidation and to identify to what extent these variables were present or absent in individual third wave countries. Consolidation success could be influenced by several factors.

First, as was pointed out earlier, in the twentieth century very few countries created stable democratic systems on their first try. It is reasonable to conclude that prior democratic experience is more conducive than none to the stabilization of third wave democracies. Extending this proposition it may also be reasonable to hypothesize that a longer and more recent experience with democracy is more conducive to demo-

TABLE 5.1
Post–World War II Democratic Experience of
Third Wave Countries

Years of Democracy Post–World War II and Pre–Third Wave	Countries
20 or more	Uruguay*, Philippines, India, Turkey, Chile*
10–19	Greece*, Ecuador, Peru, Bolivia, Korea, Pakistan, Brazil
1–9	Argentina*, Honduras, Guatemala, Hungary*, Czechoslovakia*, Grenada, Nigeria
Less than 1	Spain*, Portugal*, El Salvador, Poland*, East Germany*, Romania, Bulgaria, Nicaragua, Sudan, Mongolia

*Countries with some democratic experience before World War II.

cratic consolidation than is a shorter and more distant one. As the breakdown in Table 5.1 indicates, five countries— Uruguay, the Philippines, India, Chile, and Turkey—had twenty or more years of democratic experience after World War II before their third wave democratization, although for Turkey this was broken by brief military interventions in 1960 and 1971. At the other extreme, ten countries had no democratic experience after World War II; and six—El Salvador, Nicaragua, Romania, Bulgaria, Mongolia, and the Sudan— had no democratic experience at all before the third wave.

Second, as was also emphasized in chapter 2, a high correlation exists between level of economic development and the existence of democratic regimes. A more industrialized, modern economy and the more complex society and educated populace it entails are more conducive to the inauguration of

TABLE 5.2
Levels of Economic Development of Third Wave Countries

1987 GNP per Capita (in dollars)	Countries
5,000 and more	Spain, East Germany, Czechoslovakia, Hungary, Bulgaria
2,000–4,999	Greece, Portugal, Argentina, Uruguay, Brazil, Poland, Romania, Korea
1,000–1,999	Peru, Ecuador, Turkey, Grenada, Chile
500–999	Guatemala, El Salvador, Honduras, Nicaragua, Bolivia, Philippines
Less than 500	India, Pakistan, Nigeria, Sudan

Sources: Non-Eastern European countries: World Bank, *World Development Report 1989* (New York: Oxford University Press, 1989), pp. 164–65. Eastern European countries: Estimated from Central Intelligence Agency, "Eastern Europe: Long Road Ahead to Economic Well-Being" (Paper presented to the Subcommittee on Technology and National Security, Joint Economic Committee, United States Congress, May 16, 1990), pp. 1–6.

Note: Mongolia is omitted due to lack of data.

democratic regimes than are their opposites. It seems plausible to hypothesize that they will also be more conducive to the consolidation of new democratic regimes than will nonindustrialized societies. If GNP per capita (as of 1987) is taken as a rough index of socioeconomic development, third wave countries fall into relatively clear categories (see Table 5.2). Spain (with a per capita GNP of $6,010), East Germany, and probably Hungary, Czechoslovakia, and Bulgaria were in the top group, followed by Greece (per capita GNP of $4,020). Several other countries also were above the $2,000 mark, including Portugal, Uruguay, Korea, Brazil, and probably the three other East European countries. At the bottom were the four third wave countries with per capita GNPs less than $500. As of late 1990, two of these (Nigeria and the Sudan) had reverted to military rule, and in a third, Pakistan, the democratically elected ruler had been summarily removed from office by the head of state, reportedly at the behest of the army. In 1990, consequently, India remained the only extremely poor third wave country where democracy remained clearly intact.

Third, the international environment and foreign actors played significant roles in the creation of third wave democracies. Presumably an external environment supportive of democracy should also be conducive to its consolidation (see Table 5.3). An "external environment" here means for-

TABLE 5.3
External Environment and Democratic Consolidation in
Third Wave Countries

External Environment of Consolidation	Countries
Extremely favorable	East Germany, Spain, Portugal, Greece
Quite favorable	Czechoslovakia, Hungary, Poland, Turkey, Philippines, Guatemala, El Salvador, Honduras, Nicaragua, Grenada, Bolivia
Favorable	Peru, Ecuador, Uruguay, Korea, Chile
Indifferent/ unfavorable	Argentina, Brazil, India, Nigeria, Sudan, Romania, Bulgaria, Mongolia

Note: Classifications of the external environment are based on the author's impressionistic judgments. They rest on the assumption that both the European Community and the United States will continue to be concerned with the promotion of democracy.

eign governments and other actors that are democratic them-selves, favor the existence of democratic regimes in other countries, have close relations with the newly democratic country, and are able to exercise influence in that country. Germany's unification made the future of democracy in what had been East Germany identical with that of the stable democratic environment of what had been West Germany. Membership in the European Community is extremely desir-able for economic reasons, and democratic governance is a condition of membership; hence third wave EC members (Spain, Portugal, and Greece) have strong incentives to main-tain their democratic institutions. Other countries, such as Turkey, Hungary, Czechoslovakia, and Poland aspire to mem-bership, and that possibility provides an incentive for them to sustain their democracy. Some countries had extremely close relationships with the United States and have been heavily influenced by the United States. These include the Central American countries, Grenada, Bolivia, and the Phil-ippines. Countries where U.S. influence was present but probably less strong included Peru, Ecuador, Uruguay, Ko-rea, Turkey, Poland, and Chile. The influence of major demo-cratic powers was relatively weak in Argentina, Brazil, India, Nigeria, the Sudan, Romania, Bulgaria, and Mongolia. *

Fourth, the timing of a country's transition within the third wave may be indicative of factors that have an impact on the consolidation of democracy in that country (see Table 5.4). Countries that began a transition to democracy earlier in the

*In an analysis of the reasons why the small Caribbean countries, mostly former British colonies, have sustained democracy, Jorge I. Dominguez em-phasizes the role of the international subsystem and other Caribbean states, as well as the United States, in acting to defeat coups and other threats to democracy. The Caribbean international system has given priority to "de-mocracy over non-intervention (the opposite of what has been the more common norm in Latin America)." "The Caribbean Question: Why Has Lib-eral Democracy (Surprisingly) Flourished? A Rapporteur's Report" (Unpub-lished paper, Harvard University, Center for International Affairs, January 1991), p. 31.

TABLE 5.4

Inauguration of Democracy in Third Wave Countries

Date of Founding Election	Countries
Before 1980	Spain, Portugal, Greece, Ecuador, India, Nigeria
1980–83	Peru, Argentina, Bolivia, Honduras, Turkey
1984–87	Uruguay, Brazil, Philippines, El Salvador, Guatemala, Korea, Grenada, Sudan
1988–90	Pakistan, Poland, Hungary, East Germany, Czechoslovakia, Romania, Bulgaria, Nicaragua, Chile, Mongolia
Possible after 1990	Mexico, Soviet Union, South Africa, Taiwan, Nepal, Panama

wave did so largely as a result of indigenous causes. External influences and snowballing tended to be more significant as causes of democratization for countries that made the transition later in the wave. It seems reasonable to hypothesize that the prevalence of indigenous causes, present largely in early-in-the-wave transitions, were likely to be more conducive to democratic consolidation than were external influences, more present in later-in-the-wave transitions. To the extent that this was a factor, it favored consolidation in the southern European countries, India, Ecuador, and Peru. It should have favored consolidation in Nigeria, but clearly did not prevent an early return to authoritarianism. Presumably the forces responsible for their later transitions should make consolidation more difficult in the Eastern European countries, Korea, Pakistan, and Nicaragua, as well as those countries (such as Taiwan, South Africa, the Soviet Union, and Mexico) that as of 1990 were still in the process of liberalization.

Fifth, a crucial question obviously concerns the relation between transition processes and consolidation. Does it make a
difference for consolidation whether or not a country transits
to democracy through transformation, replacement, transplacement, or intervention? Plausible arguments can be made
for and against the helpfulness of each of these processes as
far as consolidation is concerned. A related issue concerns the
role of violence in the transition and presents similar problems. On the one hand, it can be argued that a peaceful, consensual transition favors democratic consolidation. On the
other hand, it could also be argued that a violent transition is
likely to develop among most population groups a deep aversion to bloodshed and hence to generate a deeper commitment to democratic institutions and values. Overall, it seems
more plausible to hypothesize that a consensual, less violent
transition provides a better basis for consolidating democracy
than do conflict and violence. If this is the case, negotiated
transplacements may be most supportive of consolidation;
transformations would be next; and replacements and interventions would provide the least support for consolidation
(see Table 3.1 above). It might also be hypothesized that
whatever the nature of the process, the less violence involved
in it, the more favorable are the conditions for democratic
consolidation. To the extent this is the case, it could create
problems for consolidation in El Salvador, Guatemala, Nicaragua, Grenada, Panama, Romania, and South Africa.

Sixth, it was earlier argued that consolidation of democracies was not simply a function of the number and severity of
the contextual problems they confronted. The heart of the
matter was instead how political elites and publics responded
to those problems and to the inability of the new democratic
governments to solve those problems. This was not to say,
however, that the problems confronting a new democracy
were totally irrelevant to its consolidation. The number and
nature of severe contextual problems may be one variable

along with the others that will affect democratic consolidation (see pp. 253–55 above).

Other factors in addition to these six unquestionably affect the success or failure of consolidation. The extent and direction of those influences, however, is not always easy to estimate. One would suppose, for instance, that the nature and success of the authoritarian regime might affect the consolidation prospects of its democratic successor. Is the prospect of democratic consolidation affected by whether the authoritarian regime was a military regime, a one-party system, a personal dictatorship, or a racial oligarchy? A variety of conflicting hypotheses and arguments are possible, including the argument that the nature of the predecessor authoritarian system does not have *any* significant implications for the consolidation of its democratic successor. Similarly, is democratic consolidation more likely in the wake of what might be termed relatively successful authoritarian regimes (e.g., Spain, Brazil, Taiwan, Korea, Chile) or relatively unsuccessful ones (e.g., Argentina, Philippines, Portugal, Bolivia, Romania). This distinction is obviously related to differences in transition processes, but it could also be an independent variable on its own. But in which direction? It could be argued that the reactions of elites and publics to the manifest failures of unsuccessful authoritarian regimes should be a positive force for democratic consolidation. It could also, however, be argued that nations may differ in their political capacities and that a people who made a success of authoritarianism (e.g., the Spanish) will do the same with democracy, while a people who were unable to create a successful authoritarian system (e.g., the Argentines) are likely to have no more success in consolidating a democratic one.

Democratic consolidation may also be affected by the nature of the democratic institutions that are established. Plausible arguments, for instance, have been made that a parliamentary system is more likely than a presidential system to contribute to the success of new democracies because it reduces the "all or nothing" aspect of politics, usually requires a coalition of parties to form a government, and provides an opportunity for balance between a chief of state and a chief of government.[66] These arguments are suggestive, and the desirability of shifting to a parliamentary system has been raised by several Latin Americans, including Raul Alfonsín. Evidence that parliamentary regimes contribute to democratic consolidation, however, is still scanty. A similar issue comes up with respect to the nature of the party systems in new democracies. Is democracy better served by many parties each representing a particular economic, social, regional, communal, or ideological interest? Or is it better served by two comprehensive parties, each of which will provide a plausible and responsible alternative government to the other and whose leaderships could more easily cooperate in dealing with severe economic crises, drug mafias, and threatening insurgencies? Again the evidence is lacking for a judgment one way or another.

If the factors discussed above are relevant to the consolidation of new democracies and if one makes the dubious assumption that they are equally relevant, some broad judgments emerge as to where the conditions were most favorable and least favorable for consolidation. The conclusions are not surprising. Overall, the conditions for consolidation were most favorable in the southern European countries, East Germany, Uruguay, and Turkey. For a fairly large group of countries, the conditions were less favorable but still supportive; these included Czechoslovakia, Chile, Ecuador, Bolivia, Peru, Honduras, Argentina, Brazil, the Philippines, India, Poland, and Hungary. Less favorable conditions for consolidation confronted Guatemala, Grenada, Nigeria, El Salvador, Pakistan, Nicaragua, Bulgaria, and Mongolia. Finally, the Sudan and Romania seemed especially deficient in the conditions that might support the maintenance of democracy.

Many factors will influence the consolidation of democracy

in third wave countries and their relative importance is not at all clear. It does seem most likely, however, that whether democracy in fact falters or is sustained will depend primarily on the extent to which political leaders wish to maintain it and are willing to pay the costs of doing so instead of giving priority to other goals.

CHAPTER 6

WHITHER?

DEMOCRATIZATION IN ALMOST THIRTY COUNTRIES between 1974 and 1990 and liberalization in several more focus attention on a basic issue. Were these democratizations part of a continuing and ever-expanding "global democratic revolution" that would eventually envelop virtually all countries in the world? Or were they a limited expansion of democracy, involving for the most part its reintroduction into countries that had experienced it in the past? If the third wave came to a halt, would it be followed by a significant third reverse wave eliminating many of democracy's gains in the 1970s and 1980s? Will there be a return to the situation comparable to the previous nadirs of democratization, when a fifth or less of the world's independent countries had democratic governments?

Social science cannot provide reliable answers to these questions, nor can any social scientist. It may be possible, however, to identify some of the factors that will affect the future expansion or contraction of democracy in the world and to pose the questions that seem most relevant for the future of democratization. The critical factors include: (1) the extent to which the causes of the third wave are likely to continue to operate, to gain in strength, to weaken, or to be supplemented or replaced by new forces promoting democratization; (2) the circumstances that might give rise to a significant reverse wave and the forms that reverse wave might assume; and (3) the obstacles to and opportunities for democratization that may exist in those countries that as of 1990 had not democratized. The following pages attempt to analyze these factors; the final sentences in the discussions of each topic, however, almost always end with question marks.

THIRD WAVE CAUSES: CONTINUING, WEAKENING, CHANGING?

Will the democratization trend of the 1970s and 1980s continue through the 1990s? Five general causes of the third wave were discussed in chapter 2. Two of these—the legitimacy problem of authoritarian regimes and economic development—will be discussed below in connection with potential obstacles to further democratization. This section focuses on the other three factors identified as playing a significant role in the third wave.

One was the spread of Christianity and more specifically the major changes in the doctrine, appeal, and social and political commitment of the Catholic Church that occurred in the 1960s and 1970s. The expansion of Christianity had its most noticeable impact in Korea. Are there other areas where Christianity is expanding and where, consequently, democratization may become more likely? The most obvious is Africa. The number of Christians in Africa was estimated at 236 million in 1985 and was projected to reach 400 million early in the twenty-first century. By 1990 sub-Saharan Africa was the only region of the world where substantial numbers of Catholics and Protestants lived under authoritarian regimes in a large number of countries. In 1989 and 1990 Christian leaders were actively opposing repression in Kenya and other African countries.[1] As the numbers of Christians multiply, presumable the activity of church leaders in support of democracy will not decline and their political power will increase. In 1989 Christianity was also reported to be "stirring in China, particularly among young people," although the numbers were still very small. In Singapore in 1989 perhaps 5 percent of the population was Christian, but the government was increasingly concerned about the spread of Christianity and involved in struggles over its repressive measures with the Catholic archbishop of Singapore and the executive secretary of the Catholic Archdiocesan Justice and Peace Commission.[2] The seeming end of the proscription and harassment of religion in the Soviet Union could conceivably lead to the spread of religious membership and activity, with implications for the future of democracy in that country.

By 1990 the Catholic impetus to democratization had largely exhausted itself. Most Catholic countries had democratized or, as in the case of Mexico, liberalized. The ability of Catholicism to promote further expansion of democracy without expanding itself was limited to Paraguay, Cuba, Haiti, and a few African countries such as Senegal and the Ivory Coast. In addition, to what extent would the Catholic Church continue to be the potent force for democratization that it had been in the 1970s? Pope John Paul II consistently promoted theological conservatism. Were the attitudes of the Vatican concerning birth control, abortion, women priests, and other issues consistent with the promotion of democracy in the broader society and polity?

The role of other external agents of democratization also appeared to be changing. In April 1987 Turkey applied for full membership in the European Community. One incentive was the desire of Turkish leaders to reinforce modernizing and democratic tendencies in Turkey and to contain and isolate the forces in Turkey supporting Islamic fundamentalism. Within the EC, however, little enthusiasm and some hostility (from Greece) greeted the prospect of Turkish membership. In 1990 the liberation of Eastern Europe also raised the possibility of membership for Hungary, Czechoslovakia, and Poland. The Community thus faced two issues. First, should it give priority to expanding its membership or to "deepening" the existing community by moving toward further economic and political union? Second, if it did decide to expand its membership, should priority go to European Free Trade Association members, such as Austria, Norway, and Sweden, or to the Eastern European countries, or to Turkey? Presumably the Community would only be able to absorb a limited number of countries in a given period of time.

The answers to these questions would have implications for the stability of democracy in Turkey and in the Eastern European countries. In Turkey, the lack of movement on its application reportedly was beginning to stimulate an "Islamic backlash" in 1990.[3] Given Turkey's peripheral position, Muslim heritage, past military interventions, and dubious human rights record, Turkish democracy probably needed the EC anchor at least as much as did democracy in Spain, Portugal, and Greece in the 1970s. Failure to provide that anchor would make the future of Turkish democracy more uncertain. The prospect of Community membership could also reinforce the new democracies in East Central Europe. There were, however, no countries with authoritarian governments for whom that prospect would provide an incentive to democratize.

The withdrawal of Soviet power permitted democratization in Eastern Europe. If the Soviet Union ended or drastically curtailed its support for Castro's regime, movement toward democracy might occur in Cuba. Apart from that, there seemed little more the Soviet Union could do or was likely to do to promote democracy outside its borders. The key issue was what would happen within the Soviet Union itself. With the loosening of Soviet control, it seemed likely that democracy would be reestablished in the Baltic states. Movements toward democracy also existed in other republics. Most important, of course, was Russia itself. The inauguration and consolidation of democracy in the Russian Republic, if it occurred, would be the single most dramatic gain for democracy since the immediate post–World War II years. At the end of 1990, however, conservative forces were reasserting themselves in both Russia and the Soviet Union, emphasizing the need to reimpose order and discipline, and raising the possibility of a Soviet Thermidor.

During the 1970s and 1980s the United States was a major promoter of democratization. Whether the United States continues to play this role depends on its will, its capability, and its appeal. Before the mid-1970s the promotion of democracy had not always been a top priority goal of American foreign policy. It could again subside in importance. The end of the Cold War and of the ideological competition with the Soviet Union could remove one rationale for propping up anticommunist dictators, but it could also reduce the incentives for any substantial American involvement in the Third World. By the early 1980s American policymakers had absorbed the lesson that democracies were a better bulwark against communism than were narrow-based authoritarian regimes. If the threat of communism was reduced, so also was the need to promote democracy as the most robust alternative to it. In addition, both Carter and Reagan had approached foreign policy in moralistic terms, assigning human rights and democracy a central rhetorical role and, in considerable measure, a meaningful, real role among their foreign policy objectives. President Bush, in contrast, seemed considerably more pragmatic than moralistic in his approach compared to his two predecessors. In April 1990 Secretary of State James Baker declared that "Beyond containment lies democracy. The time of sweeping away the old dictators is passing fast; the time of building up the new democracies has arrived. That is why President Bush has defined our new mission to be the promotion and consolidation of democracy." Yet other goals often seemed to get higher priority. This appeared most evident in the administration's policy toward China in 1989 and 1990. After Tiananmen Square, former President Reagan declared in eloquent Wilsonian phrases that "You cannot massacre an idea. You cannot run tanks over hope."[4] President Bush sent his national security advisor to meet secretly with Chinese leaders.

American will to promote democracy thus might or might not be sustained. American ability to do so, on the other hand, seemed likely to be constrained. Rumors of American decline in the late 1980s were often exaggerated. In fact, however, the trade and budget deficits did impose new limits on the resources that the United States could use to exercise influence in foreign countries. In addition, just as the future ability of the Catholic Church to promote democracy in authoritarian countries was greatly reduced because most Catholic countries were no longer authoritarian, so also the ability of the United States to promote democracy had in some measure run its course because it had been exercised where it could most easily be exercised. The countries in Latin America, the Caribbean, Europe, and East Asia, which were most susceptible to American influence, had, with a few exceptions, become democratic. In 1990 the one major country where the United States could still exercise significant influence on behalf of democratization was Mexico.

The undemocratic countries in Africa, the Middle East, and mainland Asia were less susceptible to American influence. In 1988, for instance, the demonstrators for democracy in Burma hailed the United States for its denunciations of government repression, "seized on every scrap of hope that the United States would intervene," and at one point were swept with enthusiasm by a report that the U.S. Navy was sailing into Burmese waters.[5] On occasion, in support of democracy, the United States Navy has sailed into the waters of the Dominican Republic, Haiti, Panama, and Grenada. It might conceivably at some point sail into Cuban waters on that mission. Burma, however, was at the utmost outer reaches of American interests and American power. There the United States only filed diplomatic protests and withheld economic aid. The ability of the United States to promote democracy among Africans and Chinese was similarly limited.

Apart from Central America and the Caribbean, the major area of the Third World where the United States has continued to have vitally important interests is the Persian Gulf. The Gulf War and the dispatch of over 500,000 American troops to that region stimulated demands for movement toward democracy in Kuwait and Saudi Arabia and delegitimated Saddam Hussein's regime in Iraq. Large American military deployments in the Gulf, if sustained over time, would be a powerful external impetus toward liberalization if not democratization, and such deployments could, in all probability, only be sustained over time if movement toward democracy occurred.

The importance of the United States to democratization involved not only the conscious and direct exercise of American power. In the 1980s movements for democracy throughout the world were inspired by and borrowed from the American example. In Rangoon supporters of democracy carried the American flag; in Johannesburg they reprinted *The Federalist*; in Prague they sang "We Shall Overcome"; in Warsaw they read Lincoln and quoted Jefferson; in Beijing they erected the Goddess of Democracy; in Moscow John Sununu advised Mikhail Gorbachev on how to organize a presidency.* The

---

*The identification of the United States with democracy was dramatically evident in the September 1988 demonstrations in Rangoon against the military regime:

Half a million euphoric Burmese paraded through the streets of Rangoon, passing deserted government offices. The center of the demonstrations was the American Embassy. When the Ambassador, Burton Levin, rode in his official car, with American flags flying on the fenders, the crowds would applaud; as the Burmese knew, the United States had been the first nation to condemn the brutal killings under Sein Lwin in early August. Every day, speeches were made in front of the Embassy. The theme of the speeches was democracy, and America became the symbol of everything the Burmese wanted and lacked. Some demonstrators carried the American flag, and at one point a group of

American democratic model was appealing in part because it stood for freedom, but also, one has to assume, in part because it conveyed an image of strength and success. As in the second wave after World War II people wanted to imitate the winning model.

What would happen, however, if the American model no longer embodied strength and success, no longer seemed to be the winning model? At the end of the 1980s many argued that "American decline" was the true reality. Others argued to the contrary. Virtually no one, however, denied that the United States faced major problems: crime, drugs, trade deficits, budget deficits, low savings and investment, decreasing productivity growth, inferior public education, decaying inner cities. People about the world could come to see the United States as a declining power, characterized by political stagnation, economic inefficiency, and social chaos. If this happened, the perceived failures of the United States would inevitably be seen as the failures of democracy. The worldwide appeal of democracy would be significantly diminished.

The impact of snowballing on democratization was clearly evident in 1990 in Bulgaria, Romania, Yugoslavia, Mongolia, Nepal, and Albania. It also affected movements toward liberalization in some Arab and African countries. In 1990, for instance, it was reported that the "upheaval in Eastern Europe" had "fueled demands for change in the Arab world" and prompted leaders in Egypt, Jordan, Tunisia, and Algeria to open up more political space for the expression of discontent. As a result of what happened in Eastern Europe, one Egyptian journalist observed, "There is no escaping from democracy now. All these Arab regimes have no choice but to earn

---

students came to the front door of the Embassy and recited the Gettysburg Address word for word in English.

Stan Sesser, "A Rich Country Gone Wrong," *New Yorker*, October 9, 1989, pp. 80–81.

the trust of their people and to become the subject of popular choice."[6]

The Eastern European example had its principal effect on the leaders of other authoritarian regimes, not on the people they ruled. The Marxist-Leninist rulers of South Yemen, for instance, were reported to have "watched with trepidation the downfall of the East European regimes, fearing the same fate," and hence moved swiftly to consummate their merger with North Yemen in order to avoid that fate. President Mobutu reacted with shocked horror at the TV pictures of the bloody corpse of his friend, Nicolae Ceausescu. A few months later, commenting that "You know what's happening across the world," he announced that he would allow two parties besides his own to compete in elections in 1993. In Tanzania, Julius Nyerere observed, "If changes take place in Eastern Europe then other countries with one-party systems and which profess socialism will also be affected." Tanzania could learn a "lesson or two" from Eastern Europe. In Nepal in April 1990 the government announced that King Birendra was lifting the ban on political parties as a result of "the international situation" and "the rising expectations of the people."[7]

In the absence of favorable conditions in the affected country, however, snowballing alone is a weak cause of democratization. The democratization of countries A and B is no reason, in and of itself, for democratization in country C, unless the conditions that favored it in countries A and B also exist in country C. In the 1980s the legitimacy of democracy as a system of government came to be accepted throughout the world. The economic and social conditions favorable to the existence of democracy, however, did not exist throughout the world. For any particular country, the "worldwide democratic revolution" could produce an external environment conducive to democratization but it could not produce the conditions within that country necessary for democratization.

In Eastern Europe the major obstacle to democratization

had been Soviet control. Once that was removed the movement to democracy developed easily. It seems unlikely that the only major obstacle to democratization in the Middle East, Africa, and Asia was the absence of the Eastern European example of democratization. Nor is it clear why, if rulers could choose authoritarianism before December 1989, they could not also, if they wished, choose it after December 1989. The snowballing effect would be real only to the extent it was real in their minds and led them to believe in the desirability and/or necessity of democratization. The Eastern European events of 1989 undoubtedly encouraged democratic opposition groups and frightened authoritarian leaders elsewhere. Given the previous weakness of the former and the long-term repression by the latter, however, some skepticism seems warranted over how much meaningful progress toward democracy the Eastern European impetus would actually produce in most of the remaining authoritarian countries.

By 1990 many of the original causes of the third wave had been significantly weakened or exhausted. Neither the White House, the Kremlin, the Vatican, nor the European Community were in a strong position to promote democracy in the countries where it did not exist in Asia, Africa, and the Middle East. It was not impossible, however, that new forces favoring democratization could emerge. In 1985 who thought that within five years Mikhail Gorbachev would be facilitating democratization in Eastern Europe? In the 1990s conceivably the IMF and the World Bank could become much more forceful than they had been in demanding political democratization as well as economic liberalization as a precondition for economic assistance. Conceivably France might become more active in promoting democracy among its former African colonies, where its influence remains substantial. Conceivably the Orthodox church could emerge as a powerful influence for democracy in the Balkans and the Soviet Union. Conceivably a Gorbachev-like supporter of a Chinese version of *glasnost* could come to power in Beijing. Conceivably a new Jeffersonian Nasser could spread a democratic version of Pan-Arabism in the Middle East. Conceivably even Japan could use its growing economic clout to encourage human rights and democracy in the poor countries to which it was making loans and grants. In 1990, none of these possibilities seemed very likely, but after the events of 1989 it would be rash to rule anything out.

A THIRD REVERSE WAVE?

By 1990 at least two third wave democracies had reverted to authoritarian rule. As suggested in chapter 5, the problems of consolidation could lead to further reversions in countries where the conditions for sustaining democracy were weak. The first and second democratic waves, however, were followed by major reverse waves that went beyond consolidation problems and during which most regime changes throughout the world were from democracy to authoritarianism. If the third wave of democratization slowed down or came to a halt, what factors might produce and characterize a third reverse wave? The experience of the first and second reverse waves may be relevant. A thorough exploration of these regime changes is beyond the scope of this study. The following generalizations, however, appear to be valid with respect to the first two reverse waves.

First, the causes of shifts from democratic to authoritarian political systems were at least as varied as and in part overlap with the causes of shifts from authoritarianism to democracy. Among the factors contributing to the first and second reverse wave transitions were

(1) the weakness of democratic values among key elite groups and the general public;

(2) economic crisis or collapse that intensified social conflict and enhanced the popularity of remedies that could only be imposed by authoritarian governments;

(3) social and political polarization often produced by leftist

governments attempting to introduce or appearing to introduce too many major socioeconomic reforms too quickly;

(4) the determination of conservative middle- and upper-class groups to exclude populist and leftist movements and lower-class groups from political power;

(5) the breakdown of law and order resulting from terrorism or insurgency;

(6) intervention or conquest by a nondemocratic foreign government;

(7) snowballing in the form of the demonstration effects of the collapse or overthrow of democratic systems in other countries.

Second, apart from those produced by foreign actors, transitions from democracy to authoritarianism were almost always produced by those in power or close to power in the democratic system. With only one or two possible exceptions, democratic systems have not been ended by popular vote or by popular revolt. In Germany and Italy in the first reverse wave, antidemocratic movements with considerable popular backing came to power and established fascist dictatorships. Nazi conquests then ended democracy in seven other European countries. In Spain in the first reverse wave and in Lebanon in the second, democracy ended in civil war.

The overwhelming majority of transitions from democracy, however, took the form of either military coups in which military officers (usually the top leadership of the armed services) ousted democratically elected leaders and installed some form of military dictatorship, or executive coups in which democratically chosen chief executives effectively ended democracy by concentrating power in themselves, usually by declaring a state of emergency or martial law. In the first reverse wave, military coups ended democratic systems in the new countries of Eastern Europe and in Greece, Portugal, Argentina, and Japan. In the second reverse wave, military coups ended democracy in many Latin American countries, Indonesia, Pakistan, Greece, Nigeria, and Turkey. Executive coups occurred in the second reverse wave in Korea, India, and the Philippines. In Uruguay civilian and military leadership cooperated to end democracy through a mixed executive-military coup.

Third, in many cases in both the first and second reverse waves, democratic systems were replaced by historically new forms of authoritarian rule. Fascism was distinguished from earlier forms of authoritarianism by its mass base, ideology, party organization, and efforts to penetrate and control most of society. Bureaucratic-authoritarianism differed from the earlier forms of military rule in Latin America by its institutional character, its assumption of indefinite duration, and its economic policies. Italy and Germany in the 1920s and 1930s and Brazil and Argentina in the 1960s and 1970s were the lead countries in introducing these new forms of nondemocratic rule and furnished the examples that antidemocratic groups in other countries attempted to emulate. Both these new forms of authoritarianism were in effect responses to social and economic development: the expansion of social mobilization and political participation in Europe and the exhaustion of the populist-based import substitution phase of economic development in Latin America.

The causes and forms of the first two reverse waves cannot generate predictions concerning the causes and forms of a possible third reverse wave. Prior experiences do suggest, however, some potential causes of a third reverse wave.

(1) Systemic failures of democratic regimes to operate effectively could undermine their legitimacy. In the late twentieth century, the major nondemocratic ideological sources of legitimacy, most notably Marxism-Leninism, became discredited. The general acceptance of democratic norms meant that democratic governments were even less dependent on performance legitimacy than they had been in the past. Yet sustained inability to provide welfare, prosperity, equity, justice, domestic order, or external security could over time undermine the legitimacy of even democratic governments. As the memories of authoritarian failures fade, irritation with democratic failures is likely to increase.

obvious causes

(2) More specifically, a general international economic collapse on the 1929–30 model could undermine the legitimacy of democracy in many countries. Most democracies did survive the Great Depression of the 1930s. Yet some succumbed and presumably some would be likely to succumb in response to a comparable economic disaster in the future.

(3) A shift to authoritarianism by any democratic or democratizing great power could trigger similar snowballing actions in other countries. A reversal of course in the direction of authoritarianism in Russia or the Soviet Union would have unsettling effects on democratization in other Soviet republics, Bulgaria, Romania, Yugoslavia, and Mongolia, and possibly in Poland, Hungary, and Czechoslovakia. It could send a message to would-be despots elsewhere: "You too can go back into business." The establishment of an authoritarian regime in India could have a significant demonstration effect on other Third World countries.

(4) Even if a major country did not revert to authoritarianism, the shift to dictatorship by several newly democratic countries because they lacked many of the usual preconditions for democracy could possibly undermine democracy in other countries where those preconditions were strong. This would be reverse snowballing.

(5) If a nondemocratic state greatly developed its power and began to expand beyond its borders, this too could stimulate authoritarian movements in other countries. This stimulus would be particularly strong if the expanding authoritarian state militarily defeated one or more democratic countries in the process of expanding. In the past, all major powers that have developed economically have also tended to expand territorially. If China retains its authoritarian system of government, develops economically in the coming decades, and expands its influence and control in East Asia, democratic regimes in East Asia could be significantly weakened.

(6) As in the 1920s and the 1960s, various forms of authoritarianism could again emerge that seem appropriate to the needs of the times. Several possibilities exist:

(a) Authoritarian nationalism could become a familiar phenomenon in Third World countries and also in Eastern Europe. Were the revolutions of 1989–90 in Eastern Europe primarily anticommunist democratic movements or anti-Soviet nationalist movements? If the latter, authoritarian nationalist regimes might return to some Eastern European countries.

(b) Religious fundamentalism has been most dramatically prevalent in Iran, but both Shi'ite and Sunni fundamentalist movements could come to power in other countries. Jewish, Hindu, and Christian fundamentalist movements have also been strong. Almost all fundamentalist movements are antidemocratic in that they would restrict political participation to those who adhere to a particular religious creed.

(c) Oligarchic authoritarianism could develop in both wealthy and poorer countries as a response to the leveling tendencies of democracy. How extreme can socioeconomic polarization get before democracy becomes impossible?

(d) Populist dictatorships could emerge in the future as they have in the past as responses to democracy's protection of property rights and other forms of privilege. In those countries where land tenancy is still an issue, the inability of democracies to put through land reforms could stimulate a resort to authoritarianism.

(e) Communal dictatorships could emerge in democracies with two or more distinct ethnic, racial, or religious groups participating in their politics. As in Northern Ireland, South Africa, Sri Lanka, and elsewhere, one group may try to establish its control of the entire society.

All of these forms of authoritarianism have existed in the past. It is not beyond the wit of humans to devise new ones in the future. One possibility might be a technocratic electronic dictatorship in which authoritarian rule was legitimated by and made possible by the ability to manipulate information, the media, and sophisticated means of communication. None of these old or new forms of authoritarianism is highly probable; it is also hard to say that any one of them is totally impossible.

FURTHER DEMOCRATIZATION: OBSTACLES AND OPPORTUNITIES

In 1990 approximately two-thirds of the countries in the world did not have democratic regimes. These countries fell largely into four geo-cultural categories:

(1) homegrown Marxist-Leninist regimes, including the Soviet Union, where liberalization occurred in the 1980s and democratic movements existed in many republics, but conservative forces remained strong;

(2) sub-Saharan African countries, which, with a few exceptions, remained personal dictatorships, military regimes, one-party systems, or some combination of these three;

(3) Islamic countries, stretching from Morocco to Indonesia, which except for Turkey and, problematically, Pakistan, had nondemocratic regimes (although in 1990 a few appeared to be liberalizing); and

(4) East Asian countries, from Burma through Southeast Asia to China and North Korea, which included communist systems, military regimes, personal dictatorships, and two semidemocracies (Thailand and Malaysia).

The obstacles to and forces for democratization in these countries can be divided into three broad categories: political, cultural, and economic.

Politics

One potentially significant political obstacle to more democratizations was the virtual absence of experience with democracy of most countries that remained authoritarian in the 1990s. Twenty-three of the twenty-nine countries that democratized between 1974 and 1990 had had some prior democratic experience. Only a small number of countries that were nondemocratic in 1990 could claim such experience. These included a few third wave backsliders (Sudan, Nigeria, Suriname, and, possibly, Pakistan), four second wave backsliders that had not redemocratized in the third wave (Lebanon, Sri Lanka, Burma, Fiji), and three first wave democratizers that had been prevented by Soviet occupation from redemocratizing at the end of World War II (Estonia, Latvia, Lithuania). Virtually all the ninety or more other nondemocratic countries in 1990 lacked significant experience with democratic rule. This obviously is not a decisive impediment to democratization or no countries would be democratic. Apart from former colonies, however, almost all the countries that de-

mocratized after 1940 had some prior experience with democracy. Will countries lacking that experience be able to democratize in the future?

One obstacle to democratization was likely to disappear in
several countries in the 1990s. As pointed out in chapter 3,
leaders who create authoritarian regimes or who remain long
in power in such regimes usually become staunch standpatters opposing democratization. Some form of leadership
change within the authoritarian system has to precede movement toward democracy. Human mortality is likely to ensure
such changes in the 1990s in some authoritarian regimes. In
1990 the long-term, controlling leaders in China, Ivory Coast,
and Malawi were in their eighties. Those in Burma, Indonesia, North Korea, Lesotho, and Vietnam were in their seven-
ties, and the long-term leaders of Cuba, Morocco, Singapore,
Somalia, Syria, Tanzania, Zaire, and Zambia were sixty or
older. The death or departure from office of these leaders
would remove one obstacle to democratization in their countries but would not make it necessary.

Between 1974 and 1990 democratization occurred in personal dictatorships, military regimes, and one-party systems.
Full-scale democratization had not occurred, however, in
communist one-party states that were the products of domestic revolution. Liberalization was under way in the Soviet
Union, and quite possibly this would lead to full-scale democratization in Russia. In Yugoslavia, movements toward
democracy were under way in Slovenia and Croatia. The Yu-
goslav communist revolution, however, had been largely a
Serbian revolution and the prospects for democracy in Serbia
were at best dubious. In Cambodia an extraordinarily brutal
revolutionary communist regime had been replaced by a less
brutal communist regime imposed by outside force. In 1990
Albania appeared to be opening up; but in China, Vietnam,
Laos, Cuba, and Ethiopia, Marxist-Leninist regimes produced
by revolutions seemed determined to remain Marxist-Leninist
regimes. The revolutions in these countries had been national

as well as communist, and hence communism and national identity were closely linked as they obviously had not been in Soviet-occupied Eastern Europe. Were the obstacles to liberalization in these countries the origins and nature of the regime, the long duration (in some cases) of their leaders in power, or their poverty and economic backwardness? One serious impediment to democratization was the absence or weakness of real commitment to democratic values among political leaders in Asia, Africa, and the Middle East. Political leaders out of office have good reason to advocate democracy. The test of their democratic commitment comes when they are in office. In Latin America democratic regimes were normally overthrown by military coups d'etat. This also, of course, happened in Asia and the Middle East. In those regions, however, elected leaders themselves were also responsible for ending democracy: Syngman Rhee and Park Chung Hee in Korea; Adnan Menderes in Turkey; Ferdinand Marcos in the Philippines; Lee Kwan Yew in Singapore; Indira Gandhi in India; Sukarno in Indonesia. These leaders won power through the electoral system and then used their power to undermine that system. They had little commitment to democratic values and practices.

More generally, even when Asian, African, and Middle Eastern leaders did more or less abide by the rules of democracy, they often seemed to do so grudgingly. Many European, North American, and Latin American political leaders in the last half of the twentieth century were ardent and articulate advocates as well as practitioners of democracy when they were in office. Asian and African countries, in contrast, did not spawn many heads of government who were also apostles of democracy. To cite for comparison eight post–World War II Latin American heads of government from eight different countries, who were the Asian, Arab, or African equivalents of Rómulo Betancourt, Alberto Lleras Camargo, José Figueres, Eduardo Frei, Fernando Belaúnde Terry, Juan Bosch, José Napoleon Duarte, and Raúl Alfonsín? Jawaharlal Nehru and Corazon Aquino were, and there may have been others, but they were few in number. No Arab leader comes to mind, and it is hard to identify any Islamic leader who made a reputation as an advocate and supporter of democracy while in office. Why is this? The question leads inevitably to culture and economics.

Culture

The argument is made that the world's great historic cultural traditions vary significantly in the extent to which their attitudes, values, beliefs, and related behavior patterns are conducive to the development of democracy. A profoundly antidemocratic culture would impede the spread of democratic norms in the society, deny legitimacy to democratic institutions, and thus greatly complicate if not prevent the emergence and effective functioning of those institutions. The cultural thesis comes in two forms. The restrictive version states that only Western culture provides a suitable base for the development of democratic institutions and democracy is, consequently, largely inappropriate for non-Western societies. In the early years of the third wave, this argument was explicitly set forth by George Kennan. Democracy, he said, was a form of government "which evolved in the eighteenth and nineteenth centuries in northwestern Europe, primarily among those countries that border on the English Channel and the North Sea (but with a certain extension into Central Europe), and which was then carried into other parts of the world, including North America, where peoples from that northwestern European area appeared as original settlers, or as colonialists, and had laid down the prevailing patterns of civil government." Democracy consequently has "a relatively narrow base both in time and in space; and the evidence has yet to be produced that it is the natural form of rule for peoples outside those narrow perimeters." Hence there is "no reason to suppose that the attempt to develop and employ democratic institutions would be the best course for many of these peoples."[8] Democracy, in short, was appropriate only for northwestern and perhaps central European countries and their settler colony offshoots.

The evidence supporting the Western culture thesis is impressive, if not totally persuasive:

(1) Modern democracy originated in the West.

(2) Since the early nineteenth century, most democratic countries have been Western countries.

(3) Outside the North Atlantic area, democracy has been most prevalent in former British colonies, countries with heavy American influence, and, more recently, former Iberian colonies in Latin America.

(4) The twenty-nine democratic countries at the depth of the second reverse wave in 1973 included twenty West European, European-settler, and Latin American countries, eight former British colonies, and Japan.

(5) The fifty-eight democratic countries in 1990 included thirty-seven West European, European-settler, and Latin American countries, six East European countries, nine former British, American, and Australian colonies, and six other countries (Japan, Turkey, South Korea, Mongolia, Namibia, and Senegal). Twenty-six of thirty countries that became democratic in the third wave were either Western countries or countries where there had been substantial Western influence.

The Western culture thesis has immediate implications for democratization in the Balkans and the Soviet Union. Historically these areas were part of the Czarist and Ottoman empires; their prevailing religions were Orthodoxy and Islam, not Western Christianity. These areas were not significantly penetrated by Western culture: they did not have the Western experiences with feudalism, the Renaissance, the Reformation, the Enlightenment, the French Revolution, and liberalism. As William Wallace has suggested, the end of the Cold War and the disappearance of the iron curtain may have shifted the critical political dividing line eastward to the boundary of Western Christendom in 1500. Beginning in the north this line runs south roughly along the border between

Finland and Russia, the eastern borders of the Baltic republics, through Byelorussia and the Ukraine separating Western Catholic Ukraine from the Eastern Orthodox Ukraine, south and then west in Romania, cutting off Transylvania from the rest of the country, and then into Yugoslavia roughly along the line separating Slovenia and Croatia from the other republics.[9] This line now may separate those areas where democracy will take root from those where it will not.

A less restrictive version of the cultural obstacle argument is not that only one culture is peculiarly favorable to democracy but that one or more cultures are peculiarly hostile to it. The two cultures most often cited are Confucianism and Islam. Three questions are relevant to determining whether these cultures pose obstacles to democratization in the late twentieth century. First, to what extent are traditional Confucian and Islamic values and beliefs hostile to democracy? Second, if they are, to what extent have these cultures in fact hampered progress toward democracy? Third, if they have done this, to what extent are they likely to continue to do so in the future?

Confucianism. Almost no scholarly disagreement exists on the proposition that traditional Confucianism was either undemocratic or antidemocratic. The only moderating element was the extent to which in the classic Chinese polity the examination system opened careers to the talented without regard to social background. Even if this was the case, however, a merit system of promotion does not make a democracy. No one would describe a modern army as democratic because officers were promoted on the basis of their abilities. Classic Chinese Confucianism and its derivatives in Korea, Vietnam, Singapore, Taiwan, and, in diluted fashion, Japan emphasized the group over the individual, authority over liberty, and responsibilities over rights. Confucian societies lacked a tradition of rights against the state; to the extent that individual rights did exist, they were created by the state. Harmony and cooperation were preferred over disagreement and

competition. The maintenance of order and respect for hierarchy were central values. The conflict of ideas, groups, and
parties was viewed as dangerous and illegitimate. Most important, Confucianism merged society and the state and provided no legitimacy for autonomous social institutions to balance the state at the national level. In "traditional China there
was no conception of the separation of the sacred from the
profane, the spiritual from the secular. Political legitimacy in
Confucian China rested on the Mandate of Heaven, which
defined politics in terms of morality." There were no legitimate grounds for limiting power because power and morality
are identical. "To think that power may be corrupt and requires institutional check and balance is a contradiction in
terms."[10]

In practice Confucian or Confucian-influenced societies
have been inhospitable to democracy. In East Asia only two
countries, Japan and the Philippines, had sustained experience with democratic government prior to 1990. In both
cases, democracy was the product of an American presence.
The Philippines, moreover, is overwhelmingly a Catholic country and Confucianism is virtually absent. In Japan Confucian
values were reinterpreted and merged with its autochthonous
cultural tradition.

Mainland China has had no experience with democratic
government, and democracy of the Western variety has been
supported over the years only by relatively small groups of
radical dissidents. "Mainstream" democratic critics have not
broken with the key elements of the Confucian tradition.[11]
The modernizers of China have been the Confucian Lenin-
ists, in Lucian Pye's phrase, of the Nationalist and Communist parties. In the late 1980s when rapid economic growth in
China produced a new series of demands for political reform
and democracy on the part of students, intellectuals, and urban middle-class groups, Communist leadership responded
in two ways. First, it articulated a theory of "new authoritarianism," based on the experience of Taiwan, Singapore, and

Korea and justified by the argument that for a country at China's stage of economic development authoritarianism was necessary to achieve balanced economic growth and to contain the unsettling consequences of development. Second, the leadership violently suppressed the democratic movement in Beijing and elsewhere in the summer of 1989.

In China economics reinforced culture in opposition to democracy. In Singapore, Taiwan, and Korea spectacular economic growth created the economic basis for democracy by the late 1980s. In these countries economics clashed with culture in shaping political development. In 1990, Singapore was the only non-oil-exporting "high-income" country (as defined by the World Bank) that did not have a democratic political system, and Singapore's leader was an articulate exponent of Confucian values as opposed to those of Western democracy. Americans, Lee Kwan Yew argued, believe in "multi-party, dissent, discussion, robust discourse, conflict— and out of conflict comes enlightenment." In fact, however, the "marketplace of ideas, instead of producing harmonious enlightenment, has, from time to time, led to riots and bloodshed." Political competition is "not the way the Japanese, or the Chinese or the Asian cultures do it. That leads to contentiousness and confusion." Adversarial politics is particularly out of place in a multiracial society such as Singapore, and in Singapore, Lee stated, "no one has the right to subvert me." In the 1980s Lee made the teaching and promulgation of Confucian values a high priority for his city-state.[12] Vigorous measures were also taken to limit and suppress dissent and to prevent the circulation of media critical of the government and its policies. Singapore was thus an authoritarian Confucian anomaly among the wealthy countries of the world. Would it remain so after Lee, who had created the state, disappeared from the political scene?

In the late 1980s both Taiwan and Korea moved in a democratic direction. Historically Taiwan had always been a peripheral part of China. It was occupied by the Japanese for fifty years, and its inhabitants rebelled in 1947 against the imposition of Chinese control. The Nationalist government arrived in 1949, humiliated by its defeat by the Communists. This defeat made it impossible "for most Nationalist leaders to uphold the posture of arrogance associated with traditional Confucian notions of authority." Rapid economic and social development further weakened the influence of traditional Confucianism. The emergence of a substantial entrepreneurial class, composed initially largely of native Taiwanese, created in very un-Confucian fashion a source of power and wealth independent of the state dominated initially by mainlanders. This produced in Taiwan a "fundamental change in Chinese political culture, which has not occurred in China itself or in Korea or Vietnam—and never really existed in Japan."[13] On Taiwan spectacular economic development thus overwhelmed a relatively weak Confucian legacy, and in the late 1980s Chiang Ching-kuo and Lee Teng-hui responded to the pressures produced by economic and social change and gradually moved to open up politics in their society.

In Korea, the classical culture included elements of mobility and egalitarianism. Yet it also contained Confucian components uncongenial to democracy, including a tradition of authoritarianism and strong-man rule. As one Korean scholar put it, "people did not think of themselves as citizens with rights to exercise and responsibilities to perform, but they tended to look up to the top for direction and for favors in order to survive." In the Confucian tradition, toleration for dissent had little place, and unorthodoxy was disloyalty. "In the Korean religious tradition," a Korean religious leader observed, "negotiation and compromise are not recognized as a social norm, but as selling out. Confucian scholars never used the word compromise. They had to maintain their purity of conscience, and that cultural trait is still here. How then can we form a democracy where compromise is a way of life?"[14] In the late 1980s, urbanization, education, the development of a substantial middle class, and the impressive spread of

Christianity all weakened Confucianism as an obstacle to democracy in Korea. Yet it remained unclear whether the struggle between the old culture and the new prosperity had been definitively resolved in favor of the latter.

The interaction of economic progress and Asian culture appeared to generate a distinct East Asian variety of democratic institutions. As of 1990, in no East Asian country except the Philippines (which is, in many respects, more Latin American than East Asian) had a turnover occurred from a popularly elected government of one party to a popularly elected government of a different party. The prototype was Japan, unquestionably a democracy, but a democracy that had not truly met the first-turnover test not to mention the second-turnover test. The Japanese model of dominant-party democracy tended, as Pye has pointed out, to spread elsewhere in East Asia. In 1990 two of the three opposition parties in Korea merged with the government party to form a political bloc that would effectively exclude the remaining opposition party, led by Kim Dae Jung and based on the Cholla region, from ever achieving national power. Korean President Roh Tae Woo justified this merger by the need to "achieve political stability" and to counter the "explosion of long-suppressed strife between different classes, generations, and regions." We must end, he said, "confrontations and splits over partisan interests."[15] In the late 1980s, democratic development in Taiwan seemed to be moving toward an electoral system in which the KMT was likely to remain the dominant party, with the Democratic Progressive party, formed in 1986, confined to a permanent opposition role. In Malaysia, the coalition of the three leading parties from the Malay, Chinese, and Indian communities first in the Alliance Party and then in the National Front similarly controlled power in unbroken fashion against all competitors from the 1950s through the 1980s. In the mid-1980s, Lee Kwan Yew's deputy and successor endorsed a similar type of party system for Singapore:

I think a stable system is one where there is a mainstream political party representing a broad range of the population. Then you can have a few other parties on the periphery, very serious-minded parties. They are unable to have wider views but they nevertheless represent sectional interests. And the mainstream is returned all the time. I think that's good. And I would not apologize if we ended up in that situation in Singapore.[16]

A first criterion for democracy is equitable and open competition for votes between political parties with an absence or minimal levels of government harassment or restriction of opposition groups. Japan clearly met this test for decades with freedom of speech, press, and assembly, and reasonably equitable conditions of electoral competition. In the other Asian dominant-party systems, for many years the playing field was tilted, often heavily, in favor of the government. At the end of the 1980s, however, conditions were becoming more equal in some countries. In 1989 in Korea the government party was unable to win control of the legislature. Presumably this failure was a major factor in its subsequent merger with two of its opponents. In Taiwan restrictions on the opposition were gradually lifted. It is thus conceivable that other East Asian countries could join Japan in having a level playing field for a game that the government always won. In 1990 the East Asian dominant-party systems covered a continuum between democracy and authoritarianism, with Japan at one extreme, Indonesia at the other, and Korea, Taiwan, Malaysia, and Singapore in between, more or less in that order.

Such a system thus could meet the formal requisites of democracy, but it would differ significantly from the democratic systems prevalent in the West. In the latter, it is assumed that political parties and coalitions not only freely and equally compete for power but also that they are likely to alternate in power. In some Western societies, such as Sweden, of course, one party has remained in power through many elections.

That, however, has been the exception. The East Asian dominant-party systems that may be emerging seem to involve competition for power but not alternation in power, and participation in elections for all, but participation in office only for those in the "mainstream" party. It is democracy without turnover. The central problem in such a system is drawing the boundaries between "the domain of the dominant party and the degree of tolerance of an opposition."[17] This type of political system represents an adaptation of Western democratic practices to serve Asian or Confucian political values. Democratic institutions work not to promote Western values of competition and change but Confucian values of consensus and stability.

Western democratic systems, as has been pointed out, are less dependent on performance legitimacy than authoritarian systems because performance failure is blamed on the incumbents rather than the system and the ouster and replacement of the incumbents lead to the renewal of the system. The East Asian societies that adopted or appear to be adopting the dominant-party model of democracy had unequaled records of economic success from the 1960s to the 1980s. What happens, however, if and when eight percent GNP growth rates disappear; unemployment, inflation, and other forms of economic distress escalate; social and economic conflicts intensify? In a Western democracy the response would be to turn the incumbents out. In a dominant-party democracy, however, that would mean a revolutionary change in a political system based on the assumption one party would always be in power and other parties always out. If the structure of political competition does not allow that to happen, unhappiness at the performance failure of the government could well lead to demonstrations, protests, riots, and efforts to mobilize popular support to overthrow the government. The government then would be tempted to respond by suppressing dissent and imposing authoritarian controls. The question thus is: To what extent does the East Asian dominant-party combination of Western procedures and Confucian values presuppose sustained substantial economic growth? Can this system last during prolonged economic downturn or stagnation?

Islam. "Confucian democracy" is clearly a contradiction in terms. It is unclear whether "Islamic democracy" is. Egalitarianism and voluntarism are central themes in Islam. The "high culture form of Islam," Ernest Gellner has argued, is "endowed with a number of features—unitarianism, a rule-ethic, individualism, scripturalism, puritanism, an egalitarian aversion to meditation and hierarchy, a fairly small load of magic—that are congruent, presumably, with requirements of modernity or modernization." [18] They are also generally congruent with the requirements of democracy. Islam, however, also rejects any distinction between the religious community and the political community. Hence there is no equipoise between Caesar and God, and political participation is linked to religious affiliation. Fundamentalist Islam demands that in a Muslim country the political rulers should be practicing Muslims, *shari'a* should be the basic law, and *ulama* should have a "decisive vote in articulating, or at least reviewing and ratifying, all governmental policy." To the extent that governmental legitimacy and policy flow from religious doctrine and religious expertise, Islamic concepts of politics differ from and contradict the premises of democratic politics.

Islamic doctrine thus contains elements that may be both congenial and uncongenial to democracy. In practice, with one exception, no Islamic country has sustained a fully democratic political system for any length of time. The exception is Turkey, where Mustafa Kemal Atatürk explicitly rejected Islamic concepts of society and politics and vigorously attempted to create a secular, modern, Western nation-state. Turkey's experience with democracy has not been an unmitigated success. Elsewhere in the Islamic world, Pakistan attempted democracy on three occasions, none of which lasted long. Turkey has had democracy interrupted by occasional military interventions; Pakistan has had bureaucratic and military rule interrupted by occasional elections. The only Arab country to sustain a form of democracy, albeit of the consociational variety, for a significant period of time was Lebanon. Its democracy, however, really amounted to consociational oligarchy, and 40–50 percent of its population was Christian. Once Muslims became a majority in Lebanon and began to assert themselves, Lebanese democracy collapsed. Between 1981 and 1990 only two of the thirty-seven countries in the world with Muslim majorities were ever rated "free" by Freedom House in its annual surveys: The Gambia for two years and the Turkish Republic of Northern Cyprus for four. Whatever the compatibility of Islam and democracy in theory, in practice they have not gone together.

Opposition movements to authoritarian regimes in southern and Eastern Europe, in Latin America, and in East Asia almost universally espoused Western democratic values and proclaimed their desire to introduce democratic processes into their societies. This does not mean that they invariably would have introduced democratic institutions if they had the opportunity to do so. At least, however, they articulated the rhetoric of democracy. In authoritarian Islamic societies, in contrast, in the 1980s movements explicitly campaigning for democratic politics were relatively weak, and the most powerful opposition tended to come from Islamic fundamentalists.

In the late 1980s domestic economic problems combined with the snowballing effects of democratization elsewhere led governments in several Islamic countries to relax their controls on opposition and to attempt to renew their legitimacy through elections. The principal initial beneficiaries of these openings were Islamic fundamentalist groups. In Algeria the Islamic Salvation Front swept the June 1990 local elections, the first free elections since the country became independent in 1962, gaining 65 percent of the popular vote and winning control of Algiers, thirty-two of forty-eight provinces, and 55 percent of 15,000 municipal posts. In the Jordanian elections in November 1989, Islamic fundamentalists won thirty-six of eighty seats in parliament. In Egypt many candidates associated with the Muslim Brotherhood were elected to parliament. In several countries Islamic fundamentalist groups reportedly were plotting insurrection against the existing regimes.[19] The electoral showings of the Islamic groups reflected in part the absence of other opposition parties, either because they had been suppressed by the government or because they boycotted the elections. Nonetheless, fundamentalism seemed to be gaining strength in Middle Eastern countries. Among the groups that appeared most sympathetic to fundamentalism were merchants and younger people. The strength of these tendencies induced secular heads of government in Tunisia, Turkey, and elsewhere to adopt policies advocated by the fundamentalists and to make gestures demonstrating their commitment to Islam.

Liberalization in Islamic countries thus enhanced the power of important social and political movements whose commitment to democracy was questionable. The position of fundamentalist parties in Islamic societies in 1990 resembled, in some respects, the position of communist parties in Western European countries in the 1940s and again in the 1970s. Comparable questions arose concerning them. Would the existing governments continue to open up their politics and hold elections in which Islamic groups could compete freely and equally? Would the Islamic groups gain majority support in those elections? If they did win the elections, would the military, which in many Islamic societies (e.g., Algeria, Turkey, Pakistan, and Indonesia) is strongly secular, allow them to form a government? If they did form a government would it pursue radical Islamic policies that would undermine democracy and alienate modern and Western-oriented elements in society?

The limits of cultural obstacles. Conceivably Islamic and Confucian cultures pose insuperable obstacles to democratic development. Several reasons exist, however, to question the severity of these obstacles.

First, similar cultural arguments have not held up in the past. As has been noted, at one point many scholars argued that Catholicism was an obstacle to democracy. Others, in the Weber tradition, argued that Catholic countries were unlikely to develop economically in the same manner as Protestant countries. Yet in the 1960s and 1970s Catholic countries became democratic and, on the average, had higher rates of economic growth than Protestant countries. Similarly, at one point Weber and others argued that countries with Confucian cultures would not engage in successful capitalist development. By the 1980s, however, a new generation of scholars saw Confucianism as a major cause of the spectacular economic growth of East Asian societies. In the longer run, will the thesis that Confucianism prevents democratic development be any more viable than the thesis that Confucianism prevents economic development? Arguments that particular cultures are permanent obstacles to development in one direction or another should be viewed with a certain skepticism.

Second, great historic cultural traditions, such as Islam and Confucianism, are highly complex bodies of ideas, beliefs, doctrines, assumptions, writings, and behavior patterns. Any major culture, including even Confucianism, has some elements that are compatible with democracy, just as both Protestantism and Catholicism have elements that are clearly undemocratic.[20] Confucian democracy may be a contradiction in terms, but democracy in a Confucian society need not be. The question is: What elements in Islam and Confucianism are favorable to democracy, and how and under what circumstances can these supersede the undemocratic elements in those cultural traditions?

Third, even if the culture of a country is at one point

an obstacle to democracy, cultures historically are dynamic rather than passive. The dominant beliefs and attitudes in a society change. While maintaining elements of continuity, the prevailing culture in a society may differ significantly from what it was one or two generations previously. In the 1950s Spanish culture was usually described as traditional, authoritarian, hierarchical, deeply religious, and oriented toward honor and status. By the 1970s and 1980s, these words had virtually no place in a description of Spanish attitudes and values. Cultures evolve, and as in Spain probably the most important cause of cultural change is economic development itself.

Economics

Few relationships between social, economic, and political phenomena are stronger than that between level of economic development and existence of democratic politics. As we have seen, shifts from authoritarianism to democracy between 1974 and 1990 were heavily concentrated in a "transition zone" at the upper-middle levels of economic development. The conclusion seems clear. Poverty is a principal and probably the principal obstacle to democratic development. The future of democracy depends on the future of economic development. Obstacles to economic development are obstacles to the expansion of democracy.

The third wave of democratization was propelled forward by the extraordinary global economic growth of the 1950s and 1960s. That era of growth came to an end with the oil price increases of 1973 and 1974. Between 1974 and 1990, democratization accelerated around the world but economic growth slowed down. The average annual rates of growth in per capita GNP for low- and middle-income countries between 1965 and 1989 were as follows:

1965–73	4.0 percent
1973–80	2.6 percent
1980–89	1.8 percent

Substantial differences in growth rates existed among regions. East Asian rates remained high throughout the 1970s and 1980s, and overall rates of growth in South Asia increased. On the other hand, growth rates in the Middle East, North Africa, Latin America, and the Caribbean declined sharply from the 1970s to the 1980s. Those in sub-Saharan Africa plummeted. Per capita GNP in Africa was stagnant during the late 1970s and declined at an annual rate of 2.2 percent during 1980s. The economic obstacles to democratization in Africa thus clearly increased during the 1980s. The prospects for the 1990s are not encouraging. Even if economic reforms, debt relief, and economic assistance materialize, the World Bank predicted an average annual rate of growth in per capita gross domestic product (GDP) for Africa of only 0.5 percent for the remainder of the century.[21] If this prediction is accurate the economic obstacles to democratization in sub-Saharan Africa will remain overwhelming well into the twenty-first century.

The World Bank was more optimistic in its predictions of economic growth for China and the nondemocratic countries of South Asia. The low levels of economic development in those countries, however, generally meant that even with annual per capita growth rates of 3–5 percent, the economic conditions favorable to democratization would still be long in coming.

In 1990 a few non-oil-exporting countries—Singapore, Algeria, South Africa, Yugoslavia—had reached levels of economic development in the upper-middle-income zone or above where transitions to democracy might be expected. Iran and Iraq, two oil exporters with substantial populations and some industrial development, were also in this zone. In these countries the economic preconditions for democratization were in some measure present but democratization had not yet occurred. Eighteen other countries with nondemocratic governments were at slightly lower levels of economic development—in the World Bank's lower-middle-income category, which included countries with a per capita GNP in 1988 from $500 to $2,200.[22] For two of these, Lebanon and Angola, no income figures were available. Nine of the remaining sixteen countries had 1988 per capita incomes between $1,000 and $2,000. These included three Arab countries (Syria, Jordan, and Tunisia), two Southeast Asian countries (Malaysia and Thailand), three Latin American countries (Panama, Mexico, and Paraguay), and one African country (Cameroon). These countries were poised for movement into the upper-middle-income political transition zone. In five of the nine (Malaysia, Jordan, Tunisia, Cameroon, and Thailand) GDP grew at an average annual rate of 3.4 percent or more between 1980 and 1988. If these rates of growth continued, the economic conditions favorable to democratization were likely to emerge in these countries some time in the 1990s. If Syria, Paraguay, Panama, and Mexico were able to achieve significantly higher growth rates than they had between 1980 and 1988, they too would be moving to levels of economic development supportive of democratization.

The seven nondemocratic countries with 1988 per capita GDP between $500 and $1,000 were the Congo, Morocco, Ivory Coast, Egypt, Senegal, Zimbabwe, and Yemen. Most of these countries had substantial rates of economic growth during the 1980s. If they could maintain those rates, they would be moving into the economic zone favorable to democratization by the early part of the twenty-first century.

The overwhelming bulk of the countries where economic conditions supportive of democratization were emerging in the 1990s were in the Middle East and North Africa. The economic well-being of many of these countries (those enclosed in parentheses in Table 6.1) was dependent on oil exports, a situation that enhanced the control of the state bureaucracy and hence provided a less favorable climate for democratization. This did not, however, mean that democratization would necessarily be impossible. The state bureaucracies of Eastern Europe, after all, exercised even more complete con-

TABLE 6.1
GNP per Capita 1988:
Upper- and Middle-Income Nondemocratic Countries

Income Level (in dollars)	Arab/ Middle East	Southeast Asia	Africa	Other
Upper income (>6,000)	(United Arab Emirates)[a] (Kuwait) (Saudi Arabia)	Singapore		
Upper-middle income (2,200–5,500)	(Iraq) (Iran) (Libya) (Oman)* Algeria*		(Gabon) South Africa	Yugoslavia
Lower-middle income (1,000–2,200)	Syria Jordan* Tunisia*	Malaysia* Thailand*	Cameroon*	Panama Mexico Paraguay
(500–1,000)	Morocco* Egypt* Yemen* Lebanon		Congo* Ivory Coast Zimbabwe Senegal* Angola	

Source: World Bank, World Development Report 1990 (New York: Oxford University Press, 1990), pp. 178–81.

[a]Parentheses indicate a country that is a major oil exporter.

*Indicates a country with an average annual GDP growth rate from 1980 to 1988 of more than 3 percent.

trol than those of the oil exporters. Conceivably at some point that control could collapse among the latter as dramatically as it did among the former. Among the other states of the Middle East and North Africa, Algeria had already reached a level conducive to democratization; Syria was approaching it; Jordan, Tunisia, Morocco, Egypt, and North Yemen were below the transition zone but grew rapidly during the 1980s. Middle Eastern economies and societies were approaching the point where they would be too wealthy and too complex for their various traditional, military, and one-party systems of authoritarian rule. The wave of democratization that had swept about the world from region to region in the 1970s and 1980s could become a dominant feature of Middle Eastern and North African politics in the 1990s. The issue of economics versus culture would then be joined: What forms of politics would emerge in these countries when economic prosperity interacted with Islamic values and traditions?

In China, the obstacles to democratization in 1990 were political, economic, and cultural; in Africa, they were overwhelmingly economic; in the rapidly developing countries of East Asia and in many Islamic countries, they were primarily cultural.

ECONOMIC DEVELOPMENT AND POLITICAL LEADERSHIP

History has proved both the optimists and the pessimists wrong on democracy, and future events will probably continue to do so. Formidable obstacles to the expansion of democracy exist in many societies. The third wave, the "global democratic revolution" of the late twentieth century, will not last forever. It may be followed by a new surge of authoritarianism constituting a third reverse wave. That, however, would not preclude a fourth wave of democratization developing some time in the twenty-first century. Judging by the past record, the two key factors affecting the future stability and expansion of democracy are economic development and political leadership.

Most poor societies will remain undemocratic so long as they remain poor. Poverty, however, is not inevitable. In the past, nations such as South Korea were assumed to be mired in economic backwardness and then have astonished the world by their ability to become prosperous quickly. In the 1980s a new consensus emerged among developmental economists on the ways to promote economic growth. The consensus of the 1980s may or may not be more lasting and more productive than the very different consensus among economists that existed in the 1950s and 1960s. Yet the new orthodoxy of neo-orthodoxy has produced significant results in many countries. Two cautions, however, are necessary. First, economic development for the very late developing countries, meaning largely Africa, may well be more difficult than it was for earlier developers because the advantages of backwardness are outweighed by the widening and historically unprecedented gap between rich countries and poor countries. Second, new forms of authoritarianism could emerge that are suitable for wealthy, information-dominated, technology-based societies. If possibilities such as these do not materialize, economic development should create the conditions for the progressive replacement of authoritarian political systems by democratic ones. Time is on the side of democracy.

Economic development makes democracy possible; political leadership makes it real. For democracies to come into being, future political elites will at a minimum have to believe that democracy is the least worse form of government for their societies and for themselves. They will also have to have the skills to bring about the transition to democracy against both radicals and standpatters who inevitably will exist and who persistently will attempt to undermine their efforts. Democracy will spread in the world to the extent that those who exercise power in the world and in individual countries want it to spread. For a century and a half after Tocqueville observed the emergence of modern democracy in America, successive waves of democratization washed up on the shore of dictatorship. Buoyed by a rising tide of economic progress, each wave advanced further and ebbed less than its predecessor. History, to shift the metaphor, does not move forward in a straight line, but when skilled and determined leaders push, it does move forward.

NOTES

Chapter 1: WHAT?

1. For descriptions of the planning and execution of the April 25 coup, see Robert Harvey, *Portugal: Birth of a Democracy* (London: Macmillan, 1978), pp. 14–20, and Douglas Porch, *The Portuguese Armed Forces and Revolution* (London: Croom Helm; Stanford: Hoover Institution Press, 1977), pp. 83–87, 90–94.

2. Quoted in Tad Szulc, "Lisbon and Washington: Behind the Portuguese Revolution," *Foreign Policy* 21 (Winter 1975–76), p. 3.

3. For further elaboration of these difficulties, see Samuel P. Huntington, "The Modest Meaning of Democracy," in *Democracy in the Americas: Stopping the Pendulum*, ed. Robert A. Pastor, (New York: Holmes and Meier, 1989), pp. 11–18, and Jeane J. Kirkpatrick, "Democratic Elections, Democratic Government, and Democratic Theory," in *Democracy at the Polls* ed. David Butler, Howard R. Penniman, and Austin Ranney (Washington: American Enterprise Institute for Public Policy Research, 1981), pp. 325–48.

4. Joseph A. Schumpeter, *Capitalism, Socialism, and Democracy*, 2d ed. (New York: Harper, 1947), chap. 21 and p. 269.

5. See Robert A. Dahl, *Polyarchy: Participation and Opposition* (New Haven: Yale University Press, 1971), pp. 1–10; Giovanni Sartori, *Democratic Theory* (Detroit: Wayne State University Press, 1962), pp. 228ff.; Kirkpatrick, "Democratic Elections," pp. 325ff.; Raymond English, *Constitutional Democracy vs. Utopian Democracy* (Washington: Ethics and Public Policy Center, 1983); G. Bingham Powell, Jr., *Contemporary Democracies* (Cambridge: Harvard University Press, 1982), pp. 2–7; Juan J. Linz, "Crisis, Breakdown, and Reequilibration," in *The Breakdown of Democratic Regimes*, ed.Juan J. Linz and Alfred Stepan (Baltimore: Johns Hopkins University Press, 1978), pp. 5–6; Guillermo O'Donnell and Philippe C. Schmitter, *Transitions from Authoritarian Rule: Tentative Conclusions about Uncertain Democracies* (Baltimore: Johns Hopkins University Press, 1986), pp. 6–14; Alex Inkeles, "Introduction: On Measuring Democracy," *Studies in Comparative International Development* 25

(Spring 1990), pp. 4–5; Tatu Vanhanen, *The Emergence of Democracy: A Comparative Study of 119 States, 1850–1979* (Helsinki: Finnish Society of Sciences and Letters, 1984), pp. 24–33.

6. For the problems of conflating stability and democracy, see Kenneth A. Bollen, "Political Democracy: Conceptual and Measurement Traps," *Studies in Comparative International Development* 25 (Spring 1990), pp. 15–17.

7. Inkeles, "On Measuring Democracy," p. 5. Bollen argues for continuous variables and continuous measures, suggesting that democracy varies in degrees as does industrialization. This is clearly not the case, however, and countries can, as the events of 1989–90 in Eastern Europe showed, quickly change from nondemocracy to democracy. They cannot quickly change from nonindustrial to industrial, and even with industrialization economists generally agree on which countries are industrialized and which are not. Bollen's own numerical index, averaging six indicators of democracy, as of 1965 groups together twenty-seven countries with scores of 90 or over at one end of a scale from 0 to 100. These included all the countries that would generally have been classified as democratic in 1965 except for West Germany, which had a score of 88.6. See Bollen, "Political Democracy," pp. 13–14, 18, 20–23. For a succinct statement of the reasons for a dichotomous approach to this issue see Jonathan Sunshine, "Economic Causes and Consequences of Democracy: A Study in Historical Statistics of the European and European-Populated English-Speaking Countries" (Ph.D. diss., Columbia University, 1972), pp. 43–48.

8. Juan J. Linz, "Totalitarian and Authoritarian Regimes," in *Macropolitical Theory*, ed. Fred I. Greenstein and Nelson W. Polsby, vol. 3 of *Handbook of Political Science* (Reading, Mass.: Addison-Wesley, 1975), pp. 175ff. See also Carl J. Friedrich and Zbigniew Brzezinski, *Totalitarian Dictatorship and Autocracy*, 2d ed. (New York: Praeger, 1965), *passim*.

9. G.P. Gooch, *English Democratic Ideas in the Seventeenth Century*, 2d ed. (New York: Harper, 1959), p. 71.

10. For similar but not identical chartings of the uneven emergence of democratic polities, see Robert A. Dahl, *Democracy and Its Critics* (New Haven: Yale University Press, 1989), chaps. 1, 2, 17; Ted Robert Gurr, Keith Jaggers, Will H. Moore, "The Transformation of the Western State: The Growth of Democracy, Autocracy, and State Power Since 1800," *Studies in Comparative Development* 25 (Spring 1990), pp. 88–95; Vanhanen, *Emergence of Democracy, passim*; Dankwart A. Rustow, "Democracy: A Global Revolution?" *Foreign Affairs* 69 (Fall 1990), pp. 75–76; Powell, *Contemporary Democracies*, p. 238; and S.P. Huntington, "Will More Countries Become Democratic?" *Political Science Quarterly* 99 (Summer 1984), pp. 195–98.

11. Jonathan Sunshine, "Economic Causes and Consequences of Democracy," pp. 48–58. According to Sunshine, the United States met the franchise criterion in 1840. Walter Dean Burnham's evidence, however, overwhelmingly supports 1828. See William N. Chambers, "Party Development and the American Mainstream," in *The American Party Systems: Stages of Political Development*, ed. William N. Chambers and Walter Dean Burnham (New York: Oxford University Press, 1967), pp. 12–13.

12. James Bryce, *Modern Democracies*, vol. 1 (New York: Macmillan, 1921), p. 24.

13. Rupert Emerson, "The Erosion of Democracy," *Journal of Asian Studies* 20 (November 1960), pp. 1–8, identifies 1958 as "the year of collapse of democratic consitutionalism in the new countries."

14. See Guillermo A. O'Donnell, *Modernization and Bureaucratic-Authoritarianism: Studies in South American Politics* (Berkeley: University of California, Institute of International Studies, 1973), and David Collier, ed., *The New Authoritarianism in Latin America* (Princeton: Princeton University Press, 1979).

15. Tun-Jen Cheng, "Democratizing the Quasi-Leninist Regime in Taiwan," *World Politics* 41 (July 1989), pp. 479–80.

16. S.E. Finer, *The Man on Horseback: The Role of the Military in Politics* 2d ed. (Harmondsworth: Penguin Books, 1976), p. 223; Sidney Verba, "Problems of Democracy in the Developing Countries," Remarks, Harvard–MIT Joint Seminar on Political Development, October 6, 1976, p. 6.

17. The shift in political development literature from a focus on democracy to a focus on stability and the highlighting of developmental contradictions and crises is briefly described in Samuel P. Huntington, "The Goals of Development," in *Understanding Political Development*, ed. Myron Weiner and Samuel P. Huntington, (Boston: Little, Brown, 1987), pp. 3ff. The concern about Western democracy is reflected in Michel Crozier, Samuel P. Huntington, and Joji Watanuki, *The Crisis of Democracy* (New York: New York University Press, 1975) and Richard Rose and B. Guy Peters, *Can Government Go Bankrupt?* (New York: Basic Books, 1978).

On February 11, 1976, at the request of CIA leaders I delivered a talk to Agency analysts on "The Global Decline of Democracy." Needless to say, I had some very persuasive theories to explain the depth and seriousness of this phenomenon. The third democratization wave was then twenty-one months old.

18. The principal multiauthor studies include the following: Juan J. Linz and Alfred Stepan, eds., *The Breakdown of Democratic Regimes* (Baltimore: Johns Hopkins University Press, 1978); Guillermo O'Donnell, Philippe C. Schmitter, and Laurence Whitehead, eds., *Transitions from Authoritarian Rule: Prospects for Democracy*, 4 vols. (Baltimore: Johns Hopkins University Press, 1986); and Larry Diamond, Juan J. Linz, and Seymour Martin Lipset, eds., *Democracy in Developing Countries*, 4 vols. (Boulder, Colo.: Lynne Rienner, 1988–89). The Linz and Stepan volume reflects the transition from the second reverse wave to the third democratization wave by including studies of the emergence as well as the breakdown of democracy.

19. Francis Fukuyama, "The End of History?" *The National Interest* 16 (Summer 1989), p. 3; Charles Krauthammer, "Democracy Has Won," *Washington Post National Weekly Edition*, April 3–9, 1989, p. 24; Marc C. Plattner, "Democracy Outwits the Pessimists," *Wall Street Journal*, October 12, 1988, p. A20. Cf. Zbigniew Brzezinski, *The Grand Failure: The Birth and Death of Communism in the Twentieth Century* (New York: Charles Scribner's Sons, 1989), *passim*.

20. Samuel P. Huntington, *Political Order in Changing Societies* (New Haven: Yale University Press, 1968), p. 1.

21. Che Guevara, *Guerrilla Warfare* (New York: Vintage Books, 1961), p. 2.

22. A considerable literature exists on the nature, extent, and possible causes of this phenomenon. See: Dean V. Babst, "A Force for Peace," *Industrial Research* 14 (April 1972), pp. 55–58; R.J. Rummel, "Libertarianism and International Violence," *Journal of Conflict Resolution* 27 (March 1983), pp. 27–71; Michael W. Doyle, "Kant, Liberal Legacies, and Foreign Affairs," *Philosophy and Public Affairs* 12 (Summer/Fall 1983), pp. 205–235, 323–353, and "Liberalism and World Politics," *American Political Science Review* 80 (December 1986), pp. 1151–69; Ze'ev Maoz and Nasrin Abdolali, "Regime Types and International Conflict, 1816–1976," *Journal of Conflict Resolution* 33 (March 1989), pp. 3–35; Bruce Russett, "Politics and Alternative Security: Toward a More Democratic, Therefore More Peaceful, World," in *Alternative Security: Living Without Nuclear Deterrence*, ed. Burns H. Weston, (Boulder, Colo.: Westview Press, 1990), pp. 107–136.

Chapter 2: WHY?

1. Dankwart A. Rustow, "Transitions to Democracy: Toward a Dynamic Model," *Comparative Politics* 2 (April 1970), pp. 337ff.

2. Gabriel A. Almond, "Approaches to Developmental Causation," in *Crisis, Choice, and Change: Historical Studies of Political Development*, ed. Gabriel A. Almond, Scott C. Flanagan, and Robert J. Mundt (Boston: Little, Brown, 1973), p. 28.

3. Rustow, "Transitions to Democracy," p. 337.

4. Myron Weiner, "Empirical Democratic Theory," *PS* 20 (Fall 1987), p. 863.

5. For comments on the impact of Allied success on democratization in some Latin American countries, see: Cynthia McClintock, "Peru: Precarious Regimes, Authoritarian and Democratic," in *Democracy in Developing Countries: Latin America*, ed. Larry Diamond, Juan J. Linz, Seymour Martin Lipset (Boulder, Colo.: Lynne Rienner, 1989), p. 344; Laurence Whitehead, "Bolivia's Failed Democratization, 1977–1980," in *Transitions from Authoritarian Rule: Latin America*, ed. Guillermo O'Donnell, Philippe C. Schmitter, and Laurence Whitehead (Baltimore: Johns Hopkins University Press, 1986), pp. 52–53; Luis A. Abugattas, "Populism and After: The Peruvian Experience," in *Authoritarians and Democrats: Regime Transition in Latin America*, ed. James M. Malloy and Mitchell A. Seligson (Pittsburgh: University of Pittsburgh Press, 1987), p. 122; Aldo C. Vacs, "Authoritarian Breakdown and Redemocratization in Argentina," in *Authoritarians and Democrats*, ed. Malloy and Seligson, p. 16.

6. Wiener, "Empirical Democratic Theory," p. 862.

7. Richard McKeon, ed., *Democracy in a World of Tensions: A Symposium Prepared by UNESCO* (Chicago: University of Chicago Press, 1951), p. 522, quoted in Giovanni Sartori, *The Theory of Democracy Revisited* (Chatham, N.J.: Chatham House Publishers, 1987), p. 3.

8. Harry Psomiades, "Greece: From the Colonels' Rule to Democracy,"

in *From Dictatorship to Democracy: Coping with the Legacies of Authoritarianism and Totalitarianism*, ed. John H. Herz (Westport, Conn.: Greenwood Press, 1982), p. 251; Scott Mainwaring and Eduardo J. Viola, "Brazil and Argentina in the 1980s," *Journal of International Affairs* 38 (Winter 1985), p. 203.

9. Gabriel Almond and Robert J. Mundt, "Crisis, Choice, and Change: Some Tentative Conclusions," in *Crisis, Choice, and Change*, ed. Almond, Flanagan, and Mundt, p. 628.

10. Arthur Zich, "The Marcos Era," *Wilson Quarterly* 10 (Summer 1986), p. 126.

11. Edward Schumacher, "Argentina and Democracy," *Foreign Affairs* 62 (Summer 1984), p. 1077.

12. Thomas C. Bruneau, "Discovering Democracy," *Wilson Quarterly* 9 (New Year's 1985), pp. 68–69; *Boston Globe*, December 3, 1984, p. 2.

13. Richard Clogg, *A Short History of Modern Greece*, 2d ed. (Cambridge: Cambridge University Press, 1986), p. 198. For an argument that the economic performance of the Greek military regime was generally unsatisfactory, see Constantine P. Danopoulos, "Military Professionalism and Regime Legitimacy in Greece, 1967–1974," *Political Science Quarterly* 98 (Fall 1983), pp. 495–98.

14. Jane S. Jaquette and Abraham F. Lowenthal, "The Peruvian Experiment in Retrospect," *World Politics* 39 (January 1987), p. 284; Thomas R. Rochon and Michael J. Mitchell, "Social Bases of the Transition to Democracy in Brazil," *Comparative Politics* 21 (April 1989), p. 309.

15. Virgilio R. Beltran, "Political Transition in Argentina: 1982 to 1985," *Armed Forces and Society* 13 (Winter 1987), pp. 214–16; Mainwaring and Viola, "Brazil and Argentina," p. 203.

16. Juan Linz and Alfred Stepan, "Political Crafting of Democratic Consolidation or Destruction: European and South American Comparisons," in *Democracy in the Americas: Stopping the Pendulum*, ed. Robert A. Pastor (New York: Holmes and Meier, 1989), p. 47; *New York Times*, July 27, 1988, p. A2, quoted in George Weigel, "Catholicism and Democracy: The Other Twentieth-Century Revolution," in *The New Democracies: Global Change and U.S. Policy*, ed. Brad Roberts (Cambridge: MIT Press, 1990), p. 33.

17. Seymour Martin Lipset, *Political Man: The Social Bases of Politics* (New York: Doubleday, 1960), pp. 45–76, and Lipset, *Political Man*, rev. ed. (Baltimore: Johns Hopkins University Press, 1981), 469–76; Robert A. Dahl, *Polyarchy: Participation and Opposition* (New Haven: Yale University Press, 1971), pp. 62–80; Seymour Martin Lipset, Kyoung-Ryung Seong, and John Charles Torres, "A Comparative Analysis of the Social Requisites of Democracy" (Unpublished paper, Stanford University, 1990).

18. Kenneth A. Bollen and Robert W. Jackman, "Economic and Noneconomic Determinants of Political Democracy in the 1960s," *Research in Political Sociology* (1985), pp. 38–39. A major study by Zehra F. Arat that questions this relation is seriously flawed by a methodology that combines into a single dependent variable changes within regimes and changes from one regime to another. See Arat, "Democracy and Economic Development: Modernization Theory Revisited," *Comparative Politics* 21 (October 1988), pp. 21–37.

19. Jonathan H. Sunshine, "Economic Causes and Consequences of Democracy: A Study in Historical Statistics of the European and European-Populated, English-Speaking Countries" (Ph.D. diss., Columbia University, 1972), pp. 109–10, 134–40.

20. David Morawetz, *Twenty-five Years of Economic Development 1950 to 1975* (Washington: World Bank, 1977), p. 12.

21. Ideally it would have been more appropriate to rank countries economically by their per capita GNPs in 1974 when the third wave started. Only limited data are, however, available for that year. The World Bank's first annual development report, issued in 1978, contains 1976 per capita figures for 125 political entities, including countries with centrally planned economies. The estimates for the latter should not be taken too seriously, and in subsequent years the bank gave up its effort to provide data on nonmembers with planned economies. These figures may be assumed to be accurate enough, however, for the purpose of classifying countries into four major groupings for this analysis. See World Bank, *World Development Report, 1978* (Washington: World Bank, 1978), pp. 76–77.

22. Phillips Cutright, "National Political Development: Measurement and Analysis," *American Sociological Review* 28 (April 1963), pp. 253–64.

23. Mitchell A. Seligson, "Democratization in Latin America: The Current Cycle," and "Development, Democratization, and Decay: Central America at the Crossroads," in *Authoritarians and Democrats*, ed. Malloy and Seligson, pp. 6–11, 173–77; Enrique A. Baloyra, "Conclusion: Toward a Framework for the Study of Democratic Consolidation," in *Comparing New Democracies: Transition and Consolidation in Mediterranean Europe and the Southern Cone*, ed. Enrique A. Baloyra (Boulder, Colo.: Westview Press, 1987), p. 297.

24. For an insightful and detailed analysis of the differing impacts of oil revenue and labor remittances on economic and political development in Saudi Arabia and North Yemen, see Kiren Aziz Chaudhry, "The Price of Wealth: Business and State in Labor Remittance and Oil Economies" (Ph.D. diss., Harvard University, 1990).

25. Alex Inkeles and Larry J. Diamond, "Personal Development and National Development: A Cross-National Perspective," in *The Quality of Life: Comparative Studies*, ed. Alexander Szalai and Frank M. Andrews, (London: Sage Publications, 1980), p. 83; Lipset, Seong, and Torres, "Social Requisites of Democracy," pp. 24–25; Ronald Inglehart, "The Renaissance of Political Culture," *American Political Science Review* 82 (December 1988), pp. 1215–20.

26. Lipset, Seong, and Torres, "Social Requisites of Democracy," pp. 25–26; World Bank, *World Development Report 1984* (New York: Oxford University Press, 1984), pp. 266–67. Cf. Dahl, *Polyarchy*, pp. 74–76.

27. Scott Mainwaring, "The Transition to Democracy in Brazil," *Journal of Interamerican Studies and World Affairs* 28 (September 1986), p. 152.

28. *New York Times*, October 8, 1984, p. A3; Sandra Burton, *Impossible Dream: The Marcoses, the Aquinos, and the Unfinished Revolution* (New York: Warner Books, 1989), p. 327.

29. Nancy Bermeo, "Redemocratization and Transition Elections: A Comparison of Spain and Portugal," *Comparative Politics* 19 (January 1987), p. 222.

30. Tun-jen Cheng, "Democratizing the KMT Regime in Taiwan." Paper prepared for Conference on Democratization in the Republic of China, Taipei, Taiwan, Republic of China, January 9–11, 1989, p. 20. For further discussion of the new middle class and its politics on Taiwan, see the special issue on this subject of the *Free China Review* 39 (November 1989) and Chu Li-Hsi, "New Generation Electorate," *Free China Review* 40 (February 1990), pp. 48–50.

31. *The Economist*, June 20, 1987, p. 39; April 15, 1989, p. 24; James Cotton, "From Authoritarianism to Democracy in South Korea," *Political Studies* 37 (June 1989), p. 252.

32. See Bermeo, *Comparative Politics* 19, 219f.; Linz and Stepan, "Political Crafting," in *Democracy in the Americas*, ed. Pastor, p. 48; Fernando H. Cardoso, "Entrepreneurs and the Transition Process: The Brazilian Case," in *Transitions from Authoritarian Rule: Comparative Perspectives*, ed. Guillermo O'Donnell, Philippe C. Schmitter, and Laurence Whitehead (Baltimore: Johns Hopkins University Press, 1986), pp. 137–53.

33. Allan Williams, *Southern Europe Transformed: Political and Economic Change in Greece, Italy, Portugal, and Spain* (London: Harper & Row, 1984), pp. 2–9; Alfred Tovias, "The International Context of Democratic Transition," in *The New Mediterranean Democracies: Regime Transition in Spain, Greece, and Portugal*, ed. Geoffrey Pridham (London: Frank Cass, 1984), p. 159; Jane S. Jaquette and Lowenthal, *World Politics* 39, p. 390; Catherine M. Conaghan, "Party Politics and Democratization in Ecuador," in *Authoritarians and Democrats*, ed. Malloy and Seligson, pp. 146–47; Burton, *Impossible Dream*, p. 283; *New York Times*, September 4, 1984, p. D1.

34. P. Nikiforos Diamandouros, "Regime Change and the Prospects for Democracy in Greece: 1974–1983," in *Transitions from Authoritarian Rule: Southern Europe*, ed. Guillermo O'Donnell, Philippe C. Schmitter, and Laurence Whitehead (Baltimore: Johns Hopkins University Press, 1986), p. 149.

35. Psomiades, "Greece," in *From Dictatorship to Democracy*, ed. Herz, p. 252.

36. Kenneth Medhurst, "Spain's Evolutionary Pathway from Dictatorship to Democracy," in *New Mediterranean Democracies*, ed. Pridham, pp. 30–31.

37. For a succinctly stated similar analysis, see Lipset, Seong, and Torres, "Social Requisites of Democracy," pp. 18–19.

38. Countries were classified religiously according to information available in *The Statesman's Yearbook 1988–1989*, ed. John Paxton (New York: St. Martin's Press, 1988). Very small countries and countries where no religion predominated were omitted from the calculations.

39. Henry Scott Stokes, "Korea's Church Militant," *New York Times Magazine*, November 28, 1972, p. 68.

40. Quoted in James Fallows, "Korea Is Not Japan," *Atlantic Monthly* 262 (October 1988), p. 30.

41. Stokes, "Korea's Church Militant," p. 105; *Washington Post*, March 30, 1986, p. A19; *New York Times*, March 10, 1986, p. A3, April 15, 1987, p. A3; Sook-Jong Lee, "Political Liberalization and Economic Development in South

Korea" (Unpublished paper, Harvard University Department of Sociology, Center for Research on Politics and Social Organization, 1988), p. 22.

42. Kenneth A. Bollen, "Political Democracy and the Timing of Development," *American Sociological Review*, Vol. 44, no. 4 (August 1979), p. 583; Lipset, Seong, and Torres, "Social Requisites of Democracy," p. 29.

43. Pierre Elliot Trudeau, *Federalism and the French Canadians* (New York: St. Martin's Press, 1968), p. 108, quoted in Lipset, Seong, and Torres, "Social Requisites of Democracy," p. 29.

44. Inglehart, *American Political Science Review* 82, pp. 1226–28.

45. Quoted in Brian H. Smith, *The Church and Politics in Spain: Challenges to Modern Catholicism* (Princeton: Princeton University Press, 1982), p. 284.

46. Juan J. Linz, "Religion and Politics in Spain: From Conflict to Consensus above Cleavage," *Social Compass* 27, no. 2/3, (1980), p. 258.

47. Jackson Diehl, *Washington Post National Weekly Edition*, Jan. 5, 1987, p. 29; Thomas P. Skidmore, *The Politics of Military Rule in Brazil, 1964–1985* (New York: Oxford University Press, 1988), p. 78 and also p. 27; Hugo Villela G., "The Church and the Process of Democratization in Latin America," *Social Compass* 26, no. 2/3 (1979), p. 264; Brian H. Smith, "Churches and Human Rights in Latin America: Recent Trends on the Subcontinent," in *Churches and Politics in Latin America*, ed. Daniel H. Levine (Beverly Hills: Sage Publications, 1979), pp. 155–93.

48. Skidmore, *Politics of Military Rule*, pp. 78, 334; Thomas C. Bruneau, *The Political Transformation of the Brazilian Catholic Church* (Cambridge: Cambridge University Press, 1974), pp. 222–23. Bruneau, pp. 182–216, details ten incidents of increasing church-state conflict in Brazil between July 1966 and early 1972.

49. Skidmore, *Politics of Military Rule*, p. 137; Mark A. Uhlig, "Pinochet's Tyranny," *New York Review of Books*, June 27, 1985, p. 38.

50. Alfred Fierro Bardaji, "Political Positions and Opposition in the Spanish Catholic Church," *Government and Opposition* 11 (Spring 1976), pp. 200–01. See also Cooper, *Catholicism and the Franco Regime*, pp. 35–44.

51. Gordon L. Bowen, "Prospects for Liberalization by Way of Democratization in Guatemala," in *Liberalization and Redemocratization in Latin America*, ed. George A. Lopez and Michael Stohl (New York: Greenwood Press, 1987), p. 38.

52. Skidmore, *Politics of Military Rule*, p. 137; Mark A. Uhlig, "Pinochet's Tyranny," *New York Review of Books*, June 27, 1985, p. 38.

53. Skidmore, *Politics of Military Rule*, p. 184.

54. Burton, *Impossible Dream*, p. 217.

55. Skidmore, *Politics of Military Rule*, p. 137.

56. See the *New York Times* reports on the relevant papal visits.

57. *Time*, December 4, 1989, p. 74; Timothy Garton Ash, "Eastern Europe: The Year of Truth," *New York Review of Books*, February 15, 1990, p. 17.

58. Feliccian Foy, ed., *1988 Catholic Almanac* (Huntington, Ind.: Our Sunday Visitor Books, 1987), p. 34.

59. *New York Times*, March 10, 1986, p. A3.

60. Rosalinda Pineda Ofrenco, "The Catholic Church in Philippine Poli-

tics," *Journal of Contemporary Asia* 17 no. 3 (1987), p. 329; *Time*, February 3, 1986, p. 34, February 17, 1986, pp. 36, 39.

61. Dahl, *Polyarchy*, p. 197. I have added Ireland to the fourteen cases Dahl specifies in his analysis.

62. Sunshine, "Economic Causes and Consequences of Democracy," pp. 134-40.

63. Frans A.M. Alting Von Geusau, "Shaping the Enlarged Community: A Survey," in *From Nine to Twelve: Europe's Destiny?* ed. J.S. Schneider (Alphen aan den Rijn: Sijthoff and Noordhoff, 1980), p. 218.

64. Susannah Verney, "Greece and the European Community," in *Political Change in Greece: Before and After the Colonels*, ed. Kevin Featherstone and Dimitrios K. Katsoudas (London: Croom Helm, 1987), p. 259.

65. Howard J. Wiarda, "The Significance for Latin America of the Spanish Democratic Transition," in *Spain in the 1980s: The Democratic Transition and a New International Role*, ed. Robert P. Clark and Michael H. Haltzel (Cambridge, Mass.: Ballinger Publishing, 1987), p. 159; Bermeo, "Redemocratization and Transition Elections," p. 218; Kenneth Maxwell, "Portugal: A Neat Revolution," *New York Review of Books*, June 13, 1974, p. 16.

66. Thomas C. Bruneau, "Portugal in 1970s: From Regime to Regime" (Paper prepared for Annual Meeting, American Political Science Association, Washington, D.C., August 28-31, 1980), pp. 15-16.

67. See Tamar Jacoby, "The Reagan Turnaround on Human Rights," *Foreign Affairs* 64 (Summer 1986), pp. 1066-86. For a short overview of U.S. human rights policy highlighting the similarities in the Carter and Reagan approaches, see Paula Dobriansky, "Human Rights and U.S. Foreign Policy," in *The New Democracies*, ed. Roberts, pp. 145-61; on Congress's role, see David P. Forsythe, *Human Rights and U.S. Foreign Policy: Congress Reconsidered* (Gainesville: University of Florida Press, 1988); and for an analysis of Carter policy, Joshua Muravchik, *The Uncertain Crusade: Jimmy Carter and the Dilemmas of Human Rights Policy* (Lanham, Md.: Hamilton Press, 1986).

68. Quoted in Muravchik, *Uncertain Crusade*, p. 214.

69. Whitehead, "Bolivia's Failed Democratization," in *Transitions from Authoritarian Rule: Latin America*, ed. O'Donnell, Schmitter, and Whitehead, pp. 66, 223; *New York Times*, November 29, 1984, p. A3, January 15, 1989, p. 6; *Time*, June 29, 1987, p. 22; *Economist*, January 21, 1989, p. 40.

70. These quotations may be found, respectively, in Osvaldo Hurtado, "Changing Latin American Attitudes: Prerequisite to Institutionalizing Democracy," in *Democracy in the Americas*, ed. Pastor, p. 101; *Boston Globe*, December 3, 1984, p. 2; Burton, *Impossible Dream*, p. 343; *New York Times*, August 1, 1980, p. A23.

71. See Luis A. Abugattas, "Populism and After: The Peruvian Experience," in *Authoritarians and Democrats*, ed. Malloy and Seligson, p. 132; Philip Mauceri, "Nine Cases of Transitions and Consolidations," in *Democracy in the Americas*, ed. Pastor, pp. 217, 229; Cynthia McClintock, "The Prospects for Democratic Consolidation in the 'Least Likely' Case: Peru," in *Democracy in Developing Countries*, ed. Diamond, Linz, and Lipset; Howard J. Wiarda, "The Dominican Republic: Mirror Legacies of Democracy and Authoritarianism,"

in *Democracy in Developing Countries: Latin America,* ed. Diamond, Linz, and Lipset, p. 437; *New York Times,* October 4, 1988, p. A6; Mark Falcoff, "The Democratic Prospect in Latin America," in *The New Democracies,* ed. Roberts, pp. 68–69.

72. Timothy Garton Ash, "Eastern Europe: The Year of Truth," *New York Review of Books,* February 15, 1990, p. 17; Michael Dobbs, "Gorbachev: Riding the Tiger," *Washington Post National Weekly Edition,* January 8–14, 1990, pp. 6–7; *Washington Post,* November 22, 1989, p. 1; "The New Germany," *Economist,* June 30, 1990, pp. 4–5; and, generally, Renée Nevers, *The Soviet Union and Eastern Europe: The End of an Era* (London: International Institute for Strategic Studies, Adelphi Paper no. 249, 1990).

73. Almond and Mundt, "Tentative Conclusions," in *Crisis, Choice, and Change,* ed. Almond, Flanagan, and Mundt, pp. 626–29; David L. Huff and James M. Lutz, "The Contagion of Political Unrest in Independent Black Africa," *Economic Geography* 50 (October 1974), pp. 352–67; Richard P.Y. Li and William R. Thompson, "The 'Coup Contagion' Hypothesis," *Journal of Conflict Resolution* 19 (March 1975), pp. 63–88; James M. Lutz, "The Diffusion of Political Phenomena in Sub-Saharan Africa," *Journal of Political and Military Sociology* 17 (Spring 1989), pp. 93–114.

74. Kenneth Maxwell, "Regime Overthrow and the Prospects for Democratic Transition in Portugal," in *Transitions from Authoritarian Rule: Southern Europe,* ed. O'Donnell, Schmitter, and Whitehead, p. 132; Jose Maravall, *The Transition to Democracy in Spain* (London: Croom Helm, 1982), p. 65.

75. *New York Times,* May 14, 1989, p. E6.

76. *Washington Post,* June 19, 1974, p. A10; Paul Preston, *The Triumph of Democracy in Spain* (London: Methuen, 1986), p. 60.

77. Falcoff, "The Democratic Prospect," in *The New Democracies,* ed. Roberts, pp. 67–68; Robert A. Pastor, "How to Reinforce Democracy in the Americas: Seven Proposals," in *Democracy in the Americas,* ed. Pastor, p. 143; Howard J. Wiarda, "The Significance for Latin America of the Spanish Democratic Transition," in *Spain in the 1980s,* ed. Clark and Haltzel, pp. 165–172.

78. *New York Times,* December 13, 1983, p. 3, January 22, 1984, p. E3; *Washington Post,* January 25, 1984, p. A5.

79. *New York Times,* March 15, 1986, p. A7; *Boston Globe,* April 5, 1986, p. 1.

80. Timothy Garton Ash, "The Revolution of the Magic Lantern," *New York Review of Books,* January 18, 1990, p. 51; *Time,* November 27, 1989, p. 41.

81. This quip apparently originated with Timothy Garton Ash. See Ash, *New York Review of Books,* January 18, 1990, p. 42.

82. *New York Times,* December 28, 1989, p. A13.

83. On leaders and their choices, see Samuel P. Huntington and Joan M. Nelson, *No Easy Choice: Political Participation in Developing Countries* (Cambridge: Harvard University Press, 1976), pp. 159–71, and Larry Diamond, "Crisis, Choice, and Structure: Reconciling Alternative Models for Explaining Democratic Success and Failure in the Third World" (Paper presented to Annual Meeting, American Political Science Association, Atlanta, Georgia,

August 31–September 3, 1989). See also chapter 3, below, for a discussion of motives for democratization.

Chapter 3: HOW? PROCESSES OF DEMOCRATIZATION

1. See, e.g., G. Bingham Powell, Jr., *Contemporary Democracies: Participation, Stability, and Violence* (Cambridge: Harvard University Press, 1982), chaps. 5–9; Juan J. Linz, "Perils of Presidentialism," *Journal of Democracy* 1 (Winter 1990), pp. 51–69.

2. Robert A. Dahl, *Polyarchy: Participation and Opposition* (New Haven: Yale University Press, 1971), pp. 33–40.

3. See Donald L. Horowitz, "Three Dimensions of Ethnic Politics," *World Politics* 23 (January 1971), pp. 232–36; Samuel P. Huntington and Jorge I. Dominguez, "Political Development," in *Handbook of Political Science*, vol. 3, ed. Fred I. Greenstein and Nelson W. Polsby (Reading, Mass.: Addison-Wesley, 1975), pp. 74–75.

4. See Martin C. Needler, "The Military Withdrawal from Power in South America," *Armed Forces and Society* 6 (Summer 1980), pp. 621–23.

5. For discussion of the terms under which military rulers arranged their exits from power, see Robert H. Dix, "The Breakdown of Authoritarian Regimes," *Western Political Quarterly* 35 (December 1982), pp. 567–68, for "exit guarantees"; Myron Weiner, "Empirical Democratic Theory and the Transition from Authoritarianism to Democracy," *PS* 20 (Fall 1987), pp. 864–65; Enrique A. Baloyra, "Conclusion: Toward a Framework for the Study of Democratic Consolidation," in *Comparing New Democracies: Transition and Consolidation in Mediterranean Europe and the Southern Cone*, ed. Enrique A. Baloyra (Boulder, Colo.: Westview Press, 1987), pp. 299–300; Alfred Stepan, *Rethinking Military Politics: Brazil and the Southern Cone* (Princeton: Princeton University Press, 1988), pp. 64–65; Philip Mauceri, "Nine Cases of Transitions and Consolidations," in *Democracy in the Americas: Stopping the Pendulum*, ed. Robert A. Pastor (New York: Holmes and Meier, 1989), pp. 225, 229; Luis A. Abugattas, "Populism and After: The Peruvian Experience," in *Authoritarians and Democrats: Regime Transition in Latin America*, ed. James M. Malloy and Mitchell A. Seligson (Pittsburgh: University of Pittsburgh Press, 1987), pp. 137–39; Aldo C. Vacs, "Authoritarian Breakdown and Redemocratization in Argentina," in *Authoritarians and Democrats*, ed. Malloy and Seligson, pp. 30–31; P. Nikiforos Diamandouros, "Transition to, and Consolidation of, Democratic Politics in Greece, 1974–83: A Tentative Assessment," in *The New Mediterranean Democracies: Regime Transition in Spain, Greece, and Portugal*, ed. Geoffrey Pridham (London: Frank Cass, 1984), p. 54; Harry J. Psomiades, "Greece: From the Colonels' Rule to Democracy," in *From Dictatorship to Democracy: Coping with the Legacies of Authoritarianism and Totalitarianism*, ed. John H. Herz (Westport, Conn.: Greenwood Press, 1982), pp. 253–54.

6. Tun-jen Cheng, "Democratizing the Quasi-Leninist Regime in Taiwan," *World Politics* 41 (July 1989), p. 496.

7. *New York Times*, March 9, 1990, pp. A1, A11, March 11, 1990, p. E3.

8. Bronislaw Geremek, "Postcommunism and Democracy in Poland," *Washington Quarterly* 13 (Summer 1990), p. 129.

9. *New York Times*, March 11, 1990, p. E3.

10. For a similar conclusion, see I. William Zartman, "Transition to Democracy from Single-Party Regimes: Lessons from North Africa" (Paper presented to Annual Meeting, American Political Science Association, Atlanta, Georgia, August 31–September 3, 1989), pp. 2–4.

11. See Richard K. Betts and Samuel P. Huntington, "Dead Dictators and Rioting Mobs: Does the Demise of Authoritarian Rulers Lead to Political Instability?" *International Security* 10 (Winter 1985–86), pp. 112–46.

12. See Raymond Carr, "Introduction: The Spanish Transition to Democracy in Historical Perspective," in *Spain in the 1980s: The Democratic Transition and a New International Role*, ed. Robert P. Clark and Michael H. Haltzel (Cambridge: Ballinger, 1987), pp. 3–4.

13. Alfred Stepan, "Introduction," in *Democratizing Brazil: Problems of Transition and Consolidation*, ed. Stepan (New York: Oxford University Press, 1989), p. ix.

14. *Ibid.*; Scott Mainwaring, "The Transition to Democracy in Brazil," *Journal of Interamerican Studies and World Affairs* 28 (Spring 1986), p. 149; Kenneth Medhurst, "Spain's Evolutionary Pathway from Dictatorship to Democracy," in *New Mediterranean Democracies*, ed. Pridham, p. 30.

15. Paul Preston, *The Triumph of Democracy in Spain* (London: Methuen, 1986), p. 93; Donald Share and Scott Mainwaring, "Transitions Through Transaction: Democratization in Brazil and Spain," in *Political Liberalization in Brazil: Dynamics, Dilemmas, and Future Prospects*, ed. Wayne A. Selcher (Boulder, Colo.: Westview Press, 1986), p. 179; Samuel P. Huntington, *Political Order in Changing Societies* (New Haven: Yale University Press, 1968), pp. 344–57.

16. Jacques Rupnik, "Hungary's Quiet Revolution," *New Republic*, November 20, 1989, p. 20; *New York Times*, April 16, 1989, p. E3.

17. Quoted by Abugattas in *Authoritarians and Democrats*, ed. Malloy and Seligson, p. 129, and by Sylvia T. Borzutzky, "The Pinochet Regime: Crisis and Consolidation," in *Authoritarians and Democrats*, ed. Malloy and Seligson, p. 85.

18. See Needler, "The Military Withdrawal," pp. 621–23 on "second phase" coups and the observation that "the military government that returns power to civilian hands is not the same one that seized power from the constitutional government in the first place."

19. Stepan, *Rethinking Military Politics*, pp. 32–40 and Thomas E. Skidmore, "Brazil's Slow Road to Democratization: 1974–1985," in *Democratizing Brazil*, ed. Stepan, p. 33. This interpretation coincides with my own impression of Golbery's intentions that I formed in 1974 working with him on plans for Brazil's democratization. For a contrary argument, see Silvio R. Duncan Baretta and John Markoff, "Brazil's *Abertura*: A Transition from What to What?" in *Authoritarians and Democrats*, ed. Malloy and Seligson, pp. 45–46.

20. Quoted in Francisco Weffort, "Why Democracy?" in *Democratizing Brazil*, ed. Stepan, p. 332.

21. Raymond Carr and Juan Pablo Fusi Aizpurua, *Spain: Dictatorship to Democracy*, 2d ed. (London: Allen & Unwin, 1981), pp. 198–206.

22. Quoted in David Remnick, "The Struggle for Light," *New York Review of Books*, August 16, 1990, p. 6.

23. See Stepan, *Rethinking Military Politics*, pp. 42–43.

24. Giuseppe Di Palma highlighted the significance of backward legitimacy in "Founding Coalitions in Southern Europe: Legitimacy and Hegemony," *Government and Opposition* 15 (Spring 1980), p. 170. See also Nancy Bermeo, "Redemocratization and Transition Elections: A Comparison of Spain and Portugal," *Comparative Politics* 19 (January 1987), p. 218.

25. Stanley G. Payne, "The Role of the Armed Forces in the Spanish Transition," in *Spain in the 1980s*, ed. Clark and Haltzel, p. 86; Stepan, *Rethinking Military Politics*, p. 36.

26. Theses presented by the Central Committee, Ninth Congress, Communist Party of Spain, April 5–9, 1978, quoted in Juan J. Linz, "Some Comparative Thoughts on the Transition to Democracy in Portugal and Spain," in Jorge Braga de Macedo and Simon Serfaty, eds., *Portugal Since the Revolution: Economic and Political Perspectives* (Boulder, Colo.: Westview Press, 1981), p. 44; Preston, *Triumph of Democracy in Spain*, p. 137.

27. Skidmore, "Brazil's Slow Road," in *Democratizing Brazil*, ed. Stepan, p. 34.

28. Virgilio R. Beltran, "Political Transition in Argentina: 1982 to 1985," *Armed Forces and Society* 13 (Winter 1987), p. 217; Scott Mainwaring and Eduardo J. Viola, "Brazil and Argentina in the 1980s," *Journal of International Affairs* 38 (Winter 1985), pp. 206–9.

29. Robert Harvey, *Portugal: Birth of a Democracy* (London: Macmillan, 1978), p. 2.

30. Gabriel A. Almond, "Approaches to Developmental Causation," in *Crisis, Choice, and Change: Historical Studies of Political Development*, ed. Gabriel A. Almond, Scott C. Flanagan, and Robert J. Mundt (Boston: Little, Brown, 1973), p. 32.

31. *Washington Post*, October 7, 1983, p. A3; Laurence Whitehead, "Bolivia's Failed Democratization, 1977–1980," in *Transitions from Authoritarian Rule: Latin America*, ed. Guillermo O'Donnell, Philippe C. Schmitter, and Laurence Whitehead (Baltimore: Johns Hopkins University Press, 1986), p. 59.

32. "Leoplitax" (identified as a "political commentator in the Polish underground press"), *Uncaptive Minds* 2 (May–June–July 1989), p. 5.

33. Steven Mufson, "Uncle Joe," *New Republic*, September 28, 1987, pp. 22–23); *Washington Post National Weekly*, February 19–25, 1990, p. 7.

34. Edgardo Boeniger, "The Chilean Road to Democracy," *Foreign Affairs* 64 (Spring 1986), p. 821.

35. Anna Husarska, "A Talk with Adam Michnik," *New Leader*, April 3–17, 1989, p. 10; Marcin Sulkowski, "The Dispute About the General," *Uncaptive Minds* 3 (March–April 1990), pp. 7–9.

36. See James Cotton, "From Authoritarianism to Democracy in South Korea," *Political Studies* 37 (June 1989), pp. 252–53.

37. *Economist*, May 10, 1986, p. 39; Alfred Stepan, "The Last Days of Pinochet?" *New York Review of Books*, June 2, 1988, p. 34.

38. Quoted by Weffort, "Why Democracy," in *Democratizing Brazil*, ed. Stepan, p. 345, and by Thomas G. Sanders, "Decompression," in *Military Government and the Movement Toward Democracy in South America*, ed. Howard Handelman and Thomas G. Sanders, (Bloomington: Indiana University Press, 1981), p. 157. As Weffort points out, this advice was somewhat beside the point in Brazil. Before starting its transformation process the Brazilian military regime had physically eliminated most of the serious radicals. The aide's advice is much more relevant in transplacement situations.

39. *Time*, June 25, 1990, p. 21.

40. Mandela quoted in Pauline H. Baker, "A Turbulent Transition," *Journal of Democracy* 1 (Fall 1990), p. 17; Botha quoted in *Washington Post National Weekly Edition*, May 14–20, 1990, p. 17.

Chapter 4: HOW? CHARACTERISTICS OF DEMOCRATIZATION

1. Enrique A. Baloyra, "Conclusion: Toward a Framework for the Study of Democratic Consolidation," in Baloyra, ed., *Comparing New Democracies: Transition and Consolidation in Mediterranean Europe and the Southern Cone*, ed. Enrique A. Baloyra (Boulder, Colo.: Westview Press, 1987), p. 299. On the Venezuelan and Colombian negotiations and agreements, see Terry Lynn Karl, "Petroleum and Political Pacts: The Transition to Democracy in Venezuela," in *Transitions from Authoritarian Rule: Latin America*, ed. Guillermo O'Donnell, Philippe C. Schmitter, and Laurence Whitehead (Baltimore: Johns Hopkins University Press, 1986), pp. 196–219; Daniel H. Levine, "Venezuela since 1958: The Consolidation of Democratic Politics," in *The Breakdown of Democratic Regimes: Latin America*, ed. Juan J. Linz and Alfred Stepan (Baltimore: Johns Hopkins University Press, 1978), pp. 93–98; Alexander W. Wilde, "Conversations among Gentlemen: Oligarchical Democracy in Colombia," in *Breakdown of Democratic Regimes*, ed. Linz and Stepan, pp. 58–67; Jonathan Hartlyn, "Colombia: The Politics of Violence and Accommodation," in *Democracy in Developing Countries: Latin America*, ed. Larry Diamond, Juan J. Linz, and Seymour Martin Lipset, (Boulder, Colo.: Lynne Rienner, 1989), pp. 306–7.

2. Jose Maravall, *The Transition to Democracy in Spain* (London: Croom Helm, 1982), pp. 42–44; Donald Share and Scott Mainwaring, "Transitions Through Transaction: Democratization in Brazil and Spain," in *Political Liberalization in Brazil: Dynamics, Dilemmas, and Future Prospects*, ed. Wayne A. Selcher, (Boulder, Colo.: Westview Press, 1986), pp. 175–79.

3. Raymond Carr, "Introduction: The Spanish Transition to Democracy in Historical Perspective," in *Spain in the 1980s: The Democratic Transition and a New International Role*, ed. Robert P. Clark and Michael H. Haltzel (Cambridge, Mass.: Ballinger, 1987), pp. 4–5.

4. Wojtek Lamentowicz, "Dilemmas of the Transition Period," *Uncaptive Minds* 2 (November–December 1989), p. 19.

5. Carr, "Introduction," in *Spain in the 1980s*, ed. Clark and Haltzel, pp. 4–5, and Richard Gunther, "Democratization and Party Building: The

Role of Party Elites in the Spanish Transition," in *Spain in the 1980s*, ed. Clark and Haltzel, pp. 54–58.

6. James Dunkerley and Rolando Morales, "The Crisis in Bolivia," *New Left Review*, no. 155 (January–February 1986), pp. 100–101; *International Herald Tribune*, April 28–29, 1990, p. 3.

7. *New York Times*, March 2, 1989, p. 1, March 24, 1989, p. A10.

8. Lamentowicz, *Uncaptive Minds* 2 (November–December 1989), p. 19.

9. Salvador Giner, "Southern European Socialism in Transition," in *The New Mediterranean Democracies: Regime Transition in Spain, Greece and Portugal*, ed. Geoffrey Pridham (London: Frank Cass, 1984), pp. 140, 155.

10. Kenneth Medhurst, "Spain's Evolutionary Pathway from Dictatorship to Democracy," in *New Mediterranean Democracies*, ed. Pridham, p. 38; Bolivar Lamounier, "Challenges to Democratic Consolidation in Brazil" (Paper presented at Annual Meeting, American Political Science Association, Washington, D.C., September 1–4, 1988), pp. 19–20; *New York Times*, August 1, 1989, p. A4.

11. For a similar statement of the compromises required, see Guiseppe Di Palma, "Government Performance: An Issue and Three Cases in Search of Theory," in *New Mediterranean Democracies*, ed. Pridham, pp. 175–77.

12. Giner, "Southern European Socialism," in *New Mediterranean Democracies*, ed. Pridham, p. 149, and P. Nikiforos Diamandouros, "Transition to, and Consolidation of, Democratic Politics in Greece, 1974–83: A Tentative Assessment," in *New Mediterranean Democracies*, ed. Pridham, p. 64.

13. Thomas E. Skidmore, "Brazil's Slow Road to Democratization: 1974–1985," in *Democratizing Brazil: Problems of Transition and Consolidation*, ed. Alfred Stepan (New York: Oxford University Press, 1989), pp. 33–34; *Economist*, September 17, 1988, p. 48.

14. Myron Weiner, "Empirical Democratic Theory and the Transition from Authoritarianism to Democracy," *PS* 20 (Fall 1987), p. 865.

15. *New York Times*, September 1, 1987, p. 1.

16. Levine, "Venezuela since 1958," in *Breakdown of Democratic Regimes: Latin America*, ed. Linz and Stepan, pp. 89–92; Philip Mauceri, "Nine Cases of Transitions and Consolidations," in *Democracy in the Americas: Stopping the Pendulum*, ed. Robert A. Pastor (New York: Holmes and Meier, 1989), p. 215.

17. "All the Spains: A Survey," *Economist*, November 3, 1979, p. 3; Gunther, "Democratization and Party Building," in *Spain in the 1980s*, ed. Clark and Haltzel, p. 58.

18. Scott Mainwaring and Eduardo J. Viola, "Brazil and Argentina in the 1980s," *Journal of International Affairs* 38 (Winter 1985), pp. 208–209.

19. Timothy Garton Ash, "The Revolution of the Magic Lantern," *New York Review of Books*, January 18, 1990, p. 51.

20. Skidmore, "Brazil's Slow Road," in *Democratizing Brazil*, ed. Stepan, pp. 9–10.

21. Luis A. Abugattas, "Populism and After: The Peruvian Experience," in *Authoritarians and Democrats: Regime Transition in Latin America*, ed. James M. Malloy and Mitchell A. Seligson (Pittsburgh: University of Pittsburgh Press, 1987), pp. 137–38.

22. Charles Guy Gillespie and Luis Eduardo Gonzalez, "Uruguay: The Survival of Old and Autonomous Institutions," in *Democracy in Developing Countries: Latin America*, ed. Diamond, Linz, and Lipset, pp. 223–24; *Economist*, December 4, 1982, p. 63; *New York Times*, December 2, 1980, p. A3, December 6, 1980, p. 3.

23. Aldo C. Vacs, "Authoritarian Breakdown and Redemocratization in Argentina," in *Authoritarians and Democrats*, ed. Malloy and Seligson, p. 16; *New York Times*, November 1, 1983, pp. 1, A14; *Washington Post*, November 1, 1983, p. A1.

24. *Time*, November 21, 1983, p. 43; *Washington Post*, November 5, 1983, p. A10; *New York Times*, November 6, 1983, p. 6.

25. *Washington Post*, February 13, 1985, pp. A1, A28.

26. Leo E. Rose, "Pakistan: Experiments with Democracy," in *Democracy in Developing Countries: Asia*, ed. Larry Diamond, Juan J. Linz, and Seymour Martin Lipset (Boulder, Colo.: Lynne Rienner, 1989), pp. 125–26.

27. Jose Luis Cea, "Chile's Difficult Return to Constitutional Democracy," *PS* 20 (Summer 1987), p. 669.

28. *New York Times*, March 28, 1989, p. 1; *Economist*, April 1, 1989, p. 39.

29. *New York Times*, June 6, 1989, p. A1; *Economist*, June 10, 1989, pp. 43–44.

30. *New York Times*, February 27, 1990, p. A12, March 1, 1990, p. A20, March 8, 1990, p. A3; *Boston Globe*, February 27, 1990; Tom Gjalten, "Let's Make a Deal," *New Republic*, March 19, 1990, p. 14; *Washington Post National Weekly Edition*, March 5–11, 1990, p. 7.

31. *New York Times*, May 29, 1990, p. A9; *Daily Telegraph* (London), May 28, 1990, p. 12; *Los Angeles Times*, July 10, 1990, p. H2.

32. *New York Times*, June 14, 1990, p. 1, June 15, 1990, p. A9; *Washington Post National Weekly Edition*, June 18–24, 1990, p. 18.

33. See Manuel Antonio Garreton, "Political Processes in an Authoritarian Regime: The Dynamics of Institutionalization and Opposition in Chile, 1973–1980," in *Military Rule in Chile: Dictatorship and Oppositions*, ed. J. Samuel Valenzuela and Arturo Valenzuela (Baltimore: Johns Hopkins University Press, 1986), pp. 173–74. An earlier plebiscite in January 1978 invited the Chilean people to rally around Pinochet in opposition to the "international aggression" against their country. It resembled plebiscites in fascist and communist countries in which governments got more than 90 percent of the vote; only 75 percent of the Chilean voters, however, supported Pinochet in this plebiscite.

34. Skidmore, "Brazil's Slow Road," in *Democratizing Brazil*, ed. Stepan, p. 23.

35. George S. Harris, *Turkey: Coping with Crisis* (Boulder, Colo.: Westview Press, 1985), p. 59.

36. Sung-joo Han, "South Korea: Politics in Transition," in *Democracy in Developing Countries: Asia*, ed. Diamond, Linz, and Lipset, pp. 283–284; Gregory Henderson, "Constitutional Changes from the First to the Sixth Republics: 1948 to 1987," in *Political Change in South Korea*, ed. Ilpyong J. Kim and Young Whan Kihl (New York: Korean PWPA, 1988), p. 38.

37. Laurence Whitehead, "Bolivia's Failed Democratization, 1977–1980," in *Transitions from Authoritarian Rule: Latin America*, ed. O'Donnell, Schmitter, and Whitehead (Baltimore: Johns Hopkins University Press, 1986), pp. 58–60.

38. Quoted in Alfred Stepan, "The Last Days of Pinochet?" *New York Review of Books*, June 2, 1988, p. 33.

39. Quoted in Constantine P. Danopoulos, "From Military to Civilian Rule in Contemporary Greece," *Armed Forces and Society* 10 (Winter 1984), pp. 236–37.

40. Sandra Burton, *Impossible Dream: The Marcoses, the Aquinos, and the Unfinished Revolution* (New York: Warner Books, 1989), p. 102; Hasan-Askari Rizvi, "The Civilianization of Military Rule in Pakistan," *Asian Survey* 26 (October 1986), pp. 1076–77; *Economist*, October 29, 1988, p. 43.

41. Karl D. Jackson, "The Philippines: The Search for a Suitable Democratic Solution, 1946–1986," in *Democracy in Developing Countries: Asia*, ed. Diamond, Linz, and Lipset, p. 253; Rizvi, "Civilianization of Military Rule," pp. 1076–77; *Economist*, June 16, 1990, p. 45; *New York Times*, June 15, 1990, p. A9.

42. Quoted in Burton, *Impossible Dream*, pp. 200–201; *Economist*, September 10, 1988, pp. 44–47.

43. *Economist*, June 29, 1985, pp. 38f.

44. Burton, *Impossible Dream*, pp. 208–11.

45. Raymond Carr and Juan Pablo Fusi Aizpurua, *Spain: Dictatorship to Democracy* (London: Allen & Unwin, 1981), p. 227.

46. Chris Hani, quoted in *Economist*, June 18, 1988, p. 46; Alvaro Cunhal, quoted in Kenneth Maxwell, "Regime Overthrow and the Prospects for Democratic Transition in Portugal," in *Transitions from Authoritarian Rule: Southern Europe*, ed. Guillermo O'Donnell, Philippe C. Schmitter, and Laurence Whitehead, (Baltimore: Johns Hopkins University Press, 1986), p. 123.

47. These figures on political deaths come primarily from press reports and should be viewed with a certain skepticism. On the one hand, the first estimates of casualties in any "incident" or "massacre" are almost always exaggerated, and are subject to later correction. See, e.g., the downgrading of initial reports of 2,700 deaths in Beijing in June 1989 and of 60,000 people killed in Bucharest in December 1989. *New York Times*, June 3, 1990, p. 20; *Economist*, January 6, 1990, p. 47. On the other hand, government reports usually underestimate the casualties their security forces have both inflicted and suffered, and many political deaths may not show up in official or independent estimates because the victims' killers or friends privately dispose of the bodies. For a sophisticated model analysis of political deaths in South Africa between 1977 and 1984, see Hendrik W. van der Merwe, "A Technique for the Analysis of Political Violence," *Politikon* 16 (December 1989), pp. 63–74. The South African Institute of Race Relations estimates 8,577 people died in political violence between September 1984 and October 1990. Wayne Safro, *Special Report on Violence against Black Town Councillors and Policemen* (Johannesburg: South African Institute of Race Relations, December 1990), p. 1.

48. See Douglas L. Wheeler, "The Military and the Portuguese Dictatorship, 1926–1974: 'The Honor of the Army,'" in *Contemporary Portugal: The Revolution and Its Antecedents*, ed. Lawrence S. Graham and Harry M. Makler (Austin: University of Texas Press, 1979), p. 215; John L. Hammond, "Electoral Behavior and Political Militancy," in *Contemporary Portugal*, ed. Graham and Makler, pp. 269–75; Douglas Porch, *The Portuguese Armed Forces and the Revolution* (London: Croom Helm, 1977), pp. 165, 228; Thomas C. Bruneau, "Discovering Democracy," *Wilson Quarterly* 9 (New Year's 1985), pp. 70–71.

49. Rafael Lopez-Pintor, "Los condicionamientos socioeconómicos de la acción politica en la transición democrática," *Revista Española de Investigaciones Sociológicas* 15 (1981), p. 21, reproduced in Jose Ignacio Wert Ortega, "The Transition from Below: Public Opinion Among the Spanish Population from 1977 to 1979," in *Spain at the Polls, 1977, 1979, and 1982: A Study of the National Elections*, ed. Howard R. Penniman and Eusebio M. Mujal-Leon (Durham, N.C.: Duke University Press, American Enterprise Institute, 1985), p. 344.

50. Timothy Garton Ash, "Eastern Europe: The Year of Truth," *New York Review of Books*, February 15, 1990, p. 18.

51. Francisco Weffort, "Why Democracy?" in *Democratizing Brazil*, ed. Stepan, pp. 341–345.

52. Mainwaring and Viola, "Brazil and Argentina," p. 208; *New York Times*, December 17, 1982, p. A6, December 18, 1982, p. 3, December 20, 1982, p. A2.

53. Ramon H. Myers, "Political Theory and Recent Political Developments in the Republic of China," *Asian Survey* 27 (September 1987), p. 1013; *New York Times*, December 1, 1986, p. A3, December 2, 1986, p. A6; *Washington Post National Weekly Edition*, January 22–28, 1990, p. 10.

54. Timothy Garton Ash, "The German Revolution," *New York Review of Books*, December 21, 1989, p. 16.

55. Ash, *New York Review of Books*, February 15, 1990, p. 19.

56. *New York Times*, September 28, 1984, p. A3.

57. *Economist*, February 17, 1990, p. 35.

58. See J. Bryan Hehir, "Papal Foreign Policy," *Foreign Policy* 78 (Spring 1990), pp. 45–46 for John Paul II's view "that violence is evil, that violence is unacceptable as a solution to problems," and that hence there can be no doctrine of "just revolution," a view not universally shared among Catholic clergy.

59. Benigno Aquino, speech prepared for delivery, August 21, 1983, Manila Airport, *New York Times*, August 22, 1983, p. A8.

60. Zbigniew Bujak, quoted in David S. Mason, "Solidarity as a Social Movement," *Political Science Quarterly* 104 (Spring 1989), p. 53; Lech Walesa, interview by Neal Conan, National Public Radio, February 5, 1985; Ash, "Eastern Europe," p. 19.

61. Chief Mangosuthu G. Buthelezi, "Disinvestment Is Anti-Black," *Wall Street Journal*, February 20, 1985, p. 32.

62. *New York Times,* January 20, 1987, p. 3; Jeffrey Herbst, "Prospects for Revolution in South Africa," *Political Science Quarterly* 103 (Winter 1988–89), pp. 681–82.

63. *Economist,* July 27, 1985, p. 26; *Washington Post National Weekly Edition,* July 21, 1986, p. 15.

64. *Washington Post,* March 28, 1984, p. A16; *New York Times,* October 30, 1984, p. A1; *Boston Globe,* October 31, 1984, p. 3, November 28, 1984, p. 17; Charles Lane, "Marcos, He Ain't," *New Republic,* July 7, 1986, p. 21.

65. *New York Times,* May 15, 1986, p. A21, June 17, 1986, p. A2, March 4, 1987, p. A3, August 4, 1987, p. A13.

66. William Flanigan and Edwin Fogelman, "Patterns of Democratic Development: An Historical Comparative Analysis," in *Macro-Quantitative Analysis: Conflict, Development, and Democratization,* ed. John V. Gillespie and Betty A. Nesvold (Beverly Hills: Sage Publications, 1971), 487–88.

Chapter 5: HOW LONG?

1. For other discussions of the problems of democratic consolidation, see Juan Linz and Alfred Stepan, "Political Crafting of Democratic Consolidation or Destruction: European and South American Comparisons," in *Democracy in the Americas: Stopping the Pendulum,* ed. Robert A. Pastor (New York: Holmes and Meier, 1989), pp. 41–61; Laurence Whitehead, "The Consolidation of Fragile Democracies: A Discussion with Illustrations," in *Democracy in the Americas,* ed. Pastor, pp. 79–95; and Charles Guy Gillespie, "Democratic Consolidation in the Southern Cone and Brazil: Beyond Political Disarticulation," *Third World Quarterly* 11 (April 1989), pp. 92–113.

2. For a thoughtful treatment of these questions, with reference to second wave and early third wave cases, see John H. Herz, "On Reestablishing Democracy after the Downfall of Authoritarian or Dictatorial Regimes," *Comparative Politics* 10 (July 1978), pp. 559–62, where Herz defined the issue as "Forgive and forget, or prosecute and purge?", and Herz, "Conclusion," in *From Dictatorship to Democracy: Coping with The Legacies of Authoritarianism and Totalitarianism,* ed. John H. Herz (Westport, Conn.: Greenwood Press, 1982), pp. 277–81. For a comparison of third wave experience in Argentina, Brazil, and Uruguay, see Alfred Stepan, *Rethinking Military Politics: Brazil and the Southern Cone* (Princeton: Princeton University Press, 1988), pp. 69–72, 107–8, 115–16, and for an excellent discussion of the political and moral issues, see the Aspen Institute, Justice and Society Program, *State Crimes: Punishment or Pardon* (Queenstown, Md.: The Aspen Institute, Papers and Report of a Conference, November 4–6, 1988, 1989).

3. These figures, which inevitably are approximate, come from a variety of sources, including those cited in connection with the estimates in chapter 4 of all those killed in democratizations. For the figures on Chile, see also *New York Times,* August 1, 1989, p. A4, March 13, 1990, p. A3, and on Brazil, *New York Times,* December 15, 1985, p. 15.

4. Quoted in Lawrence Weschler, "The Great Exception: I—Liberty," *New Yorker,* April 3, 1989, p. 84.

5. Whitehead, "Consolidation of Fragile Democracies," in *Democracy in the Americas*, ed. Pastor, p. 84.

6. Aryeh Neier, "What Should Be Done About the Guilty?" *New York Review of Books*, February 1, 1990, p. 35.

7. Vaclav Havel, New Year's Address, *Uncaptive Minds* 3 (January-February 1990), p. 2.

8. Quoted in Weschler, *New Yorker*, April 3, 1989, p. 84.

9. Neier, *New York Review of Books*, February 1, 1990, p. 35.

10. *New York Times*, August 1, 1989, p. A4, March 10, 1990, p. 4; *Boston Globe*, December 10, 1989, p. 17.

11. *New York Times*, May 29, 1983, p. E3.

12. P. Nikiforos Diamandouros, "Transition to, and Consolidation of, Democratic Politics in Greece, 1974-83: A Tentative Assessment," in *The New Mediterranean Democracies: Regime Transitions in Spain, Greece, and Portugal*, ed. Geoffrey Pridham (London: Frank Cass, 1984), p. 57.

13. Harry Psomiades, "Greece: From the Colonels' Rule to Democracy," in *From Dictatorship to Democracy*, ed. Herz, pp. 262-65. The exact number of torture trials is uncertain because they were held in a variety of jurisdictions and involved a variety of alleged crimes (assault, abuse of authority) that are difficult to distinguish from those of normal criminal cases.

14. See *Nunca Más: The Report of the Argentina National Commission on the Disappeared* (New York: Farrar Strauss Giroux, 1986), pp. 10, 51, and *passim*.

15. Diamandouros, "Democratic Politics in Greece," in *New Mediterranean Democracies*, ed. Pridham, p. 58.

16. Psomiades, "Greece," in *From Dictatorship to Democracy*, ed. Herz, pp. 263-64; *New York Times*, December 31, 1990, p. 3.

17. Peter Ranis, "The Dilemmas of Democratization in Argentina," *Current History* 85 (January 1986), p. 30; Elizabeth Fox, "Argentina: A Prosecution in Trouble," *Atlantic Monthly* 255 (March 1985), p. 42.

18. *New York Times*, December 28, 1986, p. E3, February 21, 1987, p. 4; *Economist*, December 13, 1986, p. 42.

19. *New York Times*, December 30, 1990, p. 9.

20. *International Herald Tribune*, June 27-28, 1987, p. 5.

21. James Cotton, "From Authoritarianism to Democracy in South Korea," *Political Studies* 37 (June 1989), p. 257.

22. Weschler, *New Yorker*, April 3, 1989, p. 83; Stepan, *Rethinking Military Politics*, pp. 70-71. I have relied primarily on Weschler's account for the amnesty controversy in Uruguay. His *New Yorker* articles were subsequently incorporated into a book, *A Miracle, A Universe: Settling Accounts with Torturers* (New York: Pantheon Books, 1990).

23. Danilo Arbilla, quoted in *Newsweek*, January 28, 1985, p. 23.

24. Weschler, *New Yorker*, April 3, 1989, p. 85.

25. *New York Times*, April 18, 1989, p. A8.

26. Ernesto Sabato, quoted in *Washington Post*, February 2, 1986, p. C5.

27. Neier, "What Should Be Done," p. 34; *New York Times*, June 3, 1990, p. 6, June 11, 1990, p. A4.

28. Lawrence Weschler, "The Great Exception: II—Impunity," *New Yorker*, April 10, 1989, pp. 92–93; *Boston Globe*, April 16, 1989, p. 20.

29. Neier, "What Should Be Done," p. 34.

30. Gabriel Schoenfeld, "Crimes and Punishments," *Soviet Prospects* 2 (October 1990); Janusz Bugajski, "Score Settling in Eastern Europe," *Soviet Prospects* 2 (October 1990), pp. 1–3; *New York Times*, January 1, 1990, p. A13, July 7, 1990, p. A8, November 11, 1990, p. A16; *Times* (London), May 29, 1990, p. 11.

31. "Problems in the Soviet Military," *Soviet/East European Report* 7 (September 20, 1990), pp. 1–2; *New York Times*, July 5, 1990, p. A7.

32. *New York Times*, May 11, 1989, p. A7.

33. Cynthia McClintock, "The Prospects for Democratic Consolidation in the 'Least Likely' Case: Peru," *Comparative Politics* 21 (January 1989), p. 142; Adrian Shubert, "The Military Threat to Spanish Democracy: A Historical Perspective," *Armed Forces and Society* 10 (Summer 1984), p. 535; Paul W. Zagorski, "Civil-Military Relations and Argentine Democracy," *Armed Forces and Society* 14 (Spring 1988), p. 423.

34. Psomiades, "Greece," in *From Dictatorship to Democracy*, ed. Herz, p. 207.

35. Eusebio Mujal-Leon, "The Crisis of Spanish Democracy," *Washington Quarterly* 5 (Spring 1982), p. 104; *New York Times*, Nov. 15, 1981, p. A17, Nov. 21, 1981, p. 2.

36. Thomas C. Bruneau and Alex MacLeod, *Politics in Contemporary Portugal* (Boulder, Colo.: Lynne Rienner, 1986), pp. 118–26; *Washington Post*, January 28, 1984, pp. A17, A24.

37. *New York Times*, March 11, 1990, pp. E3, E21, September 18, 1990, p. 11; *Time*, March 26, 1990, p. 26.

38. Bruneau and MacLeod, *Politics in Contemporary Portugal*, p. 24. See, generally, chaps. 1 and 6, and Walter C. Opello, Jr., *Portugal's Political Development: A Comparative Approach* (Boulder, Colo.: Westview Press, 1985), chap. 7.

39. *New York Times*, September 9, 1990, p. 6, December 6, 1990, p. A14, January 22, 1991, p. A17.

40. Henri J. Barkey, "Why Military Regimes Fail: The Perils of Transition," *Armed Forces and Society* 16 (Winter 1990), p. 187; *New York Times*, July 3, 1987, p. A5, December 4, 1990, p. A13; *Economist*, July 4, 1987, p. 47.

41. See, generally, Diamandouros, "Democratic Politics in Greece," in *New Mediterranean Democracies*, ed. Pridham, p. 60; Constantine P. Danopoulos, "From Balconies to Tanks: Post-Junta Civil-Military Relations in Greece," *Journal of Political and Military Sociology* 13 (Spring 1985), pp. 91, 95; McClintock, "Prospects for Democratic Consolidation," p. 134; Paul Heywood, "Spain: 10 June 1987," *Government and Opposition* 22 (Autumn 1987), pp. 397–98. Danopoulos uses the carrot-and-stick metaphor to describe the military policies of Karamanlis and Papendreou.

42. Shubert, *Armed Forces in Society* 10, pp. 535–37; Martin C. Needler, "Legitimacy and the Armed Forces in Transitional Spain" (Paper prepared

for Meeting, International Political Science Association, Rio de Janeiro, August 10–14, 1982), p. 16.

43. *International Herald Tribune,* May 30, 1990, p. 5; *New York Times,* March 31, 1982, p. A4; *Times* (London), March 29, 1990, p. 13.

44. Danopoulos, "From Balconies to Tanks," pp. 91–92; Salvador Giner, "Southern European Socialism in Transition," in *New Mediterranean Democracies,* ed. Pridham, p. 151; *New York Times,* March 31, 1982, p. A4.

45. Quoted in *New York Times,* July 22, 1989, p. 3.

46. "On the Edge of Europe: A Survey of Portugal," *Economist,* June 30, 1984, p. 7.

47. *New York Times,* October 28, 1983, p. A5, January 24, 1984, p. A2; *Times* (London), March 20, 1990, p. 13.

48. Danopoulos, "From Balconies to Tanks," p. 93; Zagorski, "Civil-Military Relations," p. 424.

49. Danopoulos, "From Balconies to Tanks," p. 89; Theodore A. Couloumbis and Prodromos M. Yannis, "The Stability Quotient of Greece's Post-1974 Democratic Institutions," *Journal of Modern Greek Studies* 1 (October 1983), p. 366; *New York Times,* January 15, 1989, p.6; *Economist,* Jan. 21, 1989, p. 40.

50. Danopoulos, "From Balconies to Tanks," pp. 89, 93; *New York Times,* March 31, 1982, p. A4.

51. *New York Times,* December 6, 1990, p. A14.

52. *Washington Post,* May 5, 1984, p. A17; *Washington Post National Weekly,* November 9, 1987, p. 17; Juan de Onis, "Brazil on the Tightrope Toward Democracy," *Foreign Affairs* 63 (Fall 1989), p. 128; *New York Times,* June 5, 1989, p. A9; Tzvetan Todorov, "Post-Totalitarian Depression," *New Republic,* June 25, 1990, pp. 23–25; *New York Times,* November 9, 1990, p. A1, A10.

53. Peter McDonough, Samuel H. Barnes, Antonio Lopez Pina, "The Growth of Democratic Legitimacy in Spain," *American Political Science Review* 80 (September 1986), p. 743; *New York Times,* May 7, 1989, p. 2E; Thomas C. Bruneau, "Popular Support for Democracy in Post-revolutionary Portugal: Results from a Survey," in *In Search of Modern Portugal: The Revolution and Its Consequences,* ed. Lawrence S. Graham and Douglas L. Wheeler (Madison: University of Wisconsin Press, 1983), pp. 35–36; McClintock, "Prospects for Democratic Consolidation," p. 142.

54. Larry Diamond, Juan J. Linz, Seymour Martin Lipset, "Democracy in Developing Countries: Facilitating and Obstructing Factors," in *Freedom in the World: Political Rights and Civil Liberties 1987–1988,* ed. Raymond D. Gastil (New York: Freedom House, 1988), p. 231.

55. Linz and Stepan, "Political Crafting," in *Democracy in the Americas,* ed. Pastor, pp. 46, 58–59, and Ekkart Zimmerman, "Economic and Political Reactions to World Economic Crises of the 1930s in Six European Countries" (Paper presented for convention, Midwest Political Science Association, Chicago, April 10–12, 1986), p. 51, quoted in Linz and Stepan, "Political Crafting," p. 46; Robert A. Dix, Book Review, *American Political Science Review* 83 (September 1989), p. 1055.

56. Linz and Stepan, "Political Crafting," in *Democracy in the Americas*, ed. Pastor, p. 49; McClintock, "Prospects for Democratic Consolidation," p. 127.

57. Enrique A. Baloyra, "Public Opinion and Support for Democratic Regimes, Venezuela 1973–1983" (Paper prepared for Annual Meeting, American Political Science Association, New Orleans, La., August 29–September 1, 1985), pp. 10–11.

58. Makram Haluani, "Waiting for the Revolution: The Relative Deprivation of the J-Curve Logic in the Case of Venezuela, 1968–1989" (Paper prepared for Annual Meeting, American Political Science Association, Atlanta, Georgia, August 31–September 3, 1989), pp. 9–10.

59. McDonough, Barnes, Lopez Pina, "Democratic Legitimacy in Spain," p. 751.

60. These figures on the economy and public opinion come from Linz and Stepan, "Political Crafting," in *Democracy in the Americas*, ed. Pastor, pp. 43–45.

61. See Guillermo O'Donnell, "Challenges to Democratization in Brazil," *World Policy Journal* 5 (Spring 1988), pp. 281–300.

62. McDonough, Barnes, Lopez Pina, "Democratic Legitimacy in Spain," pp. 752–753; McClintock, "Prospects for Democratic Consolidation," p. 140.

63. For these and other data on the changes in German political culture, see Kendall L. Baker, Russell J. Dalton, Kai Hildebrandt, *Germany Transformed: Political Culture and the New Politics* (Cambridge: Harvard University Press, 1981), *passim* but especially chap. 1 and pp. 273, 287; David P. Conradt, "Changing German Political Culture," in *The Civic Culture Revisited*, ed. Gabriel A. Almond and Sidney Verba (Boston: Little, Brown, 1980), pp. 212–72, and "West Germany: A Remade Political Culture?" *Comparative Political Studies* 7 (July 1974), pp. 222–38.

64. Baker, Dalton, Hildebrandt, *Germany Transformed*, pp. 68–69, 285; Warren M. Tsuneishi, *Japanese Political Style* (New York: Harper, 1966), pp. 17–21.

65. *International Herald Tribune*, May 10, 1990, p. 1, May 16, 1990, p. 1, May 21, 1990, p. 2; *Times* (London), May 11, 1990, p. 10.

66. See Juan J. Linz, "The Perils of Presidentialism," *Journal of Democracy* 1 (Winter 1990), pp. 51–70, and the follow-up articles by Donald Horowitz, Seymour Martin Lipset, and Juan J. Linz, *Journal of Democracy* 1 (Fall 1990), pp. 73–91.

Chapter 6: WHITHER?

1. For useful reports, see *Economist*, September 10, 1988, pp. 43–44, December 24, 1988, pp. 61–66, and August 5, 1989, p. 75.

2. *Economist*, May 6, 1989, p. 34, November 11, 1989, pp. 40–41; *Times* (London), April 12, 1990, p. 12; *The Observer*, May 29, 1990, p. 18.

3. *Times* (London), April 24, 1990, p. 11.

4. See Secretary James Baker, "Democracy and American Diplomacy," (Address, World Affairs Council, Dallas, Texas, March 30, 1990), and Ronald Reagan's remarks to the English-speaking Union, London, quoted in *New York Times*, June 14, 1989, p. A6.

5. Stan Sesser, "A Rich Country Gone Wrong," *New Yorker*, October 9, 1989, pp. 80–84.

6. *New York Times*, December 28, 1989, p. A13; *International Herald Tribune*, May 12–13, 1990, p. 6.

7. *Times* (London), May 27, 1990, p. A21; *Time*, May 21, 1990, pp. 34–35; *Daily Telegraph*, March 29, 1990, p. 13; *New York Times*, February 27, 1990, p. A10, April 9, 1990, p. A6.

8. George F. Kennan, *The Cloud of Danger* (Boston: Little, Brown, 1977), pp. 41–43.

9. See William Wallace, *The Transformation of Western Europe* (London: Royal Institute of International Affairs, Pinter, 1990), pp. 16–19, and Michael Howard, "The remaking of Europe," *Survival* 32 (March–April 1990), pp. 102–3.

10. Yu-sheng Lin, "Reluctance to Modernize: The Influence of Confucianism on China's Search for Political Modernity," in *Confucianism and Modernization: A Symposium*, ed. Joseph P. Liang (Taipei: Wu Nan Publishing Co., 1987), p. 25. For a somewhat different interpretation of human rights and the rule of law in the Confucian tradition, see Stephen B. Young and Nguyen Ngoc Huy, *The Tradition of Human Rights in China and Vietnam* (New Haven: Yale Center for International and Area Studies, Council on Southeast Asia Studies, 1990). They argue that there was a duality of virtue and power in the Confucian tradition, but they admit that power became increasingly concentrated in modern times.

11. See Daniel Kelliher, "The Political Consequences of China's Reforms," *Comparative Politics* 18 (July 1986), pp. 488–90, and Andrew J. Nathan, *Chinese Democracy* (New York: Alfred A. Knopf, 1985).

12. *Economist*, April 23, 1988, p. 37, November 5, 1988, p. 35; *New York Times*, May 20, 1982, p. A2, July 10, 1988, p. E2; Ian Buruma, "Singapore," *New York Times Magazine*, June 12, 1988, p. 118.

13. Lucian W. Pye with Mary W. Pye, *Asian Power and Politics: The Cultural Dimensions of Authority* (Cambridge: Harvard University Press, 1985), pp. 232–36.

14. *New York Times*, December 15, 1987, p. A14; Gregory Henderson, *Korea: The Politics of the Vortex* (Cambridge: Harvard University Press, 1968), p. 365.

15. *Economist*, January 27, 1990, p. 31; *New York Times*, January 23, 1990, p. 1.

16. Goh Chok Tong, quoted in *New York Times*, August 14, 1985, p. A13.

17. Lucian W. Pye, "Asia 1986—An Exceptional Year," *Freedom at Issue* 94 (January–February 1987), p. 15.

18. Ernest Gellner, "Up from Imperialism," *The New Republic*, May 22, 1989, pp. 35–36; R. Stephen Humphreys, "Islam and Political Values in Saudi Arabia, Egypt, and Syria," *Middle East Journal* 33 (Winter 1979), pp. 6–7.

19. *New York Times*, July 1, 1990, p. 5.

20. For a brief description of the many forms of Islamic politics, see Mahnaz Ispahani, "The Varieties of Muslim Experience," *Wilson Quarterly* 13 (Autumn 1989), pp. 63–72.

21. World Bank, *World Development Report 1990* (New York: Oxford University Press, 1990), pp. 8–11, 16, 160, and *Sub-Saharan Africa: From Crisis to Sustainable Growth* (Washington: World Bank, 1990).

22. These and subsequent figures on per capita GNP and growth rates of GNP and GDP come from World Bank, *World Development Report 1990*, pp. 178–81.

INDEX

343